THEMES IN HISTORY

PROPHECY

THE POWER OF INSPIRED
LANGUAGE IN HISTORY 1300–2000

EDITED BY
BERTRAND TAITHE
& TIM THORNTON

SUTTON PUBLISHING

We dedicate this book to Sue and Vicky

First published in 1997 by
Sutton Publishing Limited · Phoenix Mill
Thrupp · Stroud · Gloucestershire · GL5 2BU

British Library Cataloguing in Publication Data
A catalogue record for this book is available from the British Library

ISBN 0–7509–1331–2 (cased)
ISBN 0–7509–1332–0 (paperback)

Cover illustration: detail from The Garden of Earthly Delights *(c. 1500) by Hieronymous
Bosch (c. 1450–1516) (Prado, Madrid/Index/Bridgeman Art Library, London).*

ALAN SUTTON™ and SUTTON™ are the
trade marks of Sutton Publishing Limited

Typeset in 10/12pt Baskerville.
Typesetting and origination by
Sutton Publishing Limited.
Printed in Great Britain by
Hartnolls, Bodmin, Cornwall.

CONTENTS

PART THREE: PROPHECY AND SYSTEMS OF BELIEF

PART FOUR: THE ENDS OF PROPHECY

EDITORS AND SERIES EDITORS

Bertrand Taithe read history at the Sorbonne and Manchester University where he completed a thesis on the Contagious Diseases Acts and Victorian Society. He has published *The Essential Mayhew: Representing and Communicating the Poor* (1996) and is currently a lecturer in Modern French and British history at the University of Huddersfield.

Tim Thornton read history at New College, Oxford and completed a thesis on political society in early Tudor Cheshire. He is preparing books on Mother Shipton and Nixon the Cheshire prophet and is currently a lecturer in late medieval and early modern history at the University of Huddersfield.

LIST OF CONTRIBUTORS

Lesley Coote is a doctoral candidate at the Centre for Medieval Studies, University of York, where her Ph.D. thesis on prophecy and public affairs in later medieval England is in its final stages of completion. Initially trained as a historian, she has a BA in English Studies from the University of East Anglia, is married to a Hull clergyman and has a twelve-year old son.

Anne McLaren teaches at the University of Liverpool's history department. She is a cultural historian with a particular interest in queenship in the early modern period. She is currently working on a book entitled *Queen and Commonwealth: the Enactment of Sovereignty in the Reign of Elizabeth I.*

Kenneth Gibson is a doctoral candidate at Nottingham Trent University currently working on eschatology, apocalypse and millenarianism in Early Stuart England. He also teaches history at the Centre for Access and Continuing Education at the University of Derby.

Gwilym Games is a doctoral candidate at the History Department of Lancaster University. His thesis is concerned with the interaction between social, religious and political ideas in early New England.

Stephen Barnett has a Ph.D. in early modern historiography of the Church and the origins of British Enlightenment anticlericalism. He also has an interest in medieval studies. He is presently archivist to the Sedgeford Hall Archaeological Research Project (Norfolk), which is excavating a Saxon settlement.

Neil Hitchin read history and divinity in Canada. He is currently a doctoral candidate at Magdalene College, Cambridge. His research interests include eighteenth-century British divinity and political ideas. He has published in the *Anglican Theological Review.*

J.A.G. Roberts teaches Chinese and Japanese history at the University of Huddersfield. In 'Not the Least Deserving', *Monumenta Nipponica*, 44.2 (1989), he discussed the *philosophes'* understanding of the religions of Japan. He has just published *A History of China: Prehistory to c. 1800* (Sutton, Stroud, 1996) and is now working on a second volume covering the period from 1800 to the present day.

Rhodri Hayward is working as a researcher on the Wellcome Trust funded project 'The Brain and the Self: neuroscience and the public understanding of science and medicine in Britain, *c.* 1925–55.' He studied at the universities of Edinburgh and Lancaster, where he recently completed his doctoral thesis 'Popular Mysticism and the Origins of the New Psychology, 1880–1910'.

Peter Davies read politics at Swansea and completed a doctoral thesis on the French extreme right. He is currently a lecturer in Modern European History at the University of Huddersfield. He has written articles and reviews on different aspects of French history and contemporary French politics. He is currently writing a book on the *Front National,* to be published by Routledge.

ACKNOWLEDGEMENTS

Editing a collective work like this one is not an easy task and we have to thank the contributors first of all for putting up with our suggestions, editorial amendments and criticisms. We also have to thank the History Department of the University of Huddersfield which encouraged us and partially financed the conference preliminary to this volume. We have to be grateful to the various good libraries our central location enabled us to use: the Brotherton Library at Leeds University and the John Rylands Library at Manchester University. Last but not least we have to thank Roger Thorp for his support for this volume and the series *Themes in History* launched under our joint editorship.

To all many thanks.

1

THE LANGUAGE OF HISTORY: PAST AND FUTURE IN PROPHECY

B. Taithe and T. Thornton

'If history is the remembered past, it is also the expected future.' [1]

This introduction does not intend to link artificially the various contributions or to claim that this book covers all instances of prophetic utterance since 1300. In fact, the case studies represented by the following articles cover the themes we intend to lay out in this introduction. They echo each other through the ages in the way we intended for this series *Themes in History*.

There is a real paradox in attempting to write the history of what is either fundamentally a-historical or itself the motor of history. A quick glance at various University library catalogues shows how loosely the term *prophecy* has been used to sell any epic biography, scientific message or even literal readings of science-fiction writings.[2] One reason for this slippage is that the meanings of the word prophecy are multifarious. According to the Oxford English Dictionary, loosely summarized, a prophecy is 'divinely inspired utterance or discourse', which leads us to the definition of a prophet as 'one who speaks for God or for any deity, as the inspired revealer or interpreter of his will'. It is also 'sometimes applied to those who preach', as in some Protestant churches, or to 'one who predicts or foretells what is going to happen, a prognosticator'. The last meaning, of 'an omen, a portent', can be applied to an object.

These various meanings are explored in this book. Prophecy varies from being an object or a text to being the inspired reading of texts or even a radical form of preaching. Between the direct divine inspiration and the interpretation of this divine inspiration there is but a fine dividing line. The notion of inspiration, either divine or supernatural, provides the central element of the working definition of prophecy used here. We have therefore not included in this text any analysis of modern forms of prognostication or divination based on experimental rationale and extrapolation. Any spectator of the modern world will nevertheless be aware that, from the assertive economists to the tentative weather forecasters, we live in a society constantly engaged in the divination of the future and the guessing of forthcoming dangers and risks.[3] Many of the conclusions of this book undoubtedly apply by extension to science, but we could not undertake to explore this within the limits imposed. We have also limited our study to the political and public forms prophecy could take. The private interventions of chiromancers, divinatory texts, or even agricultural almanacs were beyond the reach of this book. Here again, we hope that some other team will explore them more fully in the future.

It is a paradox that, while the religious status of monarchs and their spiritual power has been explored and studied in great depth by historians since Kantorowicz's ground-breaking *Two Bodies of the King*, few studies have tried to analyse the theoretical relationship between prophets, prophecies, and the making of western politics.[4] The following essays address this issue in different ways and stress both the continuity of prophetic language in western politics and the changes in practice and understanding. The three chronological phases covered in this book are representative of the nature of these changes. Following Michel de Certeau's interpretative chronology, it can be argued that in the modern age prophecy became increasingly marginal among religious practices and increasingly contested as a system of belief.[5] Simultaneously prophecy came to be discussed in terms that were not its own. As de Certeau noted, prophecy could either be turned into an esoteric art, a lost part of our folklore, the disreputable expression of the political and religious fringe; or, as Rhodri Hayward describes in this book, an object of sceptical scientific enquiry.[6] When a prophetic movement severs its links with worldly concerns it can then offer an alternative to the world, as in the Taiping movement. In the Middle Ages, prophecy was a language of élites, and prophecies were often directly political. The following period of the Reformation centred around the analysis of divinely inspired prophecies. During the Reformation the word prophecy acquired different dimensions and a new emphasis. As noted above the definition of prophecy is flexible; as a result of the Reformation, with its inherent challenge to tradition, greater emphasis was placed on prophecy as the act of preaching, for instance among the Dissenters of New England or the Quakers.[7] More conventional prophets, keen on prognostication, could thus rub shoulders with Biblical scholars and inspired Divines under the common label of prophets. In many ways this wide understanding of the term prophecy reflected and produced the increasingly contested centrality of this system of belief in religious practice. The third period of this book, the nineteenth and the twentieth centuries, showed that prophecies had acquired a unique political potential in support of reform, offering a vision of complete transformation, even of a *tabula rasa*. Religious practice from the Welsh revival to the Toronto Blessing became increasingly the focus of scientific investigation and rationalist scepticism.[8] On the other hand, scenes of what was later termed collective hysteria were still interpreted as the outpouring of the spirit of God in the early 1800s as they are now by the believers of the Toronto Blessing or of Charismatic Catholicism.[9]

While the Taiping prophetic message appealed to the mass for political and social reasons as well as for the millennial hopes it gave rise to, the Welsh prophets, more anchored in their social and geographical context, remained unable to extend their message to the world. Finally, prophecy could take sinister apocalyptical forms, largely devoid of any religious message, and entirely based on a reading of history and an understanding of time and past omens, as the last paper on the *Front National* makes abundantly clear.

The main themes running through all the papers can be identified as prophecy as a political language, attempts to manage prophecy, and the relationship between power and prophecy.

All the chapters of this book focus on the usage of language in prophecies. Many of them provide ample evidence of the poetics involved in the writing of prophecy or its deciphering. The speaking or writing of prophecy and its interpretation are creative acts which can construct kingship, theocracy, alternative communities, or even science. Prophecy and its interpretation is a grammar which is peculiarly flexible and can produce discourse suitable to virtually any context or purpose. For instance prophecy proved to be of great importance in coping with unexpected cultural and cosmological shocks such as the discovery of the New World. As D.A. Brading has pointed out, Joachim of Fiore's prophecies could make this discovery meaningful in theology and condition Franciscan missionaries' responses, encouraging them to pursue an heterodox policy of inculturation best exemplified by the work of Bartholomé de las Casas.[10] A prophecy, or the use of prophetic language, is not solely about mystical divination or the coming of the millennium but, as Lesley Coote points out, a political language involving a critique of current political conflicts, institutions and state-making concepts like kingship. In many ways prophecies are a form of language rather than a well-established content. Anne McLaren describes how Elizabeth's prophetic role as Deborah strongly influenced the course of politics during her reign. One of the reasons for the power of prophecy in the medieval and early modern period was that it was a language shared, to some extent, by élites and the masses over which they ruled. In some cases, this discursive way of expressing alternative identities and views had its roots in the local community. As Tim Thornton explains, two local prophecies, those of Nixon and Mother Shipton, played a significant role in the formation of local responses to major events in the early modern period. This local prophecy both drew on and contributed to national and local political debates, evolving according to the nature of the demands placed on the discourse by the imperatives of the time.

Prophecy is a political grammar into which highly subversive ideas can be inserted and which is accessible to a very wide range of actors and audiences.[11] Yet at the same time, prophecy might act to reinforce authority. Prophecies can take several written forms and the body of prophecy form a corpus of texts. In itself the bibliography of prophecies makes a number of political points and enables modern historians to approach their use. The limited availability of these documents or, on the contrary, their general availability but encoded language, created an initiating process of understanding. The real or mock secrecy attached to this knowledge emphasized the values of the self-appointed, not necessarily small, élites versed in prophetic interpretation. The practice of prophecy also posed similar problems. As a result of this, one of the problems with the interpretation of William Blake's inspired work and that of many similarly inspired individuals is of tracking their tradition, their environment and the intellectual processes leading to the making of their work.[12]

The prophetic language is always remarkably a play on language itself. The Biblical inspiration of most of the prophecies discussed in this book stressed that 'In the beginning was the word and the word was God'. In this context, the use of poetics and the systematic use of images transcended the limitations of human language. One could see in the use of melodic alliterations a way of expressing more than was written. Similarly rhymes often enabled a mnemonic way of remembering the prophecy and thus transcended the need for a written text. Fundamentally it also codified the format of the prophecy. One of the implications of the careful interpretation of God's will was that nothing could be neglected and that a prophecy could be read almost literally between the lines, by using word permutations, reading vertically, or placing a greater importance on the first letter of each words. Spoken prophecies also had to be transcribed and this presented a number of difficulties. The Huguenots described in Hillel Schwartz's excellent book tried to overcome this difficulty by attempting to describe in detail the setting, tone, and gestures of the prophet in their short introductions to the message itself.[13] This difficulty of translating bodily performance and speech into written language has been identified as a consequence of the 'perennial western preference for *speech* (more easily identifiable as 'owned' by someone) over the bodiless residue of *writing*.'[14] This is perhaps why prophecy is so powerful; because unlike most other forms, its goes along with this preference.

Within the message of every prophecy the metaphors and images reminded the reader or the audience that a revelation is always beyond the intellect and is often visual and graphic. A visionary experience, often the starting point of many prophecies, could only be expressed in approximative sentences and could be best summoned up by calls to emblems and symbols. It implies a different thought-world from our own, a more evocative and more inductive one. Joan of Arc saw signs and then she understood them; could we be seeing signs and yet not understanding them?[15] The prophet may transmit his visionary experience without actually mediating or even understanding it. Experience and understanding may be rigidly divided. In the case of Nixon, his prophetic powers did not imply any understanding; in the Taiping instance the prophet also became interpreter and political leader. On the other hand the learned scholars of the late seventeenth century could still study the creation as an immense but coded message.

Umberto Eco teasingly reminds us of the attraction of obscurity. In his *Open Work* and his more recent novel, *Foucault's Pendulum*, Eco stresses the fascination of technical and encoded texts.[16] The huge success of encoded novels, where all the characters refer to living personalities, or even the popularity of word-based puzzles and crosswords are as many reminders of the human desire to be among a circle of initiates in the knowledge of secrets. Of the desire to be kept the recipient of secrets, few better examples could be given than the fact that prophetic manuscripts such as the early versions of Nixon's words or even one of the most important French versions of Merlin's Prophecy the *Merlini*, the Bodmer's manuscript of *Les Prophésies de Merlin*, were kept hidden from view in jealously guarded private collections until the mid-twentieth century.[17] The prophecy belongs to initiates; their knowledge is in itself a form of power coming either from the prognosis of future events and the ability to act upon that information, or from the certainty of acting according to the will of God and therefore securing a life after death. In fact this power is moderated by the confusion reigning over the substance of the message. This can be great because of the nature of the puzzle or because the prophecy can take an objective, physical form as well as a written one.

Beyond the corpus constituted of the various layers of prophecies and prophetic interpretations, the prophet has also a body. In some instances, such as Mother Shipton or Nixon, not to mention Merlin, the actual physical existence of the prophets is, to say the least, dubious or even unlikely. However, through the images used to illustrate the manuscripts or books containing the prophecies, they acquired a body fitting with their role. The body of other prophetic messengers like Joan of Arc could be their main message. Her youth and virginity were symbolic and therefore carried omens. The way the body is actually written upon, marked by God and cosmic forces, actually mattered. The Body of the Taiping prophet was thus opened during his Divine encounter and purified; his general outlook following his revelations also changed and became in itself a symbol of revolt. In the case of the Shawnee Prophet, a Native American leader of the beginning of the nineteenth century, his liminality and access to the other became part of his identity and of his name, 'the Open Door' (Tenskwatawa). His prophetic voice emerged after an alcohol-induced near-death experience and, like the Taiping leader's, mixed Western Christianity with a message of regeneration and rebellion against the established order.[18] The prophetic body acquired this emphasis because of its role as a bridge between the earthly world and the divine. Prophecies were often uttered from beyond the grave or on the threshold of dying. This absolute liminality is sometimes emulated at a lesser level through fasting, or in illness and madness. Shamanic practices or using music and dance or drugs also aim at establishing this absolute receptivity of the body, while weakening it.

It is one of the paradoxes of prophecy that it does not necessarily translate into earthly power. The prophet may be active in the *civitas*, be a recluse in a monastery, an itinerant preacher or the centre of his or community; the Divine or supernatural contact is not in itself the certitude of an acquisition of power. For every Taiping leader, there were many obscure prophets, labouring unceasingly the field of eschatological expectations. The power was with the prophecy, not the prophet.[19] The power of the mediators, initiates, preachers and interpreters and of the audience itself in determining the fortunes of a prophecy dwarfed the charismatic abilities of any prophet.[20]

Something of the power of prophecy can be seen from the way that kings and governments reacted to it. They were sponsors of prophecies which furthered their policies as, for example, Geoffrey of Monmouth's prophecies, especially those connected with Merlin, supported the regime of Henry II.[21] But kings were also very wary of prophecy in the wrong hands, with the most savage penalties being imposed on those who misused them. Henry II's attentions to the Arthurian myth may have positively aided the coherence of his multi-national empire, but a parallel fear of the myth led to Arthur's achievements being deliberately minimized to enhance Henry II's stature.[22] Edward I's efforts to find and re-inter Arthur may have been due as much as anything to a determination to show Arthur was dead and not about to return to lead the Welsh to victory. The Easter after Edward's first campaign in North Wales saw the opening of Arthur's tomb at Glastonbury and his reburial under a splendid monument.[23] In the following centuries, the Prophecy of the Six Kings generated intense controversy over who was the mole, or moldewarp, whose reign would end in defeat and dispossession, as recalled by Shakespeare:

> Sometimes he angers me
> With telling me of the moldwarp and the ant,
> Of the dreamer Merlin and his prophecies,
> And of a dragon, and a finless fish,
> A clip-winged griffin, and a moulten raven,
> A couching lion and a ramping cat,
> And such a deal of skimble-skamble stuff
> As puts me from my faith.[24]

It seems likely that this prophecy was written during the reign of Edward II, and that Henry IV only coincidentally became the target of the prophecy as the sixth king to follow John.[25] Yet even though the first Lancastrian king became its target by accident, the power of the prophecy of the six kings is suggested by the fact that its talk of dividing England in three inspired the idea that the Welsh and Percy rebels against Henry IV signed a tripartite indenture to split up the realm.[26] There are strong signs that Edward IV's awareness of the importance of prophecy – as a potential support and at the same time a threat to his position – broke new ground. As an usurper, his legitimacy was boosted by resort to a range of authorities, from his British ancestry to the moral tenor of his policies, and this was communicated to his subjects in the vernacular more effectively than previously. As well as pioneering the use of proclamations with explanatory and even propagandist preambles in English, Edward seems to have promoted his position through a newly invigorated prophecy tradition in the vernacular.[27] Henry Tudor's victory at Bosworth did not secure him from the prophets, although for the Welsh at least it was with Tudor that the sibyls marched to Bosworth – there were moves in the parliament of 1485–6 to outlaw prophecy, suggesting the concern with which it was viewed.[28] Henry VIII's early victories against the French and Scots, at Thérouanne, Tournai, and Flodden Field in 1513, led to celebrations once again of the English mission in European conquest.[29] Yet the repudiation of papal jurisdiction instigated by Henry VIII inevitably produced opposition to the crown's policies, some of which took the form of prophetic utterances. The most prominent example of this was Elizabeth Barton, the so-called 'Nun of Kent', who foretold drastic events should Henry win the annulification of his marriage to Katherine of Aragon. Prophecy played a major role in the Pilgrimage of Grace in the north of England in 1536–7, articulating the fears of many participants and allowing them to express their views on future developments. As prominent in the mouths of the rebels as straightforward attacks on Henry, his ministers, and his new church were a string of predictions.[30] It is not surprising that Parliament under the Tudors continued to legislate against prophecy, especially through the difficult years around the middle of the century, with acts being passed in 1541–2, 1549–50, and 1563.[31] The early seventeenth century, which witnessed an ever more intense awareness among Protestants of their special role in combating the papal antichrist, saw an increasing role for prophecy. It played a vital role in the historical system worked out by John Bale, John Foxe and others in their work on the meaning of the English Reformation experience, as Stephen Barnett and Anne McLaren emphasize. It was an important part of the role and justification for the new Protestant ministry. Without the authority of the apostolic succession possessed by their catholic predecessors, they relied on their role as interpreters of the scripture and of the experience of their flock in the world, often an explicitly prophetic task.

The dimming of the religious and political enthusiasm inspired and released by the period of the Civil War and Interregnum did not reduce the influence of prophecy. The continuing turbulence of politics, and the fears raised among many in the Protestant community by the religious views and policies of Charles II and especially his brother James, ensured a continuing currency for many of the prophecies which had first seen the light during the Civil War, such as Mother Shipton, as Tim Thornton describes. The possible return of the Old

Pretender and later of his son, Bonnie Prince Charlie, were subjects of a vigorous prophetic debate, with the Cheshire prophet Nixon, initially used by the Jacobites, being recruited for the Hanoverian cause by Oldmixon, the Whig propagandist. Although the relevance of this dynastic politics declined in the course of the eighteenth century, the French revolution produced another outburst of prophecy and prophetic interpretation. The government of the younger Pitt took the initiative in sponsoring a new trend in prophecy which identified the enemy as French and republican. If the period saw the forging of a new 'British' identity, it was a British identity that drew not just on anti-French and Protestant ideas, but which had a clear vision of its mission which was partly prophetic. As Stephen Barnett shows, this could be done in an atmosphere in which scientific discourse had attempted to accommodate itself to foreign prophetic language. It was in the early nineteenth century that prophecies like that of Mother Shipton and Nixon became most widely published and circulated. The religious revivals of the late eighteenth and nineteenth centuries all have their prophetic elements, and especially strongly in the case of Methodism. John Wesley's utterances on the French Revolution were treated as prophecy and published alongside the words of Mother Shipton and other earlier prophets.

Even at the start of the present century, the European catastrophe of the First World War produced a new outburst of prophetic speculation. The Welsh religious revival of 1904–5, as Rhodri Hayward demonstrates, had already shown how prophecy might still exert tremendous force in modern society, even if it was part of a movement which set itself against modernity. As Charles Oman observed in his presidential address to the Royal Historical Society in 1918, war tended to trigger an outburst of rumour and speculation, and this often took prophetic form.

Although some prophetic figures and their interpreters achieved their positions of authority through their sanctity, orthodoxy, or even high secular status, this was rarely the case. More frequently, the prophet was a marginal figure: poor, unorthodox, or of low status. This was because of the nature of prophetic utterance, which creates an authorial identity that denies the involvement of the earthly body of the prophet, except as a tablet upon which the source of their inspiration can inscribe the prophecy. In Middle English the prophetic mental act, *vis imaginativa* or *ymaginatif*, acquired almost an autonomous role in forcing the prophetic figures to feel or act. The body became the vessel of this force, it was written on by forces and ruled simultaneously perhaps even against the will of the prophet.[32]

In addition, because this source of inspiration was beyond conventional understanding, the liminality of the prophet's position allowed them closer contact with it. As such, prophecy is an inherently subversive political language, because it is impossible for élites to control it effectively. It always has the potential to be reclaimed by marginal individuals. Élites might attempt to control it, but the difficulty of doing this was compounded by the attractions of prophecy as a highly effective tool of manipulation of others. A whole-hearted assault on prophecy in the reign of Elizabeth I was unlikely, in spite of the statute of 1563, because of the importance of a prophetic identity to the buttressing of the queen's position.

As prophecies mediate between communities and leadership, they also deal with issues of space and relationships between the various elements in this space. They operate within geographically defined space which has specific boundaries, in this book the instance of Chester, the kingdom, or even New England. However, these boundaries can also be moving and figurative. New England could thus be a space of belief more than a clearly mapped area. To prophecies time boundaries are paramount. While the interpretation may give rise to apparent certainties in terms of number of years, dates of the second coming or lengths of reigns, the status of time is also flexible. This has historic consequences with regard to specific prognosis and the coming of the Millennium. One could thus argue that the Taiping Millennium was more figurative than real. Time is also important in the notion of revival and second coming.

In medieval and early modern thought, the idea of a steady progress into the future, with change rather than continuity as the order of the day, was profoundly alien. Time was perceived to be part of a process which was circular, understood through metaphors such as the wheel of fortune. Revolution and reformation were understood to imply circular processes, implying a departure from, and then return to, a previous state. The process of discussing and predicting the future was therefore inevitably very different from that of today. The future was to be found in the past – since it was to a past state that, for example, the reformation of the Church was intended to return religion. A revolution implied the overturning of a state of affairs before its restoration to its previous state. If the future was to be found in the past, then what more obvious than that it might be found in the minds and therefore the words and writings of people who had lived in the past? Hence the emphasis in the medieval and early modern periods on the antiquity of prophecy – texts were often attached to figures, sometimes non-existent figures from the distant past, or the evidence for the prophecy was ascribed to ancient parchments or inscriptions on stone found in ancient buildings or on sites of venerable antiquity. Acceptance of the inevitability of change produced new forms of prophecy; no longer did they inevitably have to be rooted in the past. The decline of this dependence on the past was not complete, however, even in those prophetic traditions with the least anchorage there. The Quakers, for example, or the participants in the Welsh revival of 1904–5, although they found their inspiration in a spirit which was profoundly a-historical, inevitably claimed authority for their words from a concept of the divine which was constructed around assumptions of the past of the religion and of God's previous relations with his people. Prophecy, even in the modern period, has never stopped being a story about the future written in terms of the past. The writing of history which seeks teleological explanatory causes in the distant past to explain more recent events actually abides by the same (il-)logical rules.

The social space within which prophecy operates is also extremely flexible; prophecy and the act of prophesying cannot be rigidly encoded within society. The prophet has to move from a social space on the margins to a central social role and back. This meteoric rise, by its very nature, leaves open the possibility of contestation. Inspiration is only a transient legitimacy which does not reside with the prophet but the prophecy. The difficulties of identifying a clear historical fulfilment of the prophecy always endanger the prophet's position, although an unfulfilled prophecy might paradoxically stimulate further activity.[33] Signs can always be interpreted in contradictory ways. The fate of Savonarola after his rapid emergence as a subversive force and then as a figurehead of the Florentine republic illustrates the political frailty of prophets involved in politics but unable to reshape politics around themselves. Paradoxically his death at the stake helped re-establish Savonarola as a prophet, the announcement of martyrdom being a common, often self-fulfilling, part of many prophets' message.[34]

The role of prophecy in the community is attached to the concept of identity and nationality. Prophecy gives a dynamic to Benedict Anderson's *Imagined Communities* that is not there in his mostly materialistic account. From the early texts onwards, the relatively loose notions of race were invested with eschatological purpose. This purposiveness grew in the more historically defined and idealized concepts of nations of the nineteenth and twentieth centuries. Carlyle's Prophet as Hero was not simply a mould-breaker and epoch-maker. The hero's leadership made Carlyle forget that it was the prophecy that made the community of belief, the Umma. A Mazzinian nation also acted as a unity of belief invested with an eschatological mission: 'I believe, as I have said, that where the people shall be gathered together, and prepared to receive the Spirit of God, the Spirit of God will descend.'[35] De Maistre, Maurras, Le Pen have also understood history as the sign of the prophetic fulfilment of the nation's destiny.[36] Nostradamus could thus be translated as a guide to past history, following a 'rigorous' method and combining the obscure verse with sequences of historical events. The edition by Jean Charles de Fontbrune in 1980 had a considerable media impact and revived, however tenuously, hopes of a moral and political restoration of the monarchy, a theme close to the heart of the French extreme right.[37] The final developments of prophecy may well be to be on the one hand diluted into a political movement and, on the other, focused on omen-bearing symbols like Joan of Arc. The story of Joan, fighting the invading English, became her prophetic destiny. In 1870, during the Franco-Prussian war, a number of young women tried to assume Joan's identity and to re-enact her warring postures, intending to ride horses in full plate armour, etc. The military techniques were pathetically outmoded, but the impersonation of her chivalric life granted them a minor prophetic dimension.[38]

As for individuals, Rhodri Hayward's chapter shows well that prophecies are expressed through possession, a denial of the self and the involvement of the deity or supernatural. Similarly much nationalist ideology is based on the renunciation of the self to allow a fuller participation in the whole. While the prophetic language often comes from the margins, the liminal space from which come prophets and cranks, its purpose is to be at the heart of both politics and society.[39] Seen from a 'scientific' point of view, this hegemonic propensity becomes symptomatic of collective hysteria, a problem of society or the decline of democracy. The attempt made by rationalists to diffuse the idea of prophecy as the simple manifestation of the unconscious or interiorized political factors does not hold. In any case it does not make for weaker prophecies: if anything a prophetic mission and language which are no longer the domain of the erudite but are truly integrated into the collective psyche, are precisely what the ideal of nation stands for.

While a prophecy is very important in forming imagined communities of belief and purpose, it may also break communities organized according to different principles. In times of collective crises, prophecy allowed people to express their hopes and fears about the future; it might also allow them to envision a transformation in their position as individuals and members of communities. In a sense described by Lesley Coote, the events prophesied were not an inevitable timetable, for their occurrence depended on other preconditions. These preconditions might involve the participation of those who formed the audience for the prophecy. Prophecy therefore justified vigorous action to bring about and support that change at a time when it was dangerous to question the state of society. Prophecy was not just a wish for change but a call to action. It was, in a phrase of Thomas Hobbes, 'many times the principal cause of the event foretold'.[40] Prophecies were a 'validating charter', in Keith Thomas's own more anthropological phrase, for actions that might otherwise appear unacceptably revolutionary.[41]

As a political language prophecy moved from being at the heart of western politics to being a subversive force which, because it did not participate in the common political culture, could offer unique opportunities for a complete reconstruction of the body politic. Within that political alternative the position of the prophet is never assured and leadership structures are constantly shifting out of the centre to the margins where they originated. Any political language based on prophecy implies a constant chartering of the past to understand the future. Although this historical perspective might appear to offer the ground for stability it is always a matter of conflicting interpretation and it remains for ever unstable and dynamic.

Notes

1 M. Reeves, *Joachim of Fiore and the Prophetic Future* (London, SPCK, 1976), p. 1.

2 On science fiction see A. Martin, *The Mask of the Prophet: the Extraordinary Fictions of Jules Verne* (Oxford, Clarendon Press, 1990); on earlier instances sometimes invested with prophetic meanings, E.C. Wilkie, 'Mercier's *L'An 2440*: Its Publishing History during the Author's Lifetime', *Harvard Library Bulletin*, 32 (1) (1984), 5–35.

3 T. Tinker, *Paper Prophets: a Social Critique of Accounting* (Holt, Rinehart & Winston, 1985).

4 E.H. Kantorowicz, *The King's Two Bodies: a Study in Medieval Political Theology* (Princeton and London, Princeton University Press and Oxford University Press, 1957)

5 M. de Certeau, *The Writing of History* (New York, Columbia University Press, 1988), pp. 146–205.

6 Certeau, *The Writing of History*, p. 168

7 Max Weber on the prophet: *The Sociology of Religion* (London, Methuen, 1963), pp. 46–59. In Weber the prophet is an individual bearer of charisma; it is the personal call that distinguishes him or her from the priest, who depends on sacred tradition and office. P. Mack, *Visionary Women: Ecstatic Prophecy in Seventeenth-Century England* (Berkeley, Los Angeles, London, 1992), esp. chs 5 and 10.

8 For a contemporary instance of this long tradition of rationalist reconstruction of the past see A. Cohen, 'Prophecy and Madness: Women Visionaries during the Puritan Revolution', *Journal of Psychohistory*, 11 (3) (1984), 411–30.

9 R. M'Nemar, *The Kentucky Revival or a Short History of the Late Extraordinary Outpouring of the Spirit of God in the Western States of America . . . with a brief account of the entrance and progress of what the world calls Shakerism* (1807; reprinted New York, Edwards and Jenkins, 1846), p. 31. Demonstrations of the presence of God were not dissimilar to the convulsions which agitated Jansenists in France at the cemetery of Saint-Médard. See L. Figuier, *Histoire du Merveilleux dans les Temps Modernes* (4 vols, Paris, Hachette, 1860), vol. 1, pp. 261–416.

10 D.A. Brading, *Prophecy and Myth in Mexican History*, Cambridge Latin American Miniatures 1 (Cambridge, Centre of Latin American Studies, 1984), ch. 1. J. Sala Catal and J. Vilchis Reyes, 'Apocaliptica Española y Empresa Missional en Los Primeros Franciscanos de Mexico', *Revista de Indias*, 45 (176) (1985), 421–47; on the discovery of America as a Biblical revelation see J.V. Fleming, 'Christopher Columbus as a Scriptural Exegete', *Lutheran Quarterly*, 5 (2) (1991), 187–98; P.M. Watts, 'Prophecy and Discovery: on the Spiritual Origins of Christopher Columbus's "Enterprise of the Indies"', *American Historical Review*, 90 (1) (1985), 73–102; D.J. Kagay, 'Columbus as Standardbearer and Mirror of the Spanish Reconquest', *American Neptune*, 53 (4) (1993), 254–9. On the other side of the coin, more often alluded to, see S.A. Colston, '"No Longer Will There Be a Mexico": Omens, Prophecies and the Conquest of the Aztec Empire', *American Indian Quarterly*, 9 (3) (1985), 239–58. On Bartholomé de las Casas see P. André-Vincent, *Bartholomé de las Casas: Prophète du Nouveau Monde* (Paris, Tallandier, 1980). J. Reyns, 'La Biblia de los Conquistadores y de los Vencidos', *Estudios Sociales*, 20 (70) (1987), 73–91.

11 N. Cohn, *The Pursuit of the Millennium* (London, Secker and Warburg, 1957).

12 E.P. Thompson, *Witness against the Beast: William Blake and the Moral Law* (Cambridge University Press, 1993), pp. 10–51. T.A. Hoagwood, *Prophecy and the Philosophy of the Mind: Traditions of Blake and Shelley* (University of Alabama Press, 1985); A. Lincoln, *Spiritual History: a Reading of William Blake's Vala or The Four Zoas* (Oxford, Clarendon Press, 1995).

13 H. Schwartz, *The French Prophets: the History of a Millenarian Group in Eighteenth-Century England* (Berkeley and Los Angeles, University of California Press, 1980), p. 228.

14 N. Wood, *Swift* (Brighton, The Harvester Press, 1986), pp. 6–8.

15 C. Saunders, 'The Tale of Halley's Comet: Notes on Its Prophetic Significance in South Africa', *Quarterly Bulletin of the South African Library*, 40 (3) (1986), 105–7.

16 U. Eco, *The Open Work* (London, Hutchinson Radius, 1989).

17 On Nixon see Tim Thornton's paper; on Merlin see A. Berthelot, *Les Prophésies de Merlin (cod. Bodmer* 116) (Cologny-Genève, Fondation Martin Bodmer, 1992), p. 9. The manuscript was in the hands of the Maggs Brothers, see L.A. Paton, *Les Prophécies de Merlin* (2 vols, New York & Oxford, D.C. Heath and Co., Oxford University Press, 1926–7), vol. 1, p. 9.

18 R.D. Edmunds, *The Shawnee Prophet* (Lincoln and London, University of Nebraska Press, 1983), pp. 33, 55. C.f. the prophetic movement in the Congo founded by Simon Kimbangu, with its radical offshoot of Ngunzism, which resisted colonial government and adopted the slogan of 'Africa for Africans'; and André Matswa and 'Amicalism' in French Congo, a purely political movement that became religious after his imprisonment in 1930: M.-L. Martin, *Kimbangu: An African Prophet and his Church*, translated by D.M. Moore (Oxford, Basil Blackwell, 1975); N.I. Ndiokwere, *Prophecy and Revolution: The Role of Prophets in the Independent African Churches and in Biblical Tradition* (London, SPCK, 1981), pp. 46–55.

19 On the necessity to obscure one's own historical identity to reinforce the prophetic dimensions of one's work see A.D. Chalmers, *Jonathan Swift and the Burden of the Future* (Newark, University of Delaware Press, 1995), pp. 56–7.

20 M.J. Buss, 'The Social Psychology of Prophecy' in J.A. Emerton (ed.), *Prophecy: Essays Presented to Georg Fohrer on his Sixty-Fifth Birthday, 6 September 1980* (Berlin and New York, Walter de Gruyter, 1980), pp. 1–11; T.W. Overholt, *Channels of Prophecy: The Social Dynamics of Prophetic Activity* (Minneapolis, Fortress Press, 1989).

21 J.S.P. Tatlock, *The Legendary History of Britain: Geoffrey of Monmouth's Historia Regum Britanniae and its Early Vernacular Versions* (Berkeley, University of California Press, 1950).

22 M.E. Giffin, 'Cadwalader, Arthur, and Brutus in the Wigmore Manuscript', *Speculum*, 16 (1941), 109–20, esp. p. 114.

23 Giffin, 'Cadwalader, Arthur, and Brutus', pp. 111–16; R.S. Loomis, 'Edward I, Arthurian Enthusiast', *Speculum*, 28 (1953), 114–27, esp. pp. 115–16.

24 Minot's Poems, p. 103; Shakespeare, *Henry IV*, part I.

25 T.M. Smallwood, 'The Prophecy of the Six Kings', *Speculum*, 60 (3) (1985), 571–92.

26 Smallwood, 'Six Kings', pp. 591–2, argues that the prophecy preceded the supposed plan, but does not make the leap to suggesting that the prophecy inspired the action by the rebels.

27 A. Allen, 'Yorkist Propaganda: Pedigree, Prophecy and the "British History" in the Reign of Edward IV' in C. Ross (ed.), *Patronage, Pedigree and Power in Late Medieval England* (Gloucester, Alan Sutton, 1979), pp. 171–92. C. Ross, 'Rumour, Propaganda and Popular Opinion during the Wars of the Roses' in R.A. Griffiths (ed.), *Patronage, the Crown and the Provinces in Later Medieval England* (Gloucester and New Jersey, Alan Sutton, 1981), pp.15–32.

28 *Plumpton Correspondence*, ed. T. Stapledon, Camden Society, original series, IV (London, Thomas Bowyer Nichols & Son, 1839), p. 50 (Thomas Betanson to Sir Robert Plumpton, 15 Feb. 1485–6); M. Bennett, *Lambert Simnel and the Battle of Stoke* (Gloucester and New York, Alan Sutton, 1987), p. 35.

29 A. Fox, 'Prophecies and Politics in the Reign of Henry VIII' in A. Fox and J. Guy, *Reassessing the Henrician Age: Humanism, Politics and Reform, 1500–1550* (Oxford, Blackwell, 1986), pp. 77–94.

30 S. Jansen, *Political Protest and Prophecy under Henry VIII* (Woodbridge, Suffolk, Boydell, 1991); Fox, 'Prophecies and Politics in the Reign of Henry VIII'.

31 K. Thomas, *Religion and the Decline of Magic* (Harmondsworth, Penguin, 1990), p. 397.

32 E. Kaulbach, *Imaginative Prophecy in the B-Text of Piers Plowman*, Piers Plowman Studies VIII (Cambridge, D.S. Brewer, 1993), pp. 61–7.

33 L. Festinger, H.W. Riecken, and S. Schachter, *When Prophecy Fails* (Minneapolis, University of Minnesota Press, 1956): a study of Mrs Marian Keech, who prophesied the destruction of Lake City by flood on 21 December, the information having been given to her by 'superior beings'.

34 See D. Weinstein, *Savonarola and Florence: Prophecy and Patriotism in the Renaissance* (Princeton, Princeton University Press, 1970), pp. 317–73; R. Erlanger, *Unarmed Prophet: Savonarola in Florence* (New York, McGraw-Hill, 1987); on millenarianism and prophecy after the prophet's death, see: C. Vasoli, 'Giorgio Benigno Salviati e la Tensione Profetica di fine '400', *Rinascimento*, 29 (1989), 53–78; G.C. Garfagnini, 'Giogio Benigno Salviati e Girolamo Savonarola: Note per una Lettura Delle "Propheticæ Solutionæ"', *Rinascimento*, 29 (1989), 81–123.

35 J. [sic] Mazzini, *God and the People: the Religious Creed of a Democrat, being a selection from the writings of Joseph Mazzini by Charles William Stubbs* (London, T. Fisher Unwin, 1891), p. 148. Also D. Mack Smith, *Mazzini* (New Haven, Yale University Press, 1994), pp. 192–6.

36 For a reflexive analysis of national consciousness and mission see H. Kohn, *Prophets and People: Studies in Nineteenth-Century Nationalism* (New York, The Macmillan Company, 1946), pp. 2–9, 77–104.

37 J.C. de Fontbrune, *Nostradamus, Historien et Prophète* (Monaco, Éditions du Rocher, 1980).

38 Dr L. Nass, *Le Siège de Paris et la Commune*, Essais de Pathologie Historique (Paris, Plon, 1914), pp. 60–3.

39 An example of marginal groups articulating holistic political reforms to no avail can be found in the Spencean Millenarians between 1790 and 1820. I. McCalman, *Radical Underworld: Prophets, Revolutionaries and Pornographers in London, 1795–1840* (Oxford, Clarendon Press, 1993), pp. 50–72.

40 Cited in Thomas, *Religion and the Decline of Magic*, p. 422.

41 Thomas, *Religion and the Decline of Magic*, p. 423.

Part 1

LANGUAGE OF ÉLITES, SYMBOLS OF POWER

The first part of this book is entirely devoted to prophecy from the late Middle Ages to the Reformation. This period saw the propagation of political genres of prophecies. Lesley Coote's paper and Anne McLaren's describe the prophetic language in which important political debates were encoded and discussed: in the first place, debates over the power and purpose of the monarchy in the fourteenth and fifteenth centuries, in the latter the problems of a female ruler in the sixteenth century.

Tim Thornton's paper, on the other hand, deals with local prophecies and the way in which they were used almost without interruption but with considerable variations of purpose between the sixteenth century and the modern period.

What unites all these papers is the issue of élite control of a potentially subversive culture, in the context of political societies that assumed rigid hierarchies. The language of those prophecies is also consistently about the symbols of power and their integration in the body politic. These prophecies were not therefore simply subversive, they also had potential uses for the rulers.

2

A LANGUAGE OF POWER: PROPHECY AND PUBLIC AFFAIRS IN LATER MEDIEVAL ENGLAND

L. Coote

Prophecies about public affairs in the later Middle Ages, written in Latin, English, and very rarely in French, appear chiefly in manuscript miscellanies, or as additions to older manuscripts. These texts appear to foretell future events, or provide a vision of some future state. Prophetic texts use obscure language and distinctive imagery, such as describing individuals in terms of animals, 'predictions' based on the face of a die, mathematical formulae for dates and legendary names for kings and heroes like Sextus and Brutus. They first appeared in this country in the twelfth century, the earliest being Geoffrey of Monmouth's *Prophecia Merlini*, written *c.* 1135 and incorporated into his *Historia Regum Britannie*.[1] From the middle of the thirteenth century there was a steady trickle of new texts, either written in England or imported from the Continent, which became a flood from the beginning of the fourteenth century onwards. Most new texts were created or imported in the fourteenth century. A few appeared in England in the first half of the fifteenth century, but after 1461 to the end of the century very few new texts were created or imported, although older texts were still being circulated and collected.[2] Some texts survive only in single copies, some in a few copies, but five stand out as being the most popular. These are the *Prophecia Merlini*, *The Last Kings of the English*, *The Holy Oil of St Thomas*, *Bridlington* and *Lilium regnans*.

The *Prophecia Merlini* forms part of Geoffrey of Monmouth's tale of the fall of Britain to the Saxons. The British tyrant Vortigern attempts to build a fortress on a cliff, but the walls keep falling down. Vortigern's wise men tell him that the walls will only stand if their foundations are sprinkled with the blood of a child with no father. The young man Merlin, the son of a Cornish princess and an incubus, is brought to the king. Merlin goes into a prophetic trance and tells the Britons to drain a pool they will find under the cliff. They will see two dragons in combat, one red and one white. At first the white will be triumphant, but the red will recover and defeat the white. The red dragon is the British, and the white the Saxons. At first the Saxons will be victorious, but the British will recover and defeat them in the end. There follows a series of prophecies about the future of the island kingdom; some can be fixed in Geoffrey's story, but others obviously do not refer to the *Historia*.[3] *The Last Kings of the English* is Merlin's answer to King Arthur's question about what the last kings of the English will be like. Merlin describes these kings, originally three or possibly four, to whom others were added in the course of time, in a form of animal symbolism which has become known as Galfridian, because it echoes that used by Geoffrey in the *Prophecia Merlini*.[4] Both of these texts gained a wider circulation than they might otherwise have had by virtue of their incorporation into larger works, the *Prophecia Merlini* in the *Historia Regum Britannie* and *The Last Kings of the English* in the series of chronicles known as the *Brut*. One hundred and sixty-eight copies of the English version of the latter are known to survive from the fourteenth and fifteenth centuries, a considerable number in comparison with other texts.[5]

In *The Holy Oil of St Thomas* the fugitive archbishop Becket is approached by the Virgin Mary whilst celebrating the Mass in Poitiers, and given an ampulla of holy oil with which future kings of England, specially chosen by God, will be anointed. Greatest of all will be the first king to be anointed with this oil. Whenever the king carries the eagle in which the oil has been kept in his bosom, he will not suffer defeat. Both the *Prophecia Merlini* and *The Holy Oil of St Thomas* are in Latin prose, but *The Last Kings of the English* was available to fourteenth-century readers in Latin, French and English. *The Holy Oil of St Thomas* did not exist in an English translation until the second half of the fifteenth century.[6] *Bridlington* is a long, complicated poem, mostly in Latin hexameters, which recounts conflicts of the Bull (Edward III) with the French and Scots to 1350, and then foretells the future reign of a great Cockerel (Edward the Black Prince, eldest son of Edward III), who will wear the French crown. A version was already in existence by *c.* 1340 at the Augustinian priory of Bridlington, on the coast of East Yorkshire, and this was extended around 1350, in the wake of the Black Death. John Erghome, a learned Augustinian from York, wrote a commentary in the 1360s, but this has to be viewed as a separate text. *Bridlington*, as it was known in later medieval England, was the *c.* 1350 version.[7] *Lilium Regnans* (also called by contemporaries the *Prophecia Hermerici*) is a short Latin prose text often translated as 'the Eagle, the Lily and the Son of Man'. It has three main variants; the shorter version is a précis of the more common, slightly longer one, and the expanded version is based on the common text, but is much longer. The form usually found is given below. It predicts the fall of the Lily (the king of France) and the eventual triumph of the Eagle (the Emperor) and a figure known as the 'Son of Man'.

A late medieval English writer faced at least three basic choices determining to a large extent the readership and the substance of the message. He might write in Latin, French or English, and using those languages, he might choose from a variety of different literary genres. These choices would dictate the form and style of his work, his general ordering of material, and, indeed, the type of material he might use. It is because prophecy is a discourse, not a genre, that prophetic texts appear in many different forms: Latin hexameters, lyric and alliterative poems both short and long, verse romance and prose tracts of various lengths. Because prophecy is a discourse, it has great flexibility; discourse, or language use, is not confined to the boundaries of genre.[8]

This particular type of prophecy is classifiable not by form or style, but by subject: public affairs and public policy in England, and the place of the English in Christendom and in history. In addressing this subject it projects certain ideas about kingship, and about the relationship between the king of England and his people. The nature of the discourse determines to a degree the positions which will be taken up by the writer/prophet, and the conclusions which will be reached in relation to his subject matter. This is because the discourse conditions to a large extent the nature of the connections between ideas; for example, what can stand as the cause of an effect, and what can be claimed to be the effect of a given cause. If a writer chooses to use prophetic discourse and thus assume the identity of a prophet to describe the public affairs and policy of his day, he (for they were mostly men) will also be restricted by the value judgements this discourse prescribes.[9] The assumption of a prophetic identity was influenced by factors such as patronage, social and economic position, occupation and gender; all factors outside language.[10]

The prophetic discourse of public affairs in fourteenth- and fifteenth-century England is characterized by the violence of its language, and by the way in which it treats public affairs as a series of conflicts. The object of violence is victory, resulting in the conquest, subjugation and domination of others:

The Lily, *ruling* in a noble part of the world, will stand *against* the seed of the lion and will come into the *kingdom* of the Lion and will stand in the field among the thickets of his *kingdom*. Then a son of man, carrying in his arms three wild beasts, whose *kingdom* is the *land* of the moon, *feared* throughout the entire world, will come; he will *cross* the seas *with a great army* and *enter* into the *land* of the lion lacking aid, because the beasts of his [the lion's] *kingdom* will already have *torn* his coat to *pieces*. In that year will come an eagle from eastern parts, his wings outstretched under the sun, with many of his chicks, to help the son of man. In that year *castles will be destroyed* and there will be *universal terror* in the world and in all the *regions of the lion* there will be *war* between very many *kings*. In that day there will be *rivers of blood* and the lily will *lose his crown*, with which the son of man will afterwards be *crowned*, and for four years following there will be in the world *many battles* between the followers of the faith; a great part of the world will be *destroyed*. The *head of the world* will sink to the earth. But the son of man and the eagle will *overcome* and then there will be *peace* throughout the whole world and bountiful harvests. The son of man will *take* the marvellous sign and will go over to the promised land . . . .

The Lily; the king of France. The Lion; Flanders. The Son of the Lion; the

Duke [sic] of Flanders. The Son of Man carrying *wild beasts*; the *King of England*. The Land of the Moon; *England, Wales and Ireland*. The Eagle; the *arms of the Emperor*. The Sun; *France*. The *Head of the World*; the Pope. The Marvellous Sign; the Sign of the Cross.[11]

Words in (my) italics relate to violence and authority, and demonstrate the way in which the vocabulary reflects the preoccupation of this discourse with conflict and domination. This language is totally naive in its understanding of administration and government. It is solely concerned with the fact of conquest and rule, not with how that rule is maintained. Its heroes must fight, and must fight successfully. However, the prophetic hero must not just win battles. The prophetic hero must *subjugate* peoples and lands, that is, he must win *something*. Victory alone is not enough; it must have an object. Authority over the ruled must change hands. This may be the rule over a single kingdom or region, or over a much wider area. In the text above, the *filius hominis* receives the Lily's crown. In the end, he and the eagle will overcome, and he will gain control of the *signum mirabile*, usually glossed as the Holy Cross. This introduces the element of spiritual victory and domination.

Many prophetic texts end with the hero conquering the Holy Land and freeing the Holy Places from the heathen. Often the Saracens (a corporate term for any non-Christian who cannot be classed as a Jew; no understanding of the nature of non-Christian belief is involved) will be forcibly converted to Christianity. This may also be accompanied by the forcible conversion or destruction of heretics and other schismatics. The victory is sometimes presented in a more concrete way by physical possession of the Holy Cross. The Cross was important both as a Christian symbol and as a symbol of *imperium*, or imperial rule, because of its associations with the Emperor Constantine, the originator of the Christian Roman Empire and allegedly an ancestor of the kings of England.[12] In many texts the hero is seen as the embodiment of the Christian Roman Empire. In a few cases, the hero's reward is death and burial in the Holy Land, and even elevation to the ranks of the Blessed.

The times of Sextus will endure for three times three lustres and a half
The first he will waste in wandering, towards the end he will come back
In the middle he will conquer much, turning towards the end of the second
In the remainder he will overthrow the world, he will lead the clergy back
To their original state; in the half he will renew the Holy Places
Thence, rejecting [literally: spitting out] earthly things, he will ascend, blessed,
  above the heavens.[13]

The Crusade in prophetic discourse was not solely the aim of a Christian knight, or of a king who happens to be a Christian knight. It was also associated with the Last Days. It was believed that the freeing of the Holy Places would be one of the precursors of the reign of Antichrist and the Judgement. In what Marjorie Reeves has termed 'Last World Emperor' prophecies, the emperor frees the Holy Land, converts the heathen, and then dies, handing his empire over to Christ, who then completes human history by destroying Antichrist, and ending his power.[14] In prophetic discourse this conquest, and the final sanctification of the hero, is the sign that he has God's approval, that his career of *imperium* is divinely sanctioned. This is more important than the religious act of crusading. Once again, it refers back to the nature of *imperium*, and is only one facet of the prophetic hero's career. In prophetic discourse the power conferred by successful warfare is always emphasized. This power is the aim and justification of that warfare. Prophetic discourse, therefore, is about an abstract idea of power and domination, or *imperium*, to which military victory, and the personal qualities which bring that victory, are only the means. Its subject is power relationships between kings and peoples. These relationships are defined by rise and fall, conquest and subjection; this is why prophetic discourse presents public affairs as a series of conflicts, and why it has a vocabulary which is both violent and authoritarian.

In prophetic language the emphasis is always on *moving* and *doing*. This is achieved by the use of verbs which suggest movement and action in the indicative mood, giving an impression of definiteness and purpose. We can see plainly from our text that the combination of short sentences and active verbs sets up a continual motion, leading quickly from one action to the next, punctuated with 'and' and 'then'. In other words, prophetic discourse is paratactic, using simple declarative sentences or co-ordinate main clauses, and expressing by this of a sequence of actions, perceptions or facts.[15]

Writers of prophetic texts, like Geoffrey of Monmouth, Oxford scholar and author of the *Prophecia Merlini*, did not have to write in this manner because they lacked the Latin skills needed to write in a more sophisticated way. They chose to write in this way because parataxis was also used in the writing of annals, the chronological record of events. In annalistic writing the simplicity of statements made in parataxis adds to the overall impression of 'plain truthfulness' which the writer requires, as the events he is presenting in his annal are what he perceives to have been historical truth, and he wishes the reader to share in this perception. In annals the verbs are mostly in historic tenses, but in prophetic discourse the verbs are in the future tense. The writer wishes to tell the reader that he is writing 'annals of the future', that is, he is recording future events faithfully, and that what he says is truth.

This is similar to the technique used by writers of predictions such as those in almanacs, but prophetic discourse is not ineluctably predictive. The 'future truth' recorded by prophetic writers differs from simple prediction in that the events recorded have not been immutably fixed by an outside agency like God or Fate.

They record what *should* happen, but *might* not. Prophetic discourse carries an element of responsibility. If certain conditions are not fulfilled, the hoped-for future will not happen. The timing and the favours are God's to grant, so this cannot be *fixed* truth. The writer *hopes* that it will be so. The implied condition is that others share his belief in the hero's destiny, and have the same hope as he does for the hero's, and by implication his country's, future greatness. The reader must, of course, show this by loyalty to the perceptions of king and country presented in the text. Prophetic discourse, then, does not really predict the future at all; it presents a point of view on what is happening *now*. It does this by projecting past and present events into the future, but in such a way that the reader understands that it is the present which is really being discussed. *Bridlington*, for example, features what is probably Edward III's siege of Calais in 1347, but set in the future. It would have been apparent to fourteenth-century readers that this event had already happened. *Ex eventu* prophecies, written after the event, were frequent in prophetic narratives. They helped the reader to understand contemporary events and characters to which the writer then referred. The part of *Bridlington* which actually foretold the future yet to come in the fourteenth century was very small. It consisted only of the final four short chapters, in which the glorious future reign of a hero called *gallus*, or the Cockerel, was briefly described. Because of the *ex eventu* part, we know that this must refer to a descendant of Edward III who will rule after him, in other words his eldest son Edward, the Black Prince, who was still alive in *c.* 1350, when this version of *Bridlington* was written. The writer is telling us what he thinks about Edward III and his son *in the present* and what he is *currently* hoping for.

Prophetic discourse is very vague about time, whilst appearing to be very precise. One way of dealing with time in prophetic texts is to make the events portrayed dependent upon the fulfilling of another condition, or set of conditions. Some prophetic texts do not carry references to particular times and dates at all. Others use formulae for dates and times, like the text *Mens curtor cupiunt cristi lex vera jocunda*. If we take the first letters of each word we get MCCCLVI, or 1356, the date of the battle of Poitiers. However, this might also be taken to mean 1,356 years. If this is so, the poem does not tell us exactly *when* these 1,356 years will occur.[16] The poem itself did not relate to a specific event, so it might be used in various contexts. Similarly, *ter tria lustra cum semi* is a period of forty-seven and a half years for the reign of Sextus, but we are not told when these years will occur. Thus, what appears very precise is, in fact, very flexible and open to interpretation. In *The Holy Oil of St Thomas*, the Virgin tells Becket that the first king to be anointed with the holy oil will be the great *rex futurus* who will recover his ancestors' possessions in Normandy and Aquitaine. Considering that this is the twelfth-century archbishop's future, the *rex futurus* might be anointed at any time after 1170. *Lilium Regnans* contains phrases like *illo anno, illo die* and *per quattuor annos sequentes*, which likewise give an impression of precision which is false, as the text never tells us anything precise about when these events will occur in chronological time. This use of time is one of the ways in which prophecy is a mysterious language which is also hermeneutic, that is, it asks to be interpreted. The message, for a contemporary reader, would have been obscure but stimulating interpretation. For those with a knowledge of the discourse, this interpretation would have been relatively easy.

In some prophetic texts, the people, or race, are the heroes, but such texts are relatively few and are mostly of Scots or Welsh origin. The vast majority of texts have a hero, who always, in an English context, represents the king. Some of the fifteenth-century texts of *Lilium regnans* have a 'key', which tells us 'filius hominis ferens feras rex anglie', just to make sure that the reader knows who the hero is meant to be.[17] Prophecy is not interested in giving accurate physical descriptions of heroes, like how tall they are or the colour of their hair. It is only interested in the qualities they possess which enable them to fulfil the role implied in the discourse; that is, to be successful peacekeepers at home and warriors abroad. Where heroes are presented as animals, the animals used, if not heraldic like leopards, are those which were noted for their nobility, ferocity and strength, like lions, eagles, bulls, cockerels and boars. In the prophetic texts of later medieval England it is not necessary for the hero, or his people, to be morally good. The ruler is justified and sanctified by virtue of his official, and not his private, *persona*. Thus, the prophecies present a hero who is both king and emperor, Christ-like and timeless in his kingly state. In most prophecies of English origin, and in those imported into England from the Continent (as opposed to those originating in Scotland, for example), the hero is all-important. He represents both his people and his kingdom. The people appear only in order to acclaim him; his right to rule is given by God, because God wishes to bestow it upon him. The human ruler is lifted and transformed into an almost divine figure, reminiscent of Carolingian and Ottonian ideas of imperial rule.[18] These prophetic texts are not interested in the hero's humanity. Nor is prophecy interested in the personal relationships of the people it portrays. Rulers do not display personal qualities or feelings as they do in chivalric discourse, where, for example, they embrace and kiss their wives and children; they are judged solely on the basis of how they perform their office.[19] Although the composition, collection and circulation of prophetic texts may be seen as a response to the public affairs and policies of a given time, the figure of the hero as represented in these texts does not reflect the *actual* situation or the actual attributes and abilities of the current ruler. In the 1450s Henry VI was still being described in prophetic texts as the Boar of Windsor who would 'whet his tethe upon ye yates of Paris', wear three crowns and 'conquer more [th]an euer did any of his blode', although at this time King Henry had lost all of the English conquests in France, was unable to keep the peace in his own realm of England, and was periodically incapacitated by a form of mental illness.[20]

In almost all texts, kingship is defined in terms of *imperium*, and in many texts the king of England becomes Holy Roman Emperor and ruler of the world. He receives his power directly from God, by whom he is specially chosen and awarded sacred status. Although the English people are seldom mentioned in the texts, which concentrate on the activities of the ruler, they are present in that the king represents the people. The God-given power to conquer and rule is theirs as well as his. Theirs also is the special position in Christendom and in history implied by his crusade, his recovery of the Holy Land and its relics, and his renewal of the Faith. Neither the English nor their rulers have earned this privileged status; it is a gift conferred on them by God simply because they are English, and because God wishes to prefer the English and *their* king above all other nations and their kings. The English and their rulers have been 'chosen', just like Israel and her kings in the Old Testament. Their conflictual relationship with other nations helps the English to define who they are, by defining who they are not. This is also done by allusion to the legendary past. Texts allude to the British past of Merlin, Cadwalladr and Arthur, and use names like Albania for Scotland, named after the second son of Brutus, legendary founder of Britain in the *Brut*.[21] They also use names from the imperial Carolingian past, like Gallia (France) and Allemania (the German states), the early medieval names for the western and eastern halves of Charlemagne's empire. The kings of England, as well as the kings of France, were descendants of Charlemagne, and both could therefore lay claim to his imperial, crusading heritage.

Most prophetic texts are anonymous in the sense that the actual writers are unknown. This is not necessarily an indication that the real author wishes to 'hide'.[22] Anonymity, for whatever reason, is quite common in medieval texts. Mistaken attribution is not unknown either. Attribution seems to be important to the writer and to his readership. There is no set pattern to these attributions, and it is often unclear whether they have been made by the writer or by the copier. The same text may be attributed to different 'prophets', or be attributed in one manuscript and not in another. Prophetic texts are attributed to saints and holy men like Becket and Richard Scrope (the archbishop of York executed on the orders of Henry IV in 1405), scholars like Joachim of Fiore, legendary figures like Merlin, biblical figures like Ezekiel and King David, and learned figures of the classical past like Cicero. Prophecies were also revealed and inspired through dreams or visions. The writer of *Bridlington* had a revelation in the course of a fever-induced delirium. This highlighted the fact that the text was a revelation from God, delivered to a chosen and deserving individual. This often took place in circumstances which highlight their receptivity, such as a dream, trance, or fever during the course of which the faculties of human reason are suspended. Thus God conferred a particular privilege on these people; they shared in the knowledge of his will in a way in which others did not. These were trustworthy and authoritative witnesses, and their names made the texts more believable in the eyes of the medieval reader. The privilege conferred on the original recipients of the prophetic message was then shared with those to whom the knowledge was passed. Thus the medieval writer of prophetic discourse, and his readership, shared the privilege of knowing God's will for their king and country.

Who were these privileged people? Most of the manuscripts which contain this type of text appear to have been produced by a group of hands in a professional, or semi-professional (which at this date usually means monastic) environment. As books passed in and out of religious houses by various means such as loans, donations and bequests, these manuscripts may not have remained in their original environment. A great majority of the known owners, however, were clergy. Most fourteenth-century manuscripts have a monastic provenance, but this is less true in the fifteenth century. Then the proportion of secular clergy and lay owners increases, although the majority of manuscripts are still of monastic origin. Besides monastic houses, owners included vicars like John Benet, vicar of Harlingdon, academics like John Herryson, fellow of Gonville Hall in Cambridge, laymen like London antiquarian John Shirley and Oxford burgess and university landlord Nicholas Bishop, merchants like London mercer Roger Thorney and the Wigston family, merchants of the Staple in Leicester, administrators like the clerk who collected material relating to Jack Cade's rebellion of 1450 in a small roll, and the anonymous fifteenth-century Exchequer clerk who added prophetic texts to his little reference book of statutes.[23]

Others who knew prophetic texts include the poets Laurence Minot, William Langland, John Gower, and Thomas Hoccleve, the chroniclers Thomas Walsingham, Adam of Usk, Pierre Langtoft, the anonymous writers of the *Eulogium Historiarum* and the *Gesta Edwardi*, and Andrew Horn, the London fishmonger, who died in 1328. That such prophecies, and their associated ideas, were not the preserve of the orthodox is shown by the references to them in the apocalyptic *The Last Age of the Church*, a heterodox tract produced at some time in the late fourteenth or early fifteenth century, contained in a manuscript with other 'Lollard' documents.[24] The manuscripts have no definite aristocratic or royal ownership until the later fifteenth century. The Percies were the only aristocratic family to have possible connections with a manuscript of these texts, and Richard III was the first king known to have owned, and personally looked at, a book containing an independent prophetic text. Henry VII also owned a manuscript containing some political prophecies.[25] We must add to this the audiences of the *Historia Regum Britannie*, which appears to show a similar pattern of circulation, and the *Brut*, which would have had a greater lay audience, by virtue of its use of the English language.[26]

What most of these people have in common is that they are members of what might best be described as the governing and administrative classes. They were literate, articulate and politically aware. They were neither aristocrats nor peasants, although they aspired to the lifestyle and interests of the former rather than the latter. They included, chiefly, those who had a growing interest in the conduct of England's public affairs and policies, not least because they were increasingly being asked to pay for them. All of them had received, in differing degrees, an education in English, many of them in Latin. Although prophetic texts occur in English, French and Latin in later medieval England, the majority, including all but one of the most popular ones, were only available in Latin until the second half of the fifteenth century. However, it would be unwise to dismiss the circulation of prophecies in the vernacular. As well as the prophetic content of the *Brut*, there is evidence that some prophetic texts were available in English as early as the reign of King John, and vernacular prophecies were produced throughout the later Middle Ages in England.[27]

Although the readership for these texts consisted of people who would have possessed a degree of power locally, by virtue of their social standing, education and financial circumstances, none of them possessed any actual power over the events and policies described in the prophetic texts they owned. Nor would most, if any, of them have taken part in such events. They could not be the king's councillors or be his companions-in-arms, as this required high birth or royal favour. Prophetic kings have no Council, no aristocracy, no bureaucracy. The king's person is brought close for those who did not otherwise have personal access to him. Prophecy gave these people a voice and an involvement at the centre of contemporary public affairs.[28] It was, therefore, a language of power for the unempowered in later medieval England. This power could be possessed by education, making those who were thus empowered a self-proclaimed, privileged élite. Power was conveyed by knowledge to those who understood its mysterious, hermeneutic language. By this means they could express their own ideas about what was, and should be, happening in contemporary public affairs. Prophecies were a serious activity, which represented the response of a highly articulate group within the English political nation to the public events and policies of their day. It constituted a form of political commentary which was an important part of English political consciousness.

Notes

1 For a modern edition see N. Wright (ed.), *The Historia Regum Britannie of Geoffrey of Monmouth I: Bern Burgerbibliotek MS 568* (Cambridge, D.S. Brewer, 1985), pp. 74–84. The *Prophecia Merlini* is separately dedicated to Alexander, bishop of Lincoln, and was completed and in circulation before the rest of the *Historia*, *c.* 1135. See *Historia Regum Britannie I*, p. x. It had an independent circulation in later medieval England, often appearing without the *Historia Regum Britannie*.

2 More actual manuscripts exist for this period than earlier, but this may be simply due to the production, and survival, of more manuscripts in general from the later period. Notable are some 'new' texts in English after 1461, both referring to events in and around 1483, but these are highly derivative. They appear to belong to the same tradition as that mentioned by Tim Thornton later in this volume, using similar sources, vocabulary and formulae. I have so far located forty-five separate

texts (excluding variants) for the period before 1461, of which no less than thirty-five belong to the first half of the century. This is a significantly higher proportion of texts from the earlier fifteenth century. Over half of all the surviving known texts overall, however, are of fourteenth-century origin.

3 See also A. G. Rigg, *A History of Anglo-Latin Literature, 1066–1422* (Cambridge University Press, 1992), pp. 41–7.

4 T.M. Smallwood, 'The Prophecy of the Six Kings', *Speculum*, 60 (3) (1985), 571–92, maintains that the prophecy was written originally during the final year of the reign of Edward II, although it may have been written shortly after his deposition. The text became an integral part of the *Brut* chronicle which ended with an account of the battle of Halidon Hill in 1333. See *The Brut or the Chronicles of England*, ed. F.W.D. Brie, Early English Text Society, Original Series, nos. 131, 136 (2 vols, London, Kegan Paul, Trench, Trübner and co., 1906–8), vol. I.

5 E.D. Kennedy, 'Chronicles and Other Historical Writing' in J.B. Severs and A.E. Hartung (eds), *A Manual of Writings in Middle English 1050–1500* (9 vols, New Haven, Conn., Connecticut Academy of Arts and Sciences, 1967–93), vol. 8 (1989), item no. 10, pp. 2629–37. MSS listed pp. 2818b–21a. For the *Historia Regum Britannie* see J. Crick, *The Historia Regum Britannie of Geoffrey of Monmouth III: A Summary Catalogue of the Manuscripts* (Cambridge, D.S. Brewer, 1989).

6 See T. Sandquist, 'The Holy Oil of St. Thomas of Canterbury' in T.A. Sandquist and M.R. Powicke (eds), *Essays in Medieval History presented to Bertie D. Wilkinson* (University of Toronto Press, 1969), pp. 330–44. This text is also mentioned in J.R.S. Phillips, 'Edward II and the Prophets' in W.M. Ormrod (ed.), *England in the Fourteenth Century: Proceedings of the 1985 Harlaxton Symposium* (Woodbridge, Boydell Press, 1986), pp. 189–201. The main question addressed by Sandquist is that of the connection of the text with the deposition of Richard II in 1399 and its possible invention by the Lancastrians, a link which he convincingly refutes. He uses late examples, however. Phillips compares the earliest manifestation of the text with others of the same period, the reign of Edward II, taking a valuable look at the ideas contained in the texts.

7 The scholarly works on *Bridlington* are often conflicting. The earliest major work is by Sister H.M. Peck, 'The Prophecy of John of Bridlington' (unpublished Ph.D. thesis, University of Chicago, 1930); more recently three works by M. Curley are important: 'The Cloak of Anonymity and the Prophecy of John of *Bridlington*', *Modern Philology*, 77 (1980), 361–9; 'Fifteenth-Century Glosses on the Prophecy of John of Bridlington: A Text, its Meaning and Purpose', *Medieval Studies*, 46 (1984), 321–9; and 'Versus Prophecialis: *Prophecia Johannis Bridlingtoniensis*, an edition' (unpublished Ph.D. thesis, University of Chicago, 1973), which is the only modern edition. Still the most accessible edition is T. Wright, *Political Poems and Songs relating to English History*, Rolls Series, 14 (2 vols, London, Longman, 1859–61), vol. 1, pp. 123–215. This includes John Erghome's commentary. This commentary obviously does not wholly refer to the text with which it is printed in Wright's edition, and this incongruence is taken up in A.G. Rigg, 'John of *Bridlington*'s Prophecy: A New Look', *Speculum*, 63 (1988), 596–613. Rigg postulates a date of *c.* 1350 for the printed version, and denies the theory of Curley and Peck that Erghome wrote both text and commentary. There is a summary in Rigg, *Anglo-Latin Literature*, pp. 260–8. For the earlier verses, which terminate just before Edward III's Scots campaign which climaxed at Halidon Hill, see 'Gesta Edwardi de Carnarvan, Auctorie Canonico Bridlingtoniensi, cum Continuatione ad AD 1377', *Chronicles of the Reigns of Edward I and II*, ed. W. Stubbs, Rolls Series, 76 (2 vols., London, Longman, 1882–3), vol. 2, pp. 25–131, at p. 46.

These annals were written in the first half of the fourteenth century, probably early in the reign of Edward III, by a canon of Bridlington priory.

8 This can be seen by the diversity of situations, over seven centuries, illustrated in this volume.

9 J. Barrell, *Poetry, Language and Politics* (Manchester University Press, 1988), p. 8.

10 D. Macdonell, *Theories of Discourse: an introduction* (Oxford, Blackwell, 1986); R. Hodge and G. Kress, *Language as Ideology* (London and New York, Routledge and Kegan Paul, 1979; 2nd edition, 1993).

11 Lilium *regnans* in nobile parte mundi manebit *contra* semen leonis et veniet in *terram* leonis et *stabit* in agro inter spinas *regnum* sui. Tunc veniet filius hominis ferens tres feras in brachiis suis cuius *regnum* est *terra* lune *timendus* per universum mundum cum *magno exercitu pertinebit* aquas et *ingredietur terram* leonis carentis *auxilio* quia bestie *regni sui* iam pellem eius *dilaceraverunt.* Illo anno veniet aquila parte orientali alis extensis sub sole cum multitudine pullorum suorum in adiutorum filii hominis. Illo anno *destruentur castra* et erit *terror universalis* in mundo et in quadam *parte leonis* erit *bellum* inter plures reges. Illo die erit *sanguinis diluvium* et liliam *perdit coronam* suam cum qua postmodum *coronabitur* filius hominis et per iiij^{or} annos sequentes fierit in mundo *proelia multa* inter fidem sectantes maior pars mundi *destruetur. Caput mundi* erit ad terram declinatum. Sed filius hominis et aquila *prevalebunt* et tunc erit *pax* in toto orbeterrarum et copia fructuum. Filius hominis *capiet* signum mirabile et transibit ad terram promissionis . . . .

Lilium rex francie. leo flandria. filius leonis dux [sic] flandrie. filius hominis ferens feras rex anglie. Terra lune Anglia Wallia hibernia. Aquila imperatoris arma. Sol francia. Caput mundi papa. Signum mirabile signum crucis.

Trinity College, Cambridge, MS R.3.21, f. 243r. Produced at the London workshop associated with John Shirley, in the reign of Edward IV (after Shirley's death).

12 In the fourteenth-century alliterative poem *Morte Arthure*, King Arthur speaks of:

> Seyn Constantyne, our kynsmane . . .
>
> Þat ayere was of Ynglande and Emperour of Rome,
>
> He Þat conquerid Þe crosse Þe craftez of armes
>
> That Criste was on crucifiede, Þat Kyng es of Heaven.

Arthur thus concludes that the Emperor of Rome should pay tribute to him, not ask him to pay it to the Emperor: *The Alliterative Morte Arthure: A Critical Edition*, ed. V. Krishna (New York, Franklin, 1976), p. 48, ll. 282–5.

13

> Ter tria lustra tenent cum semi tempora sexti
>
> En vagus in primo perdet, sub fine resumet
>
> Multa capit medio volutans sub fine secundi
>
> Orbem subvertet reliquo clerumque reducet
>
> Ad statum primum semi renovat loca sancta
>
> Hinc terrena spuens sanctus super ethera scandit

Gonville and Caius College, Cambridge, MS 249/277, f. 182rb. This manuscript was owned, and partly written, by John Herryson, doctor of the college and vicar of Ashwell, Hertfordshire from 1460-73. This manuscript was compiled at various dates between 1464 and 1471, that is, during the first 'reign' of Edward IV (1461–9; then 1471–83). For references see Crick, *Historia Regum Britannie III*, pp. 45–9, and P.R. Robinson, *Catalogue of Dated and Datable Manuscripts c. 737–1600 in Cambridge*

Libraries (Cambridge, D.S. Brewer, 1988), vol 1, p. 75 a, b; and for Herryson, A.B. Emden, *A Biographical Register of the University of Cambridge to 1500* (Cambridge University Press, 1963), p. 290. *Ter tria lustra* first appeared in England early in the reign of Edward III, and, although not one of the five most common prophetic texts, it is frequently found in English manuscripts of the later fourteenth and fifteenth centuries.

14 M. Reeves, *The Influence of Prophecy in the Later Middle Ages: A Study in Joachimism* (Oxford, Clarendon Press, 1969).

15 P. Field, *Romance and Chronicle* (London, Barrie and Jenkins, 1971), p. 35.

16 A *lustrum* is a period of five years, so we have a sum of 3×15, plus $2\frac{1}{2}$.

17 See above for the text. The hero is always a king, not a queen. Prophecies in the English language always refer to males at this period, and where Latin ones are translated, the third person singular is rendered as 'he'. Female characters do occur on a very few occasions in prophetic texts of the time, notably in *Bridlington* and the *Prophecia Merlini*. In the first, the female exists to tempt and threaten the hero (the Bull) with destruction, and later medieval commentators were not particularly interested in the female characters in the *Prophecia Merlini*; they preferred to speculate on the identity of the Boar of Windsor and the great hero Sextus. Women could, however, *be* prophets, such as Bridget of Sweden. The relationship between gender and prophecy can also be seen in the articles by Anne McLaren, Gwilym Games, Tim Thornton and Rhodri Hayward later in this volume.

18 For a seminal introduction to this see E. H. Kantorowicz, *The King's Two Bodies: A Study in Medieval Political Theology* (New Jersey, Princeton University Press, 1957), and the same author's *Laudes Regiae: A Study in Liturgical Acclamations and Mediaeval Ruler Worship* (Berkeley and Los Angeles, University of California Press, 1946; reprinted New York, Kraus, 1974).

19 Good examples of chivalric discourse written in a fourteenth-century English milieu are *The Life of the Black Prince by the Herald of Sir John Chandos*, ed. and trans. M.K. Pope and E.C. Lodge (Oxford, Clarendon Press, 1910), and Sir Thomas Gray, *Scalacronica*, trans. H. Maxwell (Glasgow, T. Maclehose, 1907).

20 From 'The Prophecy of Baltasar Cador', Bodleian Library, Oxford, MS Hatton 56, f. 7 rv.

21 For the legendary foundation of Britain see F.W.D. Brie, *The Brut*, vol. 1, pp. 1–12. For example, Oxford, MS Hatton 56, f. 9 v:

> Þan shall he take his cours ageyn
>
> Ouer ye se into Britayn . . .
>
> Than to Albyon he shall turne & fle . . .

22 Although this may be true in the case of the *c.* 1350 version of *Bridlington*, in which the writer appears to blame the reversal of English fortunes in the war with France on the moral failings of Edward III.

23 The manuscripts are: Trinity College, Dublin, MS 516 (Benet); Gonville and Caius College, Cambridge, MS 249/277 (Herryson); Bodleian Library, Oxford, MS Ashmole 59 (Shirley); Cambridge University Library, MS Dd.XIV.2 (Bishop); Trinity College, Cambridge, MS R 3 21 (Thorney); Society of Antiquaries, London, MS 101 (Wigston); British Library, MS Cotton Rolls ii.23 (Cade); British Library, Additional MS 20,059 (Exchequer).

24 For the *Gesta Edwardi* see n. 6. Vol. I of the same edition contains Horn's *Annales Londinienses*; for Minot see *The Poems of Lawrence Minot 1333–1352*, ed. T.B. James and J. Simons (Exeter University

Press, 1989). *Eulogium Historiarum sive Temporis*, ed. F.S. Haydon, Rolls Series, 9 (3 vols, London, Longman, 1858–65); *The Chronicle of the Reigns of Henry II and Richard I AD 1169–1192 known commonly under the name of Benedict of Peterborough*, ed. W. Stubbs, Rolls Series, 49 (2 vols, London, Longman, 1867); Pierre de Langtoft, *Chronicle*, ed. T. Wright, Rolls Series, 47 (2 vols, London, Longman, 1866–88); *Chronicon Adae de Usk AD 1377–1421*, ed. E.M. Thompson (London, H. Frowde, 1904); Thomas Walsingham, *Historia Anglicana*, ed. H.T. Riley, Rolls Series, 28i (2 vols, London, Longman, 1863–4); *The Major Latin Works of John Gower*, ed. and trans. E.W. Stockton (Seattle, University of Washington Press, 1962), for the *Tripartite Chronicle*. Hoccleve refers to Bridget of Sweden in his *Regement of Princes*, ed. F.J. Furnivall, Early English Text Society, extra series, 72 (London, Kegan Paul, Trench, & Trübner, 1897). *Piers Plowman (C Text)*, ed. D. Pearsall (London, Edward Arnold, 1978), is a good edition of Langland. *The Last Age of the Church* is contained in Trinity College, Dublin, MS 244, item 24; for a printed version see *The Last Age of the Church*, ed. J.H. Todd (Dublin University Press, 1840).

25 Manuscripts are British Library, MS Cotton Vespasian E VII (Percies); Saltykov-Schedrin State Public Library, Leningrad, MS Lat. F.IV.76 (Richard III), and British Library, MS Arundel 66 (Henry VII). Crick, *Historia Regum Britannie III*, pp. 129–30, is, as far as I am aware, the only English catalogue reference to the Leningrad manuscript, which bears (at f. 1r.) the autograph of Richard III.

26 Julia Crick notes that the largest group of owners were monastic (as might be expected), with private ownership emerging strongly in the early fourteenth century. These were mostly clergy, either secular or regular: J. Crick, *The Historia Regum Britannie of Geoffrey of Monmouth IV: Dissemination and Reception in the Later Middle Ages* (Cambridge, D. S. Brewer, 1991), pp. 215–16. Prophetic texts in vernacular works may be supposed to have had a wider appeal among the laity, however. For the manuscripts of the *Brut* see E.D. Kennedy, 'Chronicles and Other Historical Writing', item no. 10, pp. 2629–37, 2818b–21a.

27 *Benedict of Peterborough*, vol. II, p. 139, and R. Taylor, *The Political Prophecy in England* (New York, University of Columbia Press, 1911), pp. 21–2. Other vernacular prophecies passed into the local tradition featured by Tim Thornton elsewhere in this volume. The *Prophecia aquile*, or *Prophecy of the Eagle*, is the vernacular text mentioned by Benedict. Writing of the offensive against the Welsh of 1210, Ralph of Coggeshall noted that John was identified at that time with the Sextus of the *Prophecia Merlini: Ralph of Coggeshall: Chronicon Anglicanum*, ed. J. Stevenson, Rolls Series, 66 (London, Longman, 1875), p. 106.

28 It is interesting to compare this with what Anne McLaren says about the use of prophecy to create an advisory élite for Elizabeth I. In both cases direct access to the monarch is created through education.

3

PROPHECY AND PROVIDENTIALISM
IN THE REIGN OF ELIZABETH I

A.N. McLaren

As soon as it became apparent that Elizabeth Tudor would succeed Mary I as queen of England Sir Nicholas Throckmorton drew up a list of appointments he proposed she should make to fill important offices of state. At the same time he thoughtfully provided a speech she might use for her first interview with Mary's Privy Councillors. Because of the pressure of time he felt he could do no more, apologizing that 'I do at this present forbear to nominate meet persons for many other places and charges, as well because the time serveth not as also because new occasions may cause new advice, and as places shall be void and require ministers I will be ready to do as I have done.'[1] J.E. Neale finds this presumption baffling. 'We must leave it to Throckmorton's biographer', he concludes, 'to expatiate on the intimacy that must have existed between him and Elizabeth to account for his assumption that she would welcome his interference; that she would, for example, defer choosing her Privy Councillors until she received his further advice.'[2]

I do not think we need to await Throckmorton's biography, significant though that work would be. Instead I think we should see Throckmorton as engaging in a particular kind of 'political prophecy' that emerged in England with the accession of Elizabeth, a function of the reintroduction of Protestantism and contemporary beliefs concerning the dangers and inadequacy of female rule.[3] Lesley Coote argues persuasively that political prophecy as a discourse of public affairs commenting on the relationship between the king of England and his people and the nature of his kingship achieved new prominence in the first half of the fourteenth century. I would argue that it changed form in the mid-sixteenth century when, with Mary I's accession, Englishmen began to reflect on the nature of queenship, and more specifically when Elizabeth's accession promoted a providential mode of political prophecy. Especially given England's apostasy under one queen (Mary I), reading Elizabeth as the chosen of God – Deborah to the English Israelites – proved to be the most effective means of securing the political nation's allegiance to her rule.[4] As a consequence it was widely used as a strategy of legitimation, by speakers ranging from John Knox to Elizabeth herself. It also informed other kinds of utterances, like Throckmorton's.

Yet, as Coote also points out, the discourse of political prophecy is about power. Through its use individuals and groups compete with one another to establish their own interpretation of people and events as congruent with the meaning of the prophecies. Reading Elizabeth as Deborah and her governance as providentially ordained gave rise to peculiar tensions during Elizabeth's reign because of the linkage between prophecy and God's expressed will. If it constituted a powerful means of legitimating female rule in a society which defined women as spiritually deficient and lacking the capacity for political virtue, it simultaneously enhanced the political weight of those who could claim to be 'elders' or 'prophets', hence able to guide the queen and serve, in effect, as (male) interpreters of God's will in the body politic.[5] Political prophecy in Elizabeth's reign both inaugurated and reflected a continuing debate over the character of monarchical authority in 'Israel', a debate which concerned the crown's imperial supremacy as much as it did forms of ecclesiastical organization, and which featured as a continuing subtext Elizabeth's claims, as a female ruler, to monarchical prerogative.[6]

This context helps explain Throckmorton's 'presumption' in proffering his 'Advice' to the new queen. His utterance – referring to his willingness to nominate yet more 'ministers' for the 'many other places and charges' mentioned in his first schedule – also points to a conflation of the roles of 'counsellor' and 'minister' in the domain of a providentially ordained female ruler which proved to be profoundly significant during Elizabeth's reign. This chapter will consider some of the implications of this conflation for the political culture which developed during Elizabeth's reign and which provides the context for John Stubb's prophetic pronouncement of 1579, *The Discoverie of a Gaping Gulf, Whereinto England is like to be Swallowed by an other French mariage*, . . .

Throckmorton was not alone in offering advice to the new queen about how to rule as 'Deborah'. John Knox also wrote to her in the early months of her reign to clarify the position he had announced, as a prophet, in his *First Blast of the Trumpet against the Monstrous Regiment of Women*.[7] Perplexed by Elizabeth's hostile reaction to his work he wrote to explain that his strictures against female rule did not include her regiment.[8] His trumpet call was intended to awaken all men to the requisites of a godly life in this world; incidentally, in the circumstances of Mary Tudor's and Mary Stuart's ungodly regimes, this had entailed pointing out that female rule was, by God's express commands, disallowed. As he hastened to assure Elizabeth, however, the prohibition was not absolute. It was overridden when God manifestly intervened in human affairs to establish a woman in authority, as he had done in England in 1558:

And as concerning your regiment, how could I, or can I, envy that which most I have thirsted, and of the which . . . I render thanks unfeignedly to God? That is, it hath pleased Him of his eternal goodness to exalt your head (who sometimes was in danger), to the manifestation of his glory, and extirpation of idolatry?[9]

However, such legitimation was contingent. Her rule would only be continuously secure if she forswore the pomp of a worldly king to rule as 'Deborah' – a judge in Israel at a time when there were no kings. Significantly he suggests her adoption of this stance will enable him (and by implication other godly ministers and 'prophets') actively to endorse her regime, and hence maintain their flocks in due obedience:

> If . . . in God's presence ye humble yourself, as in my heart I glorify God for that rest granted to his afflicted flock within England, under you, a weak instrument, so will I with tongue and pen justify your authority and regiment, as the Holy Ghost hath justified the same in Deborah, that blessed mother in Israel. But if, these premises (as God forbid) neglected, ye shall begin to brag of your birth, and to build your authority upon your own law, flatter you who so list, your felicity shall be short. Interpret my rude words in the best part, as written by him who is no enemy to your Grace.[10]

Was this equally the interpretation of 'Deborah' which underpinned the pageant series presented by the City of London the day before Elizabeth's coronation? On that occasion too Elizabeth received advice from her loyal subjects, 'interpreted' in print in a pamphlet written by schoolmaster and author Richard Mulcaster. In the pageant series' climax Elizabeth encountered a figure representing simultaneously Deborah and Elizabeth, 'apparelled in parliament robes, with a sceptre in her hand'.[11] Flanking this figure were representatives of the three estates – two nobles, two clergymen, two commoners. This device adjured Elizabeth to follow the example of Deborah the prophetess, 'judge and restorer of Israel'. Interestingly, in his written account of the pageant Mulcaster glossed 'judgeship' as the queen's receptivity to counsel provided by such ministers, in the forum of parliament. The device revealed, he wrote, 'that it behooveth both men and women so ruling [i.e. providentially] to use advice of good counsel'.[12]

Closer to the court, John Hales, member of the think-tank which flourished during Somerset's regime, Marian exile and, under Elizabeth, Clerk of the Hanaper, proffered a similar interpretation of the divine will.[13] His reading of the national past and future under female rule shows signal affinities with John Knox's views and those of John Ponet in his *Short Treatise of Politic Power*. In *An Oration of John Hales to the Queen's Majesty, and delivered to her majesty by a certain Noble man, at her first entrance to her reign* (later included by John Foxe in his own prophetic utterance, the *Actes and Monuments*), Hales identified Elizabeth's accession as providentially ordained, a triumphant manifestation of God's omnipotence which makes England's deliverance 'far to exceed the deliverance of the children of Israel out of Egypt.'[14] Elizabeth is Deborah: 'it hath pleased [God's] divine providence to constitute your Highness to be our Deborah, to be the governess and head of the body of this realm.'

Hales also argued the new dispensation signalled a complete break with the past. Mary's reign, tyrannical because ungodly, ceased to have any standing as English history once God intervened in English affairs, '[f]or he hath not only dispatched the realm of the chief personages and head of these tyrants, but also as it were declareth, that he minded not that either they or their doings should continue.'[15] He reinforced his argument by showing how God worked both directly and through English customs and institutions to disallow the legitimacy of Mary's reign. Mary herself – 'this unnatural woman; (no, no woman, but a monster, and the devil of hell covered with the shape of a woman . . .)' – had betrayed the realm of England, as a woman and as a queen; a betrayal which culminated in the attempt to 'bring our country into the Spaniards' dominion.'[16] As a sign of his providence, however, God ensured that Mary's proceedings were not only ungodly but also contrary to English law. As a result there could be 'no disputation' that all the enactments of the reign 'were and be of none effect, force, or authority'.

Hales claimed Mary's first parliament was invalid because she allowed no 'Christian men or true Englishmen' to be elected, 'wherefore the Parliament was no Parliament, but may justly be called a conspiracy of tyrants and traitors'. By this means she prepared to have her way over her choice of Philip of Spain for a husband; the first step in the Spanish conquest. The parliament then summoned in their joint names was 'equally void and of none authority', for in the summons to this parliament Mary struck at the very heart of the imperial crown by omitting the title of supreme head of the Church of England. In language that suggests how Englishmen reworked the organic metaphor of the body politic to define their relationship to the realm and to salvation in the context of female rule, Hales argued the writs of that parliament 'cannot . . . bring forth good and sure fruit', no more than 'a woman can bring forth [a] child without a man'.[17]

Hales then demonized adherents of the legitimist position on the issue of the language of the parliamentary summons, in a move very characteristic of prophetic utterance of this period. In this case (as in many others) the status of chief demon was claimed for Mary's chancellor, Stephen Gardiner. 'That subtle serpent Gardiner' attempted to justify the omission of the words 'supreme head of the Church of England', and to legalize it in the form of statute law, by arguing that the style was in effect the ruler's personal prerogative, hence that its use was 'in the[ir] free choice, liberty, and pleasure'. For Hales – ironically in view of the controversy unleashed with Elizabeth's accession as to whether a queen, even a godly one, could be head of the Church – Gardiner's argument revealed the depravity of this unholy triumvirate. With his rebuttal he entered terrain mapped out in Ponet's *Short Treatise*, asserting the equality of all men as spiritual beings and hence the precedence of the 'common wealth' over the king:[18]

For albeit every person may by law renounce his own private right, yet may he not renounce his right in that which toucheth the common wealth . . . And this title and style more touched the common wealth, and realm of England, than the King. For . . . it was ordained for the conservation of the liberty of the whole realm, and to exclude the usurped authority of the Bishop of Rome. And therefore no king nor queen alone could renounce such title . . . .[19]

Finally, Hales turned to address Elizabeth, to inform her of the terms upon which she has been called to rule, and the means by which she may remain in authority. Like Knox, he told Elizabeth that 'it is requisite above all things, as well for [God's] glory and honour, as for your discharge, quietness and safety' that her reign should lead to a thorough reformation to preserve Protestantism and redeem the realm. But this must be real reformation, the sort inspired by God and carried out by his particular servants, not the 'piecing and patching, cobbling and botching . . . used in time past, whilst your most noble father and brother reigned'.[20] This restoration of the body politic in and to Christ was the only means by which her rule could be fully legitimated, to the extent that she herself would be redeemed from the deficiencies of her gender. In his peroration Hales prophesied what Elizabeth may become, as queen, once that restoration was effected:

All men shall confess that you are not only for proximity of blood preferred, but rather of God specially sent and ordained. And as the Queen of Sheba came from far off to see the glory of King Solomon, a woman to a man: even so shall the princes of our times come, men to a woman, and kings marvel at the virtue of Queen Elizabeth.[21]

The figure of the prophet, then, became a protean one in Elizabeth's reign. Later in this volume, Gwilym Games argues that in England and New England respected ministers could don the mantle of Old Testament prophets as effectively as religious radicals. His argument contains a necessary corrective to the view too commonly held, especially among historians of sixteenth- and seventeenth-century England, that prophecy was necessarily and inevitably the discourse of opposition and radical dissent. It also points to the affinity of prophecy and office which in important ways defined the political culture of the early years of Elizabeth's reign, when godly 'ministers' saw themselves as called to guide and direct a female ruler, whether from the pulpit or in the council chamber.[22] The conflation of the figures of prophet and councillor inaugurated with her reign can be seen in a later work by John Hales, *A Declaration of the Succession of the Crown Imperial of England*. Written in 1563 specifically to repudiate Mary Stuart's claims to the English throne, its presumption earned him Elizabeth's great displeasure as well as a spell in the Tower. Yet it was written with the full approval of at least William Cecil and Sir Nicholas Bacon among Elizabeth's Privy Councillors (if not actually at their instigation), and apparently with Bacon's active involvement.[23] In it Hales claimed the right to pronounce freely on this subject in the language of providential election; perhaps in terms that included Elizabeth's more reticent 'official' councillors as among the elect. Or did he align himself with the godly in 'Israel' – the nation at large? It is, he says, a 'great and weighty' matter he has in hand, one which 'concerneth the whole realm universally, and every one of us particularly'. He speaks as one 'chosen' to determine and enact the public good, a status ambiguously pointing in the direction of God and queen – or God and commonwealth: 'we few [are] chosen of an infinite multitude to treat and do these things, that shall be for the benefit of the commonweal, and [are] put in trust for the body of the realm.'[24]

Here, as with Hales's analysis of English history, we can see how this prophetic stance became a powerful means of opposing the queen's will over issues, pre-eminently her marriage and the related issue of the succession, consensually defined as more concerning the 'common wealth' (an entity which contains the queen as a member) than the queen as head of the body politic.[25] We can also see, in embryo, the shape of the later Elizabethan polity, as that consensus gradually eroded. As this occurred 'prophecy' itself became a term whose meaning was contested by those who saw 'Deborah's' rule as equally (and, after her providential accession, primarily) legitimated by her status as king of England; including Elizabeth and, most of the time, most of her Privy Councillors.[26] This stance came to be associated with the attempt to marginalize 'prophets' by identifying them as radicals and, in their clerical guise, 'ministers' rather than priests: the definition and marginalization of Puritans as radical sectaries which loomed so large in government policy of the 1580s and 1590s. Rather than denoting a means of spiritual illumination and a commitment to a spiritualized body politic, then, 'prophecy' increasingly came to be read as attempts by the radical few to define God's will as ordaining assaults on monarchical prerogative, and, by extension, on order and degree.

This movement left unresolved, however, the problem posed by the godly man, neither radical nor sectary, whose conscience compelled him to speak for God and the commonwealth and against the expressed will of the queen, on issues where consensus across the 'Protestant ascendancy' (but not including the queen) still prevailed.[27] The controversy over Archbishop of Canterbury Edmund Grindal's refusal, in the 1570s, to enact the queen's will over 'prophesyings' (or, as contemporaries called them, 'prophecies') provides one good example; the reaction to John Stubbs's book the *Gaping Gulf*, to which I will return in conclusion, provides another.[28] Grindal remained wedded to the view consensually held at the beginning of Elizabeth's reign of 'prophecies' as a means of national renewal, in the face of Elizabeth's decision to define them as subversive and to make the case a test of loyalty for her councillors. The Bishop of Durham's letter to Lord Burghley of 1576, written at the height of the long-running battle, reveals something of the tensions provoked by the affair, tensions which were to make 'prophecy' and 'expedience' antithetical terms in English political discourse:

> . . . truly, my good lord, I detest [Grindal's] wilfulness, and contending with the regal majesty, and obstinacy in not yielding to that which your honours [of the Privy Council] set down, the same being godly and expedient for the time, the malapertness of brainless men considered; who nowadays, if but a proclamation, a decree, or commandment come forth from her majesty, and by your honours' advice, straightways, and first in their conventicles, will call the same into question, and examine and determine whether with safe conscience they may or ought to obey the same: a thing so perilous as none can be more, and savouring of the antibaptismey; who wish a popular government.[29]

William Camden's account of Grindal's fall, written nearly forty years later, similarly illustrates the contest over the meaning of prophecies and the social standing of 'prophets' – although, writing in the context of James's reign, he vaguely referred to Grindal's 'adversaries' as winning the contest rather than the Queen herself.[30] Grindal lost favour, he says, because he was successfully portrayed as countenancing 'the conventicles of some turbulent and hot-spirited ministers, and their prophecies (as they called them)'.[31]

The prophetic mode also proved to be a double-edged sword in terms of legitimating the queen; one reason, no doubt, why Elizabeth moved against it in the 1570s. If the identification of Elizabeth with Deborah served to effect a stark antithesis between Mary I ('Jezebel') and Elizabeth in the interest of defusing hostility to female rule, it also proposed two corollaries which potentially undermined her monarchical authority once consensus across the ranks of godly Englishmen began to dissolve.[32] First, the model assumed that Elizabeth herself must be godly, and be publicly read as godly – by 'ministers' of both varieties – to maintain subjects' allegiance and obedience.[33] ('Provided that she sin not', wrote Elizabeth sarcastically on Knox's letter, or else 'upon every sin to forfeit her crown'. Nor did the identification, according to Elizabeth, serve to justify her rule as a woman, allowing men instead to plot 'to disherit both her and her issue, especially if it be a daughter, or do sin'.)[34]

Secondly it opened the door to the possibility that 'prophecy' might speak to announce that Elizabeth was not Deborah, and hence subvert her claim to exercise imperial rule on the same terms as her father had done. This is precisely what happened in a fascinating prophetic utterance of 1582, from Bury St Edmunds. There Thomas Gibson, a follower of Robert Browne and Robert Harrison – men who claimed the status of prophets – impugned Elizabeth's commitment to godly reformation by annotating the royal arms in the parish church. Beside them he had painted the following Biblical verse:

I know thy works, that thou art neither cold nor hot. I would thou wert cold or hot. Therefore because thou are lukewarm, and neither cold nor hot, it will come to pass, I will spew thee out of my mouth.

According to the seventeenth-century ecclesiastical historian John Strype, the critical words after 'I know thy works' were painted over in very short order by the more anodyne ' . . . and thy love, and service, and faith, and thy patience, and thy works; and that they are more at the last than at the first'. But Gibson, evidently willing to let godly Englishmen off the hook in this way, would only do so by re-identifying Elizabeth as Jezebel, and insisting their acceptance of Elizabeth as Deborah compromised their status as God's elect:

Notwithstanding, I have a few things against thee, that thou sufferest the woman Jezebel, which maketh herself a prophetess, to teach and to deceive my servants; and to make them commit fornication, and to eat meat sacrificed unto idols.[35]

Nor was this the end of the matter. Elizabeth herself seems to have believed that these men expressed sentiments at least comprehensible, if not widely shared, even among the ranks of her innermost councillors, and to some extent spoke as their conscience concerning religious reformation. In the end Gibson and others involved in the episode were called to the assizes held in Bury St Edmunds in 1583 and severely punished (although not executed) for denying the queen's supremacy, 'which they acknowledged only in civil matters'.[36] But the next year Elizabeth alluded to this episode, using it as a stick with which to beat her Privy Councillors, among others, for pretensions to godliness which jeopardized her tenure of the throne and hence England's Protestant identity. In an encounter which provides rich evidence of the political implications of this dynamic she identified such men as equivalent to Papists in terms of the danger they posed to the realm, for they 'join together in one opinion against me, . . . neither of them would have me to be Queen of England'.[37]

On this occasion the Queen with her principal councillors (including William Cecil, Lord Burghley) gave audience to Archbishop Whitgift and three bishops, representatives of the Lower House of Convocation, to receive their clerical subsidy. Clearly directing her remarks to her councillors at least as much as to convocation, Elizabeth 'did accept of it thankfully, and the rather that it came voluntarily and frankly, whereas the laity must be entreated and moved thereunto'. At this point Burghley responded 'Madam, these men come with mites, but we will come with pounds'; 'we' presumably meaning godly Englishmen who did not form part of the ecclesiastical hierarchy. Ignoring the interjection, Elizabeth turned to the bishops:

We understand that some of the Nether House [House of Commons] have used diverse reproachful speeches against you, tending greatly to your dishonour, which we will not suffer; and that they meddle with matters above their capacity, not appertaining unto them, for the which we will call some of them to an account. And we understand they be countenanced by some of our Council which we will redress or else uncouncil some of them.[38]

She continued by saying she had received a letter from overseas, informing her that the papists 'were of hope to prevail again in England, for that her Protestants themselves misliked her'. 'And indeed, so they do,' she said, 'for I have heard that some of them of late have said that I was of no religion – neither hot nor cold, but such a one as one day would give God the vomit.'[39] In this episode Elizabeth claimed the right to define religious orthodoxy because of the consequences for Protestantism if 'prophets' were allowed to advance their vision of the commonwealth, in terms which opposed 'bishops' to 'prophets' whose calling did not come from the queen. Burghley's response, in which he seemingly instinctively identified with 'prophets' rather than with the ecclesiastical hierarchy, is particularly revealing of deep-seated tensions between the queen and her councillors over the definition of godly rule.

Reading Elizabeth's elevation to the throne as providential entailed emphasizing the dramatic overturning, by God, of the seemingly inevitable course of human affairs, a view of history that similarly challenged her monarchical authority. It encouraged a discourse of prophecy, not necessarily or exclusively in Biblical mode, fuelled by 'prophets' eager to identify the next such revolution, or unwilling to see the drama as having only one act. In 1562, for example, men condemned of a treasonable conspiracy to proclaim Mary Stuart Queen of England argued their actions did not constitute treason because they did not plan to act before Elizabeth's death: they 'meant it not, before the queen should die; which . . . they were persuaded by Prestal, a conjuror, should be about March following.'[40] And 'prophecy' in this mode could easily elide into the practice of 'black arts' to make the prophecies come true, as the identification of Prestal as a 'conjuror' suggests. This was the reason for the passage of an Act in 1558 making the use and practice of enchantments, witchcraft and sorcery a felony: 'because conjurors and charmers, and such as invoked evil spirits, were so frequent and busy upon the queen's first coming to the crown . . . who meddled in matter of state, and endeavoured by sorcery and the black arts to deprive the queen of her kingdom.'[41]

This heightened consciousness of living in dramatic times helps explain the 'prophecies' concerning 'The Return of the King' – ambiguously Edward VI and Christ – explored by Carole Levin most recently in her book *The Heart and Stomach of a King*.[42] Although Levin is at pains to argue this kind of prophecy does not occur only in the reign of female rulers, she is quite right to assert that sex and gender as well as disputable legitimacy are significant determinants of the specific forms it takes. In Elizabeth's reign, as in Mary I's, Edward's return was prophesied in ways that expressed popular yearning for a king, yearnings that show how for many Englishmen imperial rule and redemptive capacity constituted two sides of the same (male) identity. In the popular imagination Edward (an indistinct figure because of his youth while on the throne) became on his 'return' an adult, and simultaneously St Edward and King Jesus. So for example, as Levin shows, sightings of Edward find him married to a Protestant queen and intervening in English affairs to save the commonwealth.[43] And when, in 1591, William Hacket announced himself as the new messiah, he also claimed an imperial identity as king of Europe – a claim which the authorities found perhaps more unsettling than his claim to be Christ.[44] Nicholas Bacon might well argue that Hacket and his followers were only 'blisters in some small ignoble part of the body', but it is not surprising that Elizabeth took such manifestations of dissatisfaction personally, given her own conviction that prophecy allowed men to rehearse a drama involving female rule that would climax with her own deposition.[45]

Levin notes that rumours about Edward VI's miraculous survival and imminent restoration occurred in two waves, the first petering out in the mid-1560s; the second, which she describes as more overtly expressing discontent with female rule, lasting from the mid-1580s to the end of the reign. In both cases the prophesied figure of Edward functioned as a doppelgänger for another eagerly awaited yet shadowy male figure: first the man who it was assumed would be king as Elizabeth's husband; then, from the mid-1580s, the man who would inevitably succeed her.[46] For, if Englishmen were by no means agreed, by the late 1580s, about who Elizabeth's successor was to be, there was remarkable consensus at least from that point, if not earlier, that it would be a king at all costs.[47] As the French Ambassador De Maisse noted in his Journal, 'if by chance she should die, it is certain that the English would never again submit to the rule of a woman.'[48]

If Englishmen could agree on that outcome, however, they found it impossible to achieve consensus on the subject of the queen's marriage, torn between the desire to have a king and the fear of replicating the Spanish conquest which they associated with Mary's reign. This was a 'conquest' all the more insidious because, effected from within the nation and at the level of the crown, it allowed the 'commonwealth' no redress. For contemporaries, the relationship of woman to man ensured that possession of the queen translated into possession of the realm, whatever legal steps might be taken to maintain the crown's autonomy.[49] Moreover, the charisma pertaining to a king, in the context of female rule, suggested there would always be those among the ranks of the powerful and influential willing to serve a king regardless of his religious or national identity, either to advance their own or what they perceived to be their country's interest. Much of the hatred Stephen Gardiner's memory provoked during Elizabeth's reign stemmed from his attempt to legitimate Philip of Spain, as king of England

and rightful (through divine election) emperor of Europe.[50] To do so Gardiner made extensive use of Machiavelli's *The Prince*. He also amended it for use in England under female rule by adding to Machiavelli's categories a new one, that of the matrimonial prince; an unfortunate *ad lib*, from the point of view of any Englishman arguing the necessity of marriage in Elizabeth's reign.[51]

Arguably Englishmen's failure to achieve consensus over the marriage issue constituted the main reason why, in the end, Elizabeth was able to reign in her own right despite the pressure brought to bear for various marriage schemes especially in the early decades of the reign.[52] For as the reign progressed marriage came to seem increasingly dangerous to the commonwealth, for several reasons. First, Elizabeth's advancing age made the prospect of the fervently desired (male) heir of her own body increasingly unlikely. Second, as it became increasingly clear that Elizabeth was a significant player in the political arena, with an agenda that differed in salient respects from that of the Protestant ascendancy, marriage raised the possibility of Elizabeth effecting an alliance, as queen, that would enhance her monarchical autonomy.[53] The king, in other words, might identify with the queen (like with like in regality) rather than with her councillors (like with like in reason), and hence potentially destabilize the 'commonwealth' by signally reinforcing the monarchical element of the mixed monarchy. Seemingly this was a possibility none of her councillors, whether official or unofficial, had entertained in the early years of the reign. It led to a situation in which Privy Councillors publicly urged marriage on the queen, whilst privately expressing their agonized inability to determine the best course of action to preserve the godly nation. In a letter of 1570 from Cecil to Sir Francis Walsingham, for example, Cecil took it as read that if the proposed marriage (with the duc d'Anjou) were to go forward, it should proceed as quickly as possible; Elizabeth was after all thirty-seven years old at this time. But he equally expressed his helpless sense that the matter of her marriage was so difficult that they must simply urge marriage on her and trust to God:

> That if God should permit this marriage, or any other, to take place, he [Walsingham] might well judge that no time was to be wasted, otherwise than honour might require. That he was not able to discern what was best: but that he saw no continuance of her quietness without a marriage. And that therefore he remitted the success to Almighty God.

John Strype, who transcribed the letter in the seventeenth century, added that Cecil included a postscript which revealed that councillors felt they must present a united front in favour of the marriage, both to the queen and to the nation: 'But this, [Cecil] said, he writ privately to him, as he trusted it should remain to himself [i.e., Walsingham].'[54]

Finally, as the European religious climate polarized in ways that gave new immediacy to Machiavelli's works in northern Europe, finding a Protestant prince whose commitment to the faith was more than 'politic' began to take on something of the quality of the quest for the Holy Grail, regardless of whether the prince in question was the one who was to marry the queen, or the one who was to succeed her.[55] In such difficult circumstances, what could Elizabeth's councillors do except appeal to God – and prophecy? In the same year that Cecil wrote his letter to Walsingham he had recourse to astrology, possibly as practised by his fellow Privy Councillor, Sir Thomas Smith, in an attempt to square the circle posed by the issue of the queen's marriage. The prognostication, in Latin and in Cecil's hand, suggests how difficult Elizabeth's councillors realized it would be to arrive at the desideratum of a Protestant male heir of lineal descent and a marriageable daughter, regarded as necessary to consolidate the Protestant nation at home and, through the daughter, to export godliness abroad. The castings revealed that . . .

> . . . the queen had not much inclination to marriage: yet that her wedlock would be very happy to her: that she should be somewhat elder when she entered into matrimony: . . . that she should have but one husband. Then for the quality of the man, that he should be a foreigner. . . . That she should arrive at a prosperous married estate; but slowly, and after much counsel taken, and the common rumour of it everywhere, and after very great disputes and arguings concerning it for many years by diverse persons, before it should be effected. . . . That her husband should die first; and yet she should live long with her husband, and should possess much of his estate. For children but few, yet very great hope of one son, that should be strong, famous, and happy in his mature age: and one daughter.[56]

The prophecy also reveals how, for Cecil and Smith, the queen's marriage was at least as much a matter of the 'common weal' as it was of the queen's prerogative.

In conclusion I want to examine an episode which speaks quite directly to these tensions within the Elizabethan body politic, the publication and reception of John Stubbs's 1579 book, *The Discoverie of a Gaping Gulf Whereinto England is like to be Swallowed by an other French mariage, if the Lord forbid not the bans, by letting her Maiestie see the sin and punishment thereof.*[57] The episode is significant, not least in revealing the contest over 'prophecy' between two important political players: John Stubbs, adopting the stance of a prophet to represent the Protestant ascendancy, and Elizabeth herself.[58] It also marks an important stage – arguably a turning point – in the movement from prophecy to policy as the basis of English national identity.[59]

In 1579 negotiations were again entered into concerning marriage between Elizabeth and the French and Catholic duc d'Anjou, the younger brother of the King of France. Elizabeth, in striking contrast to her reception of marriage proposals made earlier in the reign, showed every sign of enthusiasm for and commitment to this match.[60] It was, however, deeply unpopular in the country at large, xenophobia and anti-Catholic sentiment combining to make Anjou a much-reviled figure.[61] London preachers denounced the marriage from their pulpits; some organized public prayers and fastings 'for her Majesty's good estate, which they feared was now like to be in great peril'.[62] What they expressed orally – what, in fact, Elizabeth's councillors had expressed privately to the queen – John Stubbs, a lawyer educated at Lincoln's Inn and exceptionally well connected both with Elizabeth's inner ring of councillors and with godly prophets outside, put into print and published. He seems to have been encouraged by members of the Privy Council to do so. His utterance meant they could publicly (albeit equivocally) support the queen, yet mobilize public opinion against a course of action of which they could not bring themselves to approve.[63]

For his presumption he and his collaborators Hugh Singleton and William Page were sentenced to have their right hands chopped off, under a statute of Philip and Mary against publishers of seditious writings. At the same time the queen issued a proclamation which, most unusually, not only ordered the book to be suppressed but also refuted its arguments.[64] I think we are justified in regarding this as Elizabeth having recourse to print in her own right; a sign, too, of her isolation over this issue. She also mobilized her bishops to clamp down on preachers likely to echo Stubbs's arguments in their sermons, and to orchestrate a countervailing broadside from the pulpit attacking Stubbs as seditious. (And, lest that view appear merely politic, Archbishop Grindal was brought out of his enforced semi-retirement to lend the lustre of prophetic authority to the counter-attack).[65]

Stubbs's pamphlet witnesses the re-emergence in English political debate of arguments against female rule which had been articulated by John Knox and Christopher Goodman under Mary Tudor. In it he explores the consequences for England once Elizabeth loses her status as Deborah and rules merely as a female ruler. This will happen, he says, because of the 'sin' she will commit in allying herself and her people to France, a 'den of idolatry'.[66] He argues first that she will inevitably be drawn toward Catholicism. A 'weaker vessel', she will be powerless to resist her husband's superior strength:

> And if woman, that weaker vessel, be strong enough to draw man through the advantage which the Devil hath within our bosom (I mean our natural corruption and proneness to idolatry), how much more forcibly shall the stronger vessel pull weak woman, considering that with the inequality of strength there is joined as great or more readiness to idolatry and superstition? And if the husband, which is the head, be drawn aside by his wife, over whom nevertheless he hath authority and rule, how much more easily shall the wife be perverted by her husband, to whom she is subject by the law of God and

oweth both awe and obedience, howsoever the laws by prerogative or her place by pre-eminence may privilege her?[67]

Moreover, her declension will lead England – 'a kingdom of light, confessing Christ and serving the living God' – into the realms of darkness, as happened in the Old Testament, when the sins of Jeroboam 'caused all Israel to sin against the Lord'.[68]

In the matter of her marriage she cannot be a private person: she is the 'goodwife' of England, a relationship that means that she cannot in good conscience 'conclude her marriage before she parle in Parliament with her subjects, before she consult with the laws and call the commonweal as it were to common council . . . forasmuch as it also is to be married with her and in sort to be governed by him that shall be her governor'.[69] Stubbs does not doubt that the godly will speak with one voice on this issue. 'We do not love her,' he announces, 'whatsoever we say, when . . .

. . . flattering her, perhaps, in other vanities, we do not fall down before her with tears, bewailing the wrath of God kindled against her, if by her advised permission, and by means of her marriage, God should be so highly dishonoured in this kingdom wherewith he hath honoured her. Look not the word of God in your mouths, you that breathe such lukewarm counsel, halt no more on both sides.'[70]

And if God withdraws his blessing from Elizabeth because she asserts her prerogative over and against the 'commonweal' in the matter of her marriage, then Stubbs intimates that her subjects are removed from their duty of obedience to the queen:

. . . to alter our good religion or give any permission to so wicked idolatry [as Anjou would introduce] takes away God's blessing from the state, whose providence it is whereby rulers reign and states do stand. And let him . . . that holds himself the best politic, hold this with me for a cornerstone: . . . to bring in and hold true religion procureth God's protection and worketh subjects' obedience of heart far above all other laws or fear of laws.[71]

Englishmen's obedience to God has sustained her rule, for, as he reminds her, it has been only His ongoing providence which has overridden His prohibition against female rule:

And sith the Lord for his own son's sake and of his love to the gospel which we have among us hath weakened the hand of our foreign enemies and broken the devices of their heads hitherto, since he hath engraven such a fearing love in her subjects' hearts as children bear to their mother, and such a reverent note of sovereignty in her person as he is wont to set on them whom he calls by his own names and are his ordinances, insomuch as it may be said of her most truly, it is the Lord by whom kings reign. . . .[72]

Elizabeth was, understandably, 'much incensed' by Stubbs's book, and presumably deeply frightened. Surely she had John Knox's strictures against female rule in *The First Blast of the Trumpet Against the Monstrous Regiment of Women* in mind when she termed it 'a trump of sedition secretly sounding in every subject's ear', designed to 'set all at liberty for some monstrous, secret innovation'.[73] For it was a dangerous move to reintroduce legislation passed during her sister's ungodly reign to buttress her own monarchical authority. The risk she ran is suggested by William Camden's description of the sentencing of Stubbs, Singleton and Page in his *History of . . . Princess Elizabeth*:

Against [the three] sentence was given, that their right hands should be cut off, according to an act of Philip and Mary against the authors and publishers of seditious writings. Though some lawyers muttered that the sentence was erroneous and void by reason of the false noting of the time wherein the law was made; and that the act was only temporary, and died with Queen Mary. Of this number, Dalton, who bawled it out openly, was committed to the Tower; and Monson, a judge in the Court of Commonpleas, was so strongly reprehended that he resigned his place: forasmuch as Wray, Lord Chief Justice of England, made it appear that there was no mistake in noting the time; and proved by the words of the act, that the act was made against those who should abuse the king by seditious writings, and that the king of England never dieth; yea, that that act was renewed *anno primo Elizabethae*, to be in force during the life of her and the heirs of her body.[74]

Stubbs's mutilation made a profound impact on contemporaries, perhaps as glaring confirmation that by the 1580s in England political expediency or 'necessity' held the whip hand. Later historians have read Stubb's ejaculation at the time – he is reported to have shouted out 'God save the queen' after his hand was chopped off – as evidence of unconditional loyalty to the queen on the part of her subjects. Yet from this vantage point it looks more like a statement about the limitations of subjects' obedience to a female ruler, delivered by a man defined by himself and by others as a godly man and a prophet, and standing in a privileged position relative to some of the greatest men in the land.[75] As such it also speaks volumes about the tensions in Elizabethan England inseparable from the fact of female rule.

In the end Chief Justice Wray sided with the queen (as did her Privy Councillors), in the interests of stability and perpetuity. These key concepts also featured prominently in Elizabeth's defence of her regiment in her proclamation against the *Gaping Gulf*. In conjunction with her decision not to proceed with the marriage, they proved enough to stabilize the ship of state.[76] Whether or not she was Deborah, her rule was at least (as the Bishop of Durham said about the decision to abolish prophecies) 'godly and expedient for the time.' Perhaps it was this conviction which enabled Wray to proceed against Thomas Gibson and the prophets at Bury St Edmunds in a few years' time. The exchange did not, however, resolve the tensions between prophecy and policy in Elizabeth's realm. It only signalled the point from which prophecy could be successfully labelled what Elizabeth called it in her proclamation: 'fanatical divinations' calculated to appeal to 'every most meanest person of judgment', in the interest of destabilizing the realm rather than reforming the commonweal.[77]

Notes

1 J. Neale, 'Sir Nicholas Throckmorton's Advice to Queen Elizabeth on Her Accession to the Throne', *English Historical Review*, LXV (1950), 91–8; my emphasis.

2 Neale, 'Sir Nicholas Throckmorton', p. 92.

3 For contemporary views about female rule see M. Weisner, *Women and Gender in Early Modern Europe* (Cambridge University Press, 1993), ch. 8.; for their intersection with reforming Protestant views see D. Kelley, *The Beginning of Ideology: Consciousness and Society in the French Reformation* (Cambridge University Press, 1981), pp. 73–4.

4 J. Dawson, 'Revolutionary Conclusions: The Case of the Marian Exiles', *History of Political Thought*, XI (2) (1990), 257–72; p. 257. Jane Dawson points out England enjoyed the unique distinction of being the only European country during this period to return from Protestantism to Catholicism.

5 See T. Dughi, 'The Breath of Christ's Mouth: Apocalyptic and Prophecy in Early Reformation Ideology'(unpublished PhD thesis, The Johns Hopkins University, 1989).

6 J. Guy, 'The Henrician Age' in J. Pocock (ed.), *The Varieties of British Political Thought, 1500–1800* (Cambridge University Press, 1993), pp. 13–44; p. 43.

7 J. Knox, *The First Blast of the Trumpet against the Monstrous Regiment of Women*, ed. E. Arber (London, Archibald Constable and Co., 1895), p. 10. Knox is more forthright about his membership among the prophetic elect in his account of his calling, in D. Laing (ed.), *The Works of John Knox* (6 vols, Edinburgh, T. Constable for the Bannatyne Club, 1846–64), vol. 6, p. 230.

8 For the significance of Knox's views and his role in English political affairs at this point see A. McLaren, 'Delineating the Elizabethan Body Politic: Knox, Aylmer and the Definition of Council 1558–1588', *History of Political Thought*, XVII (2) (1996), 224–55.

9 Laing, *John Knox*, vol. 6, pp. 48–9.

10 Laing, *John Knox*, pp. 50–1.

11 R. Mulcaster, *The Quenes Majesties Passage Through the Citie of London to Westminster the Day before her Coronation*, ed. J.M. Osborn (New Haven, Yale University Press, 1960), p. 55. D. Bergeron, 'Elizabeth's Coronation Entry, 1559: New Manuscript Evidence', *English Literary Renaissance*, 8 (1978), 3–8. Bergeron suggests the Deborah figure may have been wearing a costume designed to be similar

to Elizabeth's costume on the day; if that were the case, he notes, 'symbol and reality would have fused' (p. 7).

12 Mulcaster, *Quenes Majesties Passage*, p. 55.

13 For Hales's career and significance in Edward VI's reign see M. Bush, *The Government Policy of Protector Somerset* (London, Arnold, 1975).

14. J. Hales, *An Oration of John Hales to the Queenes Majestie, and delivered to her Majestie by a certain noble man, at her first entrance to her reign* in J. Foxe, *Ecclesiastical History: Containing the Actes and Monuments of Martyrs* (6 vols, London, Company of Stationers, 1641), vol. 3, pp. 976–9; p. 977.

15 Hales, *Oration*, p. 978.

16 Hales, *Oration*, p. 976.

17 Hales, *Oration*, p. 977.

18 Ponet was not alone, nor was Hales. For the genesis and persistence of this understanding of the relationship between king and commonwealth see G. Bowler, '"An Axe or an Act": The Parliament of 1572 and Resistance Theory in Early Elizabethan England', *Canadian Journal of History*, 19 (3) (1984), 349–59, and 'Marian Protestants and the Idea of Violent Resistance to Tyranny' in P. Lake and M. Dowling (eds), *Protestantism and the National Church in Sixteenth-Century England* (London, Croom Helm, 1987), pp. 124–43. See also J.A. Dawson, 'Revolutionary Conclusions', p. 272.

19 Hales, *Oration*, p. 978.

20 Hales, *Oration*, p. 979.

21 Hales, *Oration*, p. 979.

22 McLaren, 'Delineating', pp. 21–5.

23 J. Strype, *Annals of the Reformation and Establishment of Religion and other various occurrences in the Church of England during Queen Elizabeth's Happy Reign; together with an appendix of original papers of state, records and letters* (4 vols, Oxford, Clarendon Press, 1824), vol. I (ii), pp. 117–21.

24 J. Hales, *A Declaration of the Succession of the Crown Imperial of England* (1563) in F. Hargrave (alias George Harbin), *The Hereditary Right of the Crown of England Asserted* (London, printed by G. James for Richard Smith, 1713), pp. xx–xlii; p. xx.

25 See the discussion of 'good order' and commonwealth in 'The Concept of Order and the Northern Rising, 1569' in M.E. James, *Society, Politics and Culture: Studies in Early Modern England* (Cambridge University Press, 1986), pp. 280–5.

26 This category includes, pre-eminently, Elizabeth herself. For her ultimately successful attempts to proclaim herself 'king' at least linguistically see L. Marcus, 'Erasing the Stigma of Daughterhood: Mary I, Elizabeth I, and Henry VIII' in L.E. Boose and B.S. Flowers (eds), *Daughters and Fathers* (Baltimore, The Johns Hopkins University Press, 1989), pp. 400–17.

27 P. Collinson, 'The Monarchical Republic of Queen Elizabeth I', *Bulletin of the John Rylands University Library of Manchester*, 69 (2) (1986–7), 394–424.

28 P. Collinson, 'The Downfall of Archbishop Grindal and its Place in Elizabethan Political and Ecclesiastical History' in *Godly People: Essays on English Protestantism and Puritanism* (London, Hambledon Press, 1983), pp. 371–98.

29 Strype, *Annals*, vol. II (ii), pp. 110–11.

30 Collinson, 'Archbishop Grindal', shows that one remarkable feature of the episode is that there were no adversaries about. For Camden's tailoring of his *Annals* to James I's political requirements see

D. Woolf, 'Two Elizabeths? James I and the Late Queen's Famous Memory', *Canadian Journal of History*, 20 (2) (1985), 167–91.

31 W. Camden, *The History of the Most Renowned and Victorious Princess Elizabeth Late Queen of England*, ed. W. MacCaffrey (University of Chicago Press, 1970), pp. 161–2.

32 P. Corts, 'Governmental Persuasion in the Reign of Elizabeth I, 1558–1563' (unpublished Ph.D. dissertation, Indiana University, 1971), argues persuasively that Elizabeth's image was fabricated with some care and by a process of negotiation between Elizabeth and her 'inner' councillors; see ch. 2.

33 M. Christian, 'Elizabeth's Preachers and the Government of Women: Defining and Correcting a Queen', *Sixteenth Century Journal*, XXIV (3) (1993), 561–76; and see my unpublished paper, '"To Be Deborah": The Political Implications of Providentialism in the Reign of Elizabeth I'.

34 Letter from Knox to Elizabeth 20 July 1559, annotated by Elizabeth: British Library, Additional MS 32,091, ff. 167–9.

35 Strype, *Annals*, vol. III (i), p. 269.

36 Strype, *Annals*, vol. III (i), p. 269.

37 J. Neale recounts this episode in *Elizabeth I and Her Parliaments* (2 vols, London, Cape, 1953), vol. II, pp. 69–71.

38 Neale, *Elizabeth I and Her Parliaments*, vol. II, p. 69.

39 Neale, *Elizabeth I and Her Parliaments*, vol. II, p. 71.

40 Strype, *Annals*, vol. I (i), p. 546.

41 Strype, *Annals*, vol. I (i), p. 88.

42 C. Levin, *The Heart and Stomach of a King: Elizabeth I and the Politics of Sex and Power*, (Philadelphia, University of Pennsylvania Press, 1994), ch. 5, pp. 92–118.

43 Levin, *Heart and Stomach*, p. 118.

44 Levin, *Heart and Stomach*, p. 116.

45 Levin, *Heart and Stomach*, p. 115.

46 Corts, *Governmental Persuasion*, pp. 153–5, 171, argues the issue of Elizabeth's marriage, which historians traditionally relate to the question of the succession, was equally if not more strongly associated with the attempt to enact a religious settlement at the beginning of the reign, and specifically because of the issue of the Supreme Headship. In his view it is no coincidence that as soon as the settlement of 1559 was drafted a joint committee of the two houses met to decide what authority was to be vested in the queen's husband.

47 In the early years of the reign the Spanish ambassador reported 'the cry is that they do not want any more women rulers'. He also claimed William Cecil himself supported the claims of Lord Hastings to the throne over those of Katherine Grey, declaring that 'no woman should succeed'. *Calendar of State Papers Spanish*, Eliz., I, p. 176; A. Shephard, 'Gender and Authority in Sixteenth Century England: The Debate About John Knox's *First Blast of the Trumpet Against the Monstrous Regiment of Women*' (unpublished PhD dissertation, University of Lancaster, 1990), p. 26.

48 Quoted in L. Montrose, '"Shaping Fantasies": Figurations of Gender and Power in Elizabethan Culture' in S. Greenblatt (ed.), *Representing the English Renaissance* (Berkeley, University of California Press, 1988), pp. 31–64; p. 50.

49 See, for example, *Certain Questions Demanded and Asked by the Noble Realm of England, of her true natural children and Subjects of the Same* (Wesel, 1555; Short Title Catalogue, 9981). One of the questions

asks 'whether the realm of England belong to the Queen, or to her subjects' (fol. Av.ᵛ). And see G. Bowler's discussion of this and other similar Marian literature in 'Marian Protestants'.

50 S. Gardiner, *A Discourse on the Coming of the English and Normans to Britain* (tr. into Italian by George Rainsford, pub. 1556), edited and translated by P. Donaldson as *A Machiavellian Treatise* (Cambridge University Press, 1975), p. 108.

51 Gardiner, *Discourse*, Introduction p. 25; text p. 145.

52 S. Doran, *Monarchy and Matrimony: The Courtships of Elizabeth I* (New York, Routledge, 1996). The issue of whether or not Elizabeth chose to remain unmarried remains an open one. I incline to the view that she chose that course and was able to stick to it because no suitable Protestant suitor presented himself at the right time; just as she was able to maintain her position as queen because of the dearth of Protestant males with strong claims to the throne.

53 J. Guy, 'The 1590s: The Second Reign of Elizabeth I?' in J. Guy (ed.), *The Reign of Elizabeth I: Court and Culture in the Last Decade* (Cambridge University Press, 1995), pp. 1–19; p. 13.

54 Strype, *Annals*, vol. II (i), p. 22.

55 For Machiavelli's career see D. Kelley, 'Murd'rous Machiavel in France: A Post Mortem', *The Political Science Quarterly*, 85 (2) (1970), 545–59. James VI, for example, did not firmly position himself as a Protestant prince until the 1590s, as it became increasingly clear both that England was within his grasp and that this identity was a pre-condition of his succession.

56 Stubbs, *Annals*, vol. II (i), p. 23.

57 L. Berry (ed.), *John Stubbs's 'Gaping Gulf' with Letters and Other Relevant Documents*, Folger Documents of Tudor and Stuart Civilization (Charlottesville, University Press of Virginia, 1968).

58 Berry, *John Stubbs's 'Gaping Gulf'*. On the title page Stubbs quotes from Psalms 20: 9 to identify himself in this role: 'Save Lord, let the King hear us in the day that we call.'

59 J. Guy, *Tudor England* (Oxford University Press, 1988), esp. chs 11 and 13.

60 S. Doran's *Monarchy and Matrimony* is a valuable up-to-date treatment of the subject which sheds light on the tensions between the queen and her councillors over the issue. In what follows I am much indebted to her account of the reception of Stubbs's book.

61 See D. Adler, 'Imaginary Toads in Real Gardens', *English Literary Renaissance*, 11 (1981), 235–60, for the highly creative ways in which this hatred was disguised and expressed.

62 J. Strype, *Historical Collections of the Life and Acts of John Aylmer* (Oxford, Clarendon Press, 1821); quoted in Doran, *Monarchy and Matrimony*, p. 166.

63 Doran, *Monarchy and Matrimony*, pp. 166–74; for information on Stubbs see the entry in the *Dictionary of National Biography* (Oxford University Press, 1995) and Berry, *John Stubbs's 'Gaping Gulf'*, Preface and Introduction.

64 Doran, *Monarchy and Matrimony*, p. 168.

65 Doran, *Monarchy and Matrimony*, p. 166.

66 Berry, *John Stubbs's 'Gaping Gulf'*, p. 7.

67 Berry, *John Stubbs's 'Gaping Gulf'*, p. 11. It is interesting that Stubbs amends traditional Aristotelian reasoning. Anjou possesses superior authority, as a man, because of his superior physical strength. He has lost his claim to superiority based on a larger measure of reason because of his commitment to the 'idolatry and superstition' of Rome.

68 Berry, *John Stubbs's 'Gaping Gulf'*, pp. 6, 15.

69 Berry, *John Stubbs's 'Gaping Gulf'*, pp. 68–9.

70 Berry, *John Stubbs's 'Gaping Gulf'*, p. 17.

71 Berry, *John Stubbs's 'Gaping Gulf'*, p. 39.

72 Berry, *John Stubbs's 'Gaping Gulf'*, p. 85.

73 P. Hughes and J. Larkin (eds), *Tudor Royal Proclamations vol.II: The Later Tudors* (New Haven, Yale University Press, 1969), pp. 448–9.

74 W. Camden, *History*, p. 138. S. Doran, *Monarchy and Matrimony*, notes that the Earls of Leicester and Bedford – both Privy Councillors – were patrons of Singleton, Page, Dalton and Monson: p. 167.

75 Doran, *Monarchy and Matrimony*, p. 167.

76 Doran, *Monarchy and Matrimony*, suggests that at one point Elizabeth seriously considered admitting four Catholics to the Privy Council as well as possibly dismissing Sir Francis Walsingham, whom she saw as particularly implicated in the business: pp. 173–4. Whether or not she would have been able to effect this 'palace revolution' is, of course, another matter.

77 Hughes and Larkin, *Tudor Royal Proclamations*, vol. II, pp. 448–9.

4

RESHAPING THE LOCAL FUTURE: THE DEVELOPMENT AND USES OF PROVINCIAL POLITICAL PROPHECIES, 1300–1900

T. Thornton

The late sixteenth and early seventeenth centuries saw a transformation in the media of political debate in England. The success of printing meant that it became possible to produce printed books and pamphlets in large numbers, relatively quickly, and at very low prices. Texts could be published and republished, and responses and commentaries could be produced far more quickly and with far greater impact on a wider audience than before. A host of political and religious topics, from the qualities of the crown's ministers to an axe-murder in Shropshire, were discussed.[1] In particular the English Civil War produced an explosion of printed material of a political and religious nature, and among this was a large body of text which may be described as prophetic.[2] Lesley Coote has already outlined some of the reasons for the importance of prophecy as a language of political debate in the late middle ages, and Anne McLaren has described how prophecy came to play an important role in shaping the queenship of Elizabeth I. This chapter discusses two prophetic traditions that appeared in the seventeenth century, those attributed to Nixon, the Cheshire prophet, and Mother Shipton. It considers the portrayal of the alleged authors of the prophetic texts, placing them in the context of a prophetic culture that judged validity through a variety of measures, especially antiquity, oral and written transmission, and the marginal position of the individual authors. It then considers the language and form of the texts, and especially the importance of these prophecies in defining and redefining locality and community through their narratives of collective past and future. This then supports a discussion of the control and use of the texts, demonstrating that far from becoming the victim of scepticism among the political élite, prophecy remained a political language which that élite attempted to use and control. Yet its control could never be total, because of the flexibility of the prophetic language and the liminality of its supposed and actual prophet authors, and the challenge to rationality and hierarchy they represented.

Both Nixon and Mother Shipton initially appear unpromising subjects for study in a collection of essays such as this. Shipton's reputation appears to be built mainly upon a group of prophecies, apparently relating to the invention of the motor car, the end of the world in 1881 or 1981, and so on, which were revealed soon after their publication at the end of the last century to be forgeries.[3] Nixon's fame has been almost completely eroded by the passage of time, so that his most lasting memorial is a derogatory reference in Dickens to a 'red faced Nixon' as typical of worthless cheap chapbooks.[4] Yet both Nixon and Shipton have a far more complex past than this would suggest.

The relative lack of interest in prophecy among political historians of the early modern period has not been shared by literary scholars. Employing the early modern emphasis on prophecy as any form of utterance directly inspired by God, as in its contemporary Protestant meaning, Diane Purkiss and Nigel Smith have recently described the way that women prophets of the 1650s and later used the action and form of prophecy as a means to negotiate a space for themselves to speak.[5] Through the display of their bodies as a vehicle for God's words, these women challenged established orders and hierarchies. Their activity threatened ideas of the masculinity of God, and of the enclosure and privacy proper for the female person. Purkiss has described as characteristic of these women prophets fasting and other forms of less deliberately induced bodily weakness, proximity to or feigning of death or infancy, and aspects of motherhood and reproduction.[6] This effacement of the human body can also be seen in some manifestations of the Nixon and Shipton traditions. Although the external force operating through Nixon and Shipton was not clearly the Christian God (always the power behind the women prophets discussed by Purkiss), in most versions of his text Nixon's body is clearly used and overwhelmed by the power that produces his predictions. Only in his masculinity is Nixon not weak, powerless, and marginal, and even then no mention is ever made of him marrying, producing children, or running his own household. He is a younger brother, poor, short, ugly, drivelling, violent, cruel and irrational in his actions, and he rarely speaks; when he does so his words are barely comprehensible except when he is prophesying.[7]

It is intriguing, however, that in the earliest versions of Nixon's prophecy, the writers of the texts did not feel the need to emphasize his social, physical and mental marginality.[8] It is also significant that the women prophets of the 1650s and 1660s described by Purkiss operated in the context of wide public knowledge of Mother Shipton, a prophetess who exhibited few of the characteristics of marginality. Shipton was permitted her voice in 1641 very specifically through the display of her body alongside the printing of her words, yet without recourse to any of these devices referred to by Purkiss, such as fasting or bodily weakness. The portrayal of the prophetess on the frontispiece of the first edition is simply that of a young woman dressed with some splendour in the clothes of perhaps forty years before. And the text and descriptions of Shipton imply nothing unusual about her in terms of her health, diet, or reproductive functions. The only signs of the kind of negotiation which Purkiss deems necessary for her prophetesses are that Shipton is probably meant to be old; her association with motherhood, although this lies only in the title of the prophecy and not in its text; and the fact that, like these later prophetesses, she is dismissed as a witch. This charge is levelled, however, by only one player in the drama, Cardinal Wolsey, who does not occupy a position of authority or moral superiority in the text. It is only in the editions of the 1650s that the image of Shipton begins to change, with, for example, frontispiece portrayals that bear more of the hallmarks of witchcraft – a trend which in the seventeenth century reaches its culmination with the 1686 edition.[9] This may be an example of the process whereby the mid-seventeenth century saw a reduction rather than an expansion of the opportunities for women to act as powerful voices and actors in political life.[10] Given the almost certainly largely male authorship of the Shipton prophecy, it is interesting that although a woman's voice was chosen to utter the portentous words, it was a woman's voice pure and simple. More broadly, it might be suggested that it was only from the 1650s that female prophetic authors were forced into positions of marginality, and that this marginality paradoxically then became another element to their validation.

Nixon and Shipton were, therefore, rather more powerful images than was usual in early modern prophecy. It is therefore interesting that in neither case did they unequivocally act as vehicle for the words of a Christian God. Unlike virtually every other prophet or prophetic tradition discussed in this volume, the authority behind their words remained obscure.

Given the power and authority with which Shipton and Nixon were made to speak, it is intriguing to consider them in the light of the currently accepted historiographical orthodoxy on prophecy in the early modern period. A clear chronology is apparent in Keith Thomas's influential discussion of prophecy;[11] it provides two elements to Thomas's argument which are highly debatable. The first is that Thomas's account is a modernization narrative, telling how the grip of prophecy on the minds of English people was once strong but grew ever weaker in the early modern period, allegedly part of the emancipation of the English from the past. Yet Thomas devoted little time to the implications of this theory. In a remarkable passage, following twenty-six pages documenting the continuing popularity of prophecy as late as the eighteenth century, he wrote:

> . . . the number of surviving chap-books of this kind might make one think that there was no difference between the seventeenth century and the nineteenth so far as the cult of ancient prophecy was concerned. Nevertheless, the evidence suggests that after the seventeenth century such prophecies were not usually taken seriously by educated persons. They continued to be issued and read, especially at times of excitement, but their general prestige had substantially diminished. It is hard to demonstrate this conclusion, but few acquainted with this period of history are likely to challenge it.[12]

The second debateable element to Thomas's account is a consequence of the first. Thomas does not examine how prophecy developed and grew in the early modern period, only how it declined. For Thomas, prophecy is a given. Thomas also identifies prophecy as declining from a position of national dominance, perhaps with local variations but with an essentially national focus. Prophecy is seen to operate on the national level and address national issues.

Yet prophecy did not die out as Thomas suggests. Its flexibility allowed it a continued role in English political life. It was flexible because of its deliberate obscurity and intentionally concealed meaning. There were three methods of concealing meaning: animal symbols, number and letter symbols, and painted scrolls.[13] All are very indirect means of reference. The flexibility of prophecy was also enhanced by the identification of prophecy with particular prophet-authors, whereby the prophet was the source of authority rather than the text: a particular text could be emphasized among the body of his or her work, or new texts could be 'discovered' and added to the corpus. This flexibility further allowed 'editors' to add prefaces and introductions that provided more interpretations and meanings. And this flexibility allowed prophecy to be used by a very broad spectrum of the population, which is an important factor in explaining how the political nation in England in the late medieval and early modern period was far broader and more inclusive than is usually assumed.

The local prophecies of Nixon, the Cheshire prophet, and Mother Shipton, the Yorkshire prophetess showed remarkable vitality during the period when according to Thomas they should have been in decline; and they allow us to see in detail the way that traditions were created, grew, and were sustained. Humphrey Newton of Pownall in Cheshire, a gentleman who died in 1536, kept a commonplace book which allows us to see the Nixon prophecy tradition in its early stages. In a memorandum, probably added to the book no later than the mid-1520s, he recorded that

Thomas Perkynson sang a song of Thomas Ersholedon & the quene of ffeiree Rehersyng the batell of Stoke fild & the batell at Branston of deth of the kynges of Scotts[.][14]

After describing the song of Erceldoun, Stoke and Flodden, Newton's visitor went on to say:

a lion shuld come out of walys & also a dragon & lond in werall that eny woman shuld have rowme to milke her cowe w[i]t[h] mony thousands & on a wennysday after to drive don Chester walls & after to feght in the fforest delamar w[i]t[h] a kyng of the southe which shuld have hundreds of m¹ & that shu[ld] feght ii or iii days & then ther shuld come a plogh of yew w[i]t[h] clubbez & clot chone & take parte & wyn alle & ther the kyng shuld be kylled w[i]t[h] many an other to the nowmber of lxi m[1] & never kyng after bot iiii wardens unto domysday[.]

This blend of Erceldoun and local material on Cheshire is precisely the form that Nixon's prophecy takes when Nixon first appears explicitly in a manuscript of the late sixteenth or early seventeenth century.[15] This text then formed the basis for the first printed edition in about 1713.[16]

Shipton also emerged late, with a printed edition in 1641.[17] Yet both prophets grew rapidly to immense popularity. Eighteen editions of Shipton are listed in the *Short Title Catalogue* for 1641 to 1700.[18] As for Nixon, once he received his first print publication, editions came thick and fast. By 1719 the prophecy was in its sixth edition, suggesting that the excitement around the Jacobite rebellion of 1715 had supported more than one edition a year. There was then a lull, but the seventh and tenth editions appeared in 1740. The threat from the Young Pretender produced another rush of editions in the 1740s. Fifteenth, eighteenth, and twenty-first editions are all recorded in 1745.[19] There was also an early tradition of publication of Nixon in Scotland. An edition appeared in Edinburgh in 1730, followed by two in Glasgow, one in 1738 and another perhaps in 1740.[20] Glasgow and Edinburgh were soon joined by many others. Significantly, as will be argued below, there was a consistently strong and creatively fertile tradition of publication in towns such as Chester itself, Warrington, Manchester, and Liverpool, in and near Nixon's home territory.[21] But the prophecy also spread far and wide: it was taken up by publishers in Derby, Gainsborough, Birmingham, Aylesbury, Hull, Penrith, Diss, and Halifax further afield.[22] In the early nineteenth century, the prophecy also began to be published in Welsh, with an edition, *Daroganau a phrophwydoliaeth hynod*, by J. Usher.[23] The same broad spread of influence is also true of Shipton's prophecy: in the 1660s, versions of the prophecy of Shipton even appeared in Dutch.[24] Both traditions addressed issues in which non-English speakers were interested, and the prophecies were able to cross linguistic barriers.

The Shipton and Nixon prophecies undoubtedly developed and flourished in the early modern period. Was this growth spontaneous, or was it organized, and if so by whom? The language and the form of publication of both traditions might initially suggest that this was material of interest to only the mass of the semi- or even un-educated poor. Both traditions expressed their hopes and fears for the future in a language which was uncomplicated, even crude: a predominance of active verbs, a distinct paucity of adjectives, and a sentence structure simple to the point of being basic. There was no complex analysis of motive or explanation of context.

Peckforton mill shall be removed to Ludington-hill,
And three days blood shall turn Noginshire mill.[25]

The time shall come when England shall tremble and quake for fear of a dead man that shall be heard to speak, then will the Dragon give the Bull a great snap, and when the one is down they shall go to London Town[.][26]

Equally, the format of publication is almost exclusively in the form of octavo or smaller chapbooks, usually of no more than sixteen or at most thirty-two pages. Where evidence of their cost survives for the eighteenth and nineteenth centuries, it usually suggests that the texts sold for sixpence or less.[27] Yet there are immediate reasons to question the assumption of marginality in readership. If the works were cheaply produced, it only meant that they were accessible to the poor, not that they were inevitably ignored by the rich. And there were other possible reasons for the form of the apparently uncouth language that the prophecy texts adopted. A deliberate archaism may have helped to give the texts the apparent antiquity upon which much of their reliability depended. Both Nixon and Shipton were placed initially in the early part of the sixteenth century, and it was necessary for the language to approximate to the style a reader might expect from work of such a vintage.[28] In the case of the Cheshire material, there also seems to have been an inheritance from the local poetic tradition of alliterative verse, a style which persisted in Cheshire and the North West into the seventeenth century, and which lends an archaic quality to the text, even where it had lost an overtly verse form.[29] This may in part have been due to the unconscious assimilation of this style by those who compiled the texts, but it may also have been a deliberate attempt to identify the work with a local tradition. The apparent crudity of the language may therefore be due to more than the illiteracy of the publishers and readers. While the texts of Nixon's prophecy itself, for example, were expressed in crude language, the commentaries which formed the major part of the publications of his prophecy included sophisticated and sceptical discussion that showed awareness of Camden and other English historians, and of comparable cases on the continent.[30] An ironic reference in Oldmixon's commentary on Nixon suggests its amused engagement with the style of the prophecies:

I know your prophets are generally for Raw-head and Bloody-bones, and therefore do not mind it much; or I might add, that Oulton mill shall be driven with blood instead of water: But these soothsayers are great butchers, and every hall is with them a slaughter-house.[31]

Some of the reasons for the survival and success of these prophecies lay in the texts themselves. The texts of the prophecies vary but have a demonstrable development. In each case, there was a considerable constituent of the tradition that was clearly drawn from earlier prophecies, some of which had been circulating for some time. Nixon's prophecy, for example, in its earliest manuscript version appeared alongside prophecies attributed to Bede and Thomas of Erceldoun alias the Rhymer.[32] By the time of its first printing, the different prophecies had been merged into one text, the Cheshire material intermingling with other prophecies such as the Cock of the North. Shipton also drew on earlier traditions, although to a lesser extent than Nixon: there were echoes, for example, of the idea that the kingdom should be placed under three governors, found in the prophecy of the Six Kings.[33] By the 1680s, the Shipton tradition had incorporated material from the White King prophecy tradition relevant to Charles I.[34] Despite the inclusion of this material, both prophecies also incorporated clearly original local sections. The earliest text of Nixon's prophecy included many references to an area of Cheshire around the abbey and house of Vale Royal, places such as the forest of Delamere, Acton Bridge, Darnhall Park and Pool, Northwich, and Windle Pool. Geographically, the area covered was very small. Local figures also appeared, such as John Hareware, abbot of Vale Royal.[35] Shipton's prophecy concerned a visit by three Tudor noblemen to York to question her, and included mentions of important York figures such as the lawyer Reginald Beasley.[36] After this, the text became a recitation of prophecies centred on York:

before that Owes Bridge and Trinitie Church meet, they shall build on the day, and it shall fall in the night, untill they get the highest stone of Trinitie Church, to be the lowest stone of Owes bridge, then the day will come when the North shall rue it wondrous sore, but the South shall rue it for evermore[37]

The alleged chronology of the prophets and their prophecies is significant in this connection. In spite of their widely different publication dates, the uttering of both prophecies was located by the traditions to a very similar time, during the reigns of Henry VII and Henry VIII. The most clearly dateable elements to the Nixon prophecy related to the end of the Cheshire monasteries and especially Vale Royal. Abbot Hareware, the last abbot of Vale Royal, and Sir Thomas Holcroft, the man who obtained the site of the monastery for his new house, were the main characters named in the prophecy.[38] Shipton's prophecy was introduced in the context of Wolsey's final journey northwards just before his death. Lords Darcy, Northumberland, and Suffolk were described visiting Shipton at the instance of the Cardinal after Wolsey heard Shipton's prophecy that he would never enter York in company with the king. Reginald Beasley, the other important figure to appear, is first noticed in 1530, became clerk of the city and castle of York before 1555, and died in the early 1560s.[39]

Partly because it could accommodate such derivative or local material, prophecy of this kind showed an ability to adapt to new conditions. Although much late medieval prophecy was connected more or less closely with the Catholic Church, for example, the Reformation was accompanied by the creation of Protestant prophecy and the adaptation of older prophecy to Protestant ends. Even Merlin ended up as a crypto-Protestant. In the same way, the English Civil War, unprecedented as it was, could be seen as the fulfilment of many of the dire warnings of earlier prophecies. Shipton, Nixon, and other new prophecies responded to these events. Shipton, who first arrived on the national scene during the Civil War, proved particularly adapatable. Developments of the text and the commentary on the text allowed reference to be made to contemporary events and aspirations. Shipton's text was recruited to the Protestant cause: Richard Lownds, its first publisher, specialized in radical Protestant pamphlets, producing a defence of the destruction of altar rails and an edition of John Pym's speech to the House of Lords in November 1641, a crucial statement of the radical Protestant cause.[40] *Mother Shipton's prophesies*, printed by one T.P. for Francis Coles in 1663, was prefaced by a print of 'The Pope suppressed by K. Henry the Eight', extracted directly from Foxe's *Actes and Monuments*.[41] The Shipton prophecy was, however, particularly relevant in 1641–2 because of its references to the North and to Scottish invasion.[42]

The Nixon prophecy provides a good example of continuing flexibility and adaptability after 1660. Although apparently well known in Cheshire, the prophecy had not in 1688 yet achieved a wider fame. There are signs, however, that it was seized upon by Jacobites in Cheshire to support the idea that William of Orange's triumph would be short-lived and that the Old Pretender would soon return: at least one Jacobite version and one reference to a Jacobite interpretation survive.[43] Partly in response to this and partly due to the literary entrepreneurism of two Whig publicists, John Oldmixon and Arthur Mainwaring, the prophecy was translated to the national stage. Arthur Mainwaring was well connected to the Cholmondeleys and their house at Vale Royal, where the earliest manuscript of the prophecy was preserved: his mother was the daughter of Charles Cholmondeley of Vale Royal, the heir whose miraculous birth one of the most famous Nixon prophecies foretold. Mainwaring's was an originally Tory or Jacobite family, but he had become an important member of the Whig regime, serving as secretary to the Duchess of Marlborough and receiving the lucrative post of auditor of the imprests from Godolphin in 1705.[44] Mainwaring had a very close working relationship with John Oldmixon, who was the author of such famous works as the *Critical History of England*, and it was in an edition by Oldmixon that Nixon was printed, in about 1713.[45] Mainwaring wrote the first editions of the *Examiner*, the newspaper set up to counter the Tory paper of the same name, but he brought in Oldmixon to write the *Medley*, its successor. Oldmixon repaid the debt incurred through this patronage many times over: he was a great admirer of Mainwaring, always stressing his ancient Cheshire ancestry – 'We find his Ancestors in the Rolls of the Conqueror' – and remained, after Mainwaring's death in 1712, a strong defender of his patron's politics and morals. The manner of his death caused comment, not least because of his notorious relationship with an actress, Mrs Oldfield, but Oldmixon was strenuous in his insistence that Mainwaring had not died of a sexually transmitted disease. It was Oldmixon who acted as Mainwaring's literary executor.[46] Oldmixon therefore served a patron who grew up in circles within which the prophecy was familiar currency. Yet Mainwaring was not the only member of the Whig élite who could supply Oldmixon with material on Nixon: according to his edition, Oldmixon worked from a copy of the prophecy in the possession of Lady Cowper, the politically active and highly opinionated wife of the man who was to become George I's first Lord Chancellor. Her other literary activity, for example the translation, for the benefit of the new non-English speaking king, of her husband's tract on the politics of Great Britain, is better known. Yet she also supported this publication of prophecies.[47] Given these two powerful Whig sponsors, it is not surprising that Oldmixon used the introduction he wrote to the prophecy to stress that the text supported the claim of George I to the throne, and that it predicted doom for invasions by foreign pretenders. He even silently changed the name of the king who would rule peacefully and long, which appears as Richard, son of Richard, in some versions,[48] to George, son of George.[49]

Behind this élite intervention in a popular tradition lies the extremely complex but nonetheless highly polarized politics of Cheshire from the Restoration to the middle of the eighteenth century.[50] In particular, the seizure by the Whig élite of the Nixon prophecy was permitted by the changing loyalties of many connected to the Cholmondeley family of Vale Royal. After the Restoration, many had been strident supporters of the Church and had, at best, grudgingly tolerated William of Orange. But after the Assassination Plot of 1696, they shifted towards acceptance of the removal of James II and even, eventually, of the inevitability of the Hanoverian succession. The Cholmondeleys' loyalty was significant because they were known to possess the original text of the prophecy, and this gave them some control over the tradition, a control they were keen to preserve. Their move to the Whigs provided, through the medium of Arthur Mainwaring, the possibility of a Whig interpretation of Nixon. As this change took place it became possible, and indeed necessary, to provide Whig and Hanoverian versions and interpretations of the prophecy. We should not, however, attribute this to cynical manipulation of plebeian credulity alone. It is notable that even in the nineteenth century the Cholmondeleys denied possession of the manuscript – to the Lysons, for example.[51] Yet there is no doubt that they kept it at Vale Royal, and there is every sign that they believed its contents, even keeping eagles in a special aviary to ensure that the family should never want for an heir.[52] In July 1943, with the new post-war world coming into sight, Lord Delamere finally acknowledged possession of the manuscript, depositing it in the Cheshire Record Office.[53] But not long after, the house was lost, and when it was photographed for *Cheshire Life* in 1947 the aviary stood ominously empty.[54] There was a degree of credulity in the minds of those in the Cheshire élite who guarded the tradition for what we might think were otherwise cynical political motives.

Shipton's tradition never seems to have had this element of élite control, and its early sponsors do not appear to have had the kind of official backing enjoyed by Nixon. Richard Lownds produced the first edition of Mother Shipton in London in 1641, *The Prophesie of Mother Shipton*:[55] his previous work, on the destruction of altar rails and an account of the speech of Pym to the Lords in November 1641, was unofficial. He seems to have catered to the market for anti-Arminian texts among many of London's population. Only in 1648 did a publisher with official connections begin producing editions of Shipton; Francis Coles also produced many official pamphlets and proclamations. Lownds's edition was noted by Thomason as appearing in December 1641. This was a time of serious crisis and, significantly, shortly after the king's return from Scotland, in the course of which he travelled through Yorkshire. Charles had left London on 10 August 1641. On his way north, he received a splendid reception in York, where he was greeted by the mayor and aldermen in full regalia, and by the city waits, at Bootham Bar.[56] After his visit to Scotland, Charles returned to London on 25 November, but the crisis returned and worsened. On 15 December there was a bitter debate on the printing of the Grand Remonstrance, and on 22 December the convicted murderer and papist Colonel Lunsford was appointed Lieutenant of the Tower of London. The period 27–9 December saw the city in tumult against the bishops.[57] During 1642 several editions of the prophecy were produced. After the abortive attempt on the five members, Charles again went north, arriving back in York on 18 March 1642. Although the response he received was now relatively low-key, the king stayed there until he moved to Nottingham to raise his standard on 22 August.[58] Another edition of Lownds's version followed in 1642 hard on the heels of the first,[59] and the text soon reappeared in other volumes of prophecy, such as *Two Strange Prophesies*, noted by Thomason in March 1642.[60] *Four Severall Strange Prophesies*, printed for Richard Harper, 1642, must be after 2 July, but not long after, because of the 'strange newes from Oundle in Northamptonshire' of that date appended to it,[61] and later still in the year came *Six Strange Prophecies*, 1642.[62] *A True Coppy of Mother Shiptons Last Prophecies*, printed for one T.V., also appeared in 1642.[63] No volume of prophecy was complete without Shipton's words, including for example also from 1642, *A True Coppie of a Prophesie which was found in [an] old ancient house of one Master Truswell. . . . Whereunto is added Mother Shipton's Prophesies*.[64]

There followed, interestingly, a pause in the flood of Shipton publications, until the crisis surrounding the Second Civil War, the disbanding of the army, and the execution of the king. *Twelve Strange Prophesies*, [sic] *besides Mother Shiptons*, newly printed for Francis Coles, was noted by Thomason in May 1648, following Charles's signature of the Engagement with the Scots in the December of the previous year, and soon after the outbreak of the Second Civil War.[65] *Thirteen* . . .

and *Foureteene Strange Prophesies, besides Mother Shipton's,* followed in 1648 and early in the following year.[66] Crucially, the Scots had re-entered the political stage as a threat to England. There were then two editions of the prophecy in the early 1650s, as the Scots were defeated by Cromwell,[67] and, as the collapse of the protectorate approached, another edition of *Shiptons Prophesie* in 1659.[68] The 1660s saw few editions, only *Mother Shipton's Prophesies,* 1663,[69] and *Mother Shiptons Christmas Carrols,* 1668.[70] It was the exclusion crisis that produced the next major group of publications of Shipton's words. A new edition of the 1663 *Mother Shipton's Prophesies* appeared in 1678.[71] The same period also produced *Fore-warn'd, Fore-arm'd; By a collection of five prophetical predictions, published by Mr William Lilly forty years ago . . . and one of Mother Shipton's,* 1682,[72] and another edition of *Mother Shipton's Prophesies,* 1685.[73] Richard Head's *The Life and Death of Mother Shipton* had editions in 1684 and 1687.[74] Head's purpose was clear: he explained Shipton's alleged words 'But tell's what's next, Oh cruel fate! / A King made martyr at his gate' as meaning 'the Execrable murther of that most excellent Prince Charles the First'.

There is therefore a clear contrast between the two prophecies. Shipton's prophecy emerged on the national stage in the 1640s and gained wide currency through printers with no official links. Nixon's prophecy, although probably in existence for at least as long in its Cheshire birthplace, only came to national attention through its printing in the early eighteenth century, and then with official sponsorship. One reason for this has already been suggested – the greater suitability of some prophecy texts to particular circumstances. A second important reason is the relative integration of local political cultures into the national political culture. Shipton's prophecy entered national debate earlier because the Yorkshire tradition from which it sprang was more quickly integrated into the national culture, partly due to the movement of people and ideas consequent on civil war. Nixon's Cheshire prophecy remained outside the national debate for so long because of the peculiar autonomy of Cheshire's political culture, consequent on a variety of constitutional and political factors as well as relative geographical and social isolation. Within the region of the north-west, even in the years 1590 to 1642, John Morrill found that 75 per cent of heads or heirs of major gentry families married partners from within the region.[75] Chester was a palatinate, with its own courts through the sixteenth and seventeenth centuries, and outside the English parliament until the 1540s.[76] Although Yorkshire was obviously distant from Westminster, and in the North Riding in particular had many jurisdictionally independent areas, it lay more clearly within the English political mainstream.[77]

This paper has attempted to demonstrate the continuing currency of political prophecy into the eighteenth century. It has shown senior political figures and important political writers were behind their publication. The reason for this is partly continuing credulity, but also, it should be noted, the potential for continuous reinterpretation of the texts. This made them relevant to the events of the middle and later seventeenth century and eighteenth centuries, a time in which events occurred that could never have been foreseen at the time the prophecy traditions originated. But it also shows the flexibility of political culture in the British Isles. Local areas were able to draw on traditions circulating nationally and develop them to apply to local circumstances; and then the newly formed prophecy could re-emerge to a national audience. This re-emergence was conditioned by the nature of the prophecy; Mother Shipton applied particularly well to a time when the main threat to England – all of England, including the south – was from the north, which had not been the case for at least sixty and effectively three hundred years. But it was also conditioned by the relative permeability of divisions between different local political cultures – not too difficult a transmission between Yorkshire and London, harder between London and Cheshire.

Notes

1 J. Loach, 'Pamphlets and Politics, 1553–8', *Bulletin of the Institute of Historical Research*, XLVIII (1975), 31–44; J. Loach, 'The Marian Establishment and the Printing Press', *English Historical Review*, 100 (1986), 138–51; J.N. King, 'Freedom of the Press, Protestant Propaganda, and Protector Somerset', *Huntington Library Quarterly*, 40 (1) (1976), 1–9; D. Cressy, *Literacy and the Social Order* (Cambridge University Press, 1980); N.Z. Davis, 'Printing and the People', in her *Society and Culture in Early Modern France* (London, Duckworth, 1975), pp. 189–226; T. Watt, *Cheap Print and Popular Piety, 1550–1640* (Cambridge University Press, 1991); P. Collinson, *The Birthpangs of Protestant England* (London and Basingstoke, Macmillan, 1988); S. Clark, *The Elizabethan Pamphleteers: Popular Moralistic Pamphlets, 1580–1640* (London, Athlone Press, 1983); L.B. Wright, *Middle-Class Culture in Elizabethan England* (Chapel Hill, North Carolina, University of North Carolina Press, 1958); P. Lake, 'Deeds against Nature: Cheap Print, Protestantism and Murder in Early Seventeenth-Century England', in K. Sharpe and P. Lake (eds), *Culture and Politics in Early Stuart England* (London and Basingstoke, Macmillan, 1994), pp. 257–83; P. Croft, 'The Reputation of Robert Cecil: Libels, Political Opinion and Popular Awareness in the Early Seventeenth Century', *Transactions of the Royal Historical Society*, 6th series, 1 (1991), 43–69; F.J. Levy, 'How Information Spread Among the Gentry', *Journal of British Studies*, 21 (2) (1982), 11–34; K. Sharpe, *Criticism and Compliment: The Politics of Literature in the England of Charles I* (Cambridge University Press, 1987); T. Cogswell, 'Politics and Propaganda: Charles I and the People in the 1620s', *Journal of British Studies*, 29 (3) (1990), 187–215; R. Cust, 'News and Politics in Early Seventeenth Century England', *Past and Present*, 112 (1986), 60–90; A. Bellany, '"Raylinge Rymes and Vauntinge Verse": Libellous Politics in Early Stuart England', in Sharpe and Lake (eds), *Culture and Politics in Early Stuart England*, pp. 285–310. c.f., for a continental perspective, R. Darnton's *The Literary Underground of the Old Regime* (Cambridge, Massachusetts, Harvard University Press, 1982); E. Eisenstein, *The Printing Press as an Agent of Change* (Cambridge University Press, 1980).

2 H. Rusche, 'Merlini Anglici: Astrology and Propaganda from 1641 to 1651', *English Historical Review*, 80 (1965), 322–33; H. Rusche, 'Prophecies and Propaganda, 1641 to 1651', *English Historical Review*, 84 (1969), 752–70; J. Friedman, *Miracles and the Pulp Press during the English Revolution: The Battle of the Frogs and Fairford's Flies* (London, UCL Press, 1993). One of William Lilley's prophecies sold over

1,800 copies in three days and went through several editions, eventually selling over 4,500 copies: Friedman, *Miracles and the Pulp Press*, p. 74; H.R. Plomer, 'A Printer's Bill in the Seventeenth Century', *The Library*, new series, 7 (1906).

3 W.H. Harrison, *Mother Shipton Investigated. The Result of Investigation in the British Museum Library, of the Literature Pertaining to the Yorkshire Sybil* (London, W.H. Harrison, 1881); *DNB, sub nomine.*

4 C. Dickens, *The Pickwick Papers*, ed. J. Kinsley, The Clarendon Dickens (Oxford, Clarendon Press, 1986), ch. 43, p. 668; c.f. the scepticism with regard to prophecy of e.g. C. Mackay, *Memoirs of Popular Delusions* (3 vols, London, Bentley, 1841), vol. I, pp. 196–201.

5 D. Purkiss, 'Producing the Voice, Consuming the Body: Women Prophets of the Seventeenth Century', in I. Grundy and S. Wiseman (eds), *Women, Writing, History, 1640–1740* (London, Batsford, 1992), pp. 139–58; N. Smith, *Literature and Revolution in England, 1640–1660* (New Haven and London, Yale University Press, 1994), p. 125; N. Smith, *Perfection Proclaimed: Language and Literature in English Radical Religion, 1640–1660* (Oxford, Clarendon Press, 1989), *passim*, esp. chapter 1.

6 Purkiss, 'Producing the Voice', pp. 141–53.

7 Nixon, later editions.

8 Cheshire County Record Office (hereafter CCRO), DDX 123, ff. 23r.–25r.

9 *The Strange and Wonderful History of Mother Shipton, Plainly Setting out her Prophecy, Birth, Life, Death, and Burial, with an excellent Collection of all her famous Prophecys more complete than ever yet before published* (London, for W.H., 1686), frontispiece; reproduced in *Mother Shipton's Prophecies: the Earliest Printed Editions of 1641, 1684 and 1686, together with an Introduction, to which is added the Story of Knaresborough* (Maidstone, George Mann, 1978), p. xxxii.

10 c.f. the contemporary pamphlet debate on the nature of woman: L. Woodbridge, *Women and the English Renaissance: Literature and the Nature of Womankind* (Brighton, Harvester, 1984); and, related specifically to prophecy, P. Mack, *Visionary Women: Ecstatic Prophecy in Seventeenth-Century England* (Berkeley, Los Angeles, London, 1992).

11 Thomas, *Religion and the Decline of Magic*, chapter 13.

12 Thomas, *Religion and the Decline of Magic*, p. 415.

13 Thomas, *Religion and the Decline of Magic*, p. 390.

14 Bodleian Library, Oxford, MS Lat. misc. c.66, f. 104. On Newton, D. Marsh, 'Humphrey Newton of Newton and Pownall (1466–1536): a gentleman of Cheshire and his commonplace book' (unpublished Ph.D. thesis, Keele University, 1995); D. Marsh, '"I See by Sizt of Evidence": Information Gathering in Late Medieval Cheshire', in D.E.S. Dunn (ed.), *Courts, Counties and the Capital in the Later Middle Ages*, The Fifteenth Century Series, no. 4 (Stroud, Sutton, 1996), pp.71–92.

15 CCRO, DDX 123, ff. 23r.–25r. is the Nixon text itself; ff. 1r.–2v. is material ascribed to Thomas 'Arseldoin'. Whitegate saw the baptisms, marriages and burials of many Nixons: e.g. 9 Aug. 1594, baptism of William Nicson, son of Thomas Nicson and Joanne his wife. Strangely there are no Robert Nixons to be found in this period. The appearance of the name John Walker several times on the last folio of CCRO, DDX 123 suggests a possible involvement of the production of the text with the John Walker who married Elizabeth Maddocke on 25 April 1591 at Whitegate parish church, the parish church for the Cholmondeleys of Vale Royal: CCRO, DDX 123, f. 27v.; P52/1/1 (Whitegate parish register, 1565–1753).

16 *The Cheshire Prophesy with historical and political remarks* (second edition, London, printed and sold by J. Roberts, *c.* 1713) (BL c.175 i.16(6.)) is apparently the earliest surviving printed version.

17 *The Prophesie of Mother Shipton in the raigne of King Henry the Eighth, fortelling the death of Cardinall Wolsey* (London, Richard Lownds, 1641) (BL, E. 181. (15.)); facsimile reprint: London, John Tuckett, 1869; Occasional Facsimilie reprints, no. 6 (an edition of 100 copies).

18 D.G. Wing, *Short-Title Catalogue of Books Printed in England, Scotland, Wales, and British America, 1641–1700*, III, p. 364.

19 J. Oldmixon, *Nixon's Cheshire Prophecy at Large . . . . Also his Life* (15th edition, London, 1745) (BL, 8610. aaa. 18. (1.)); J. Oldmixon, *Nixon's Cheshire Prophecy at Large . . . . Also his Life* (18th edition, London, 1745) (John Rylands University Library, Manchester, R 16917); J. Oldmixon, *Nixon's Cheshire Prophecy at Large . . . . Also his Life* (21st edition, London, 1745) (BL, 8630. f. 25.).

20 *A Wonderful Prophecy by one called Nixon . . . . With a Short Description of that Prophet* (Edinburgh, 1730) (BL, 1078. k. 15. (1.)); *A Wonderful Prophecy by one called Nixon . . . . With a Short Description of that Prophet* (Glasgow, 1738) (BL, 1076. l. 10. (6.)); *A Wonderful Prophecy by one called Nixon . . . . With a Short Description of that Prophet* (Glasgow, [1740?]) (BL, 1078. k. 26. (8.)).

21 J. Oldmixon, *The Original Predictions of Robert Nixon, commonly called the Cheshire Prophet; in doggrel verse . . . also some particulars of his Life* (Chester, W. Minshull, [1800?]) (BL, 8631. bb. 49.); *The Life and Prophecies of R. Nixon* ('55th edition', Warrington, 'for the travelling stationers', [1815?]) (BL, 1078. i. 23. (15.)); *The Life and Prophecies of Robert Nixon, of the Bridge House near the Forest of Delamere in Cheshire* (Manchester, J. Swindells, [1830?]) (BL, 11621. b. 16. (19.)); *Prophecies of Robert Nixon, commonly called the Cheshire Prophet, taken from a very ancient and authentic Manuscript, with Remarks on several instances wherein they have been fulfilled, to which is prefixed the life of this remarkable man* (Liverpool, J. Hopper & Son) (CCRO, H 13.3K).

22 *Nixon's Original Cheshire Prophecy in Doggerel Verse . . . To which is . . . added the Prophecy at large from Lady Cowper's Correct Copy . . . also some particulars of his life, likewise Jurieu's Prophecy of the French Revolution* (Gainsborough, Henry Mozley, [1800?]) (BL, 8630. a. 53. (1.)); *Nixon's Cheshire Prophecy at Large* (Aylesbury, [1820?]) (BL, 1078. i. 26. (8.)); *Nixon's Cheshire Prophecy at Large* (Birmingham, [1820?]) (BL, 8610. a. 60.); *Nixon's Cheshire Prophecy at Large* (Hull, [1820?]) (BL, 11621. c. 9. (2.)); *Prophecies of R. Nixon . . . from Lady Cowper's Correct Copy. . . . Also an account of his Life and Death* (Penrith, [1820?]) (BL, 1078. k. 7. (12.)); *Nixon's Original Cheshire Prophecy* (Diss, [1845?]) (BL, 8631. b. 37. (2.)); *Nixon's Original Cheshire Prophecy. . . . Likewise Jurieu's Prophecy of the French Revolution* (Halifax, [1850?]).

23 BL, 872. e. 29. (8.).

24 *Moeder Schiptons Prophecyen van Engelant . . . Uyt het Engelsch overgeset . . .* ('s Gravenhage, 1667) (BL, T. 1720. (30.)).

25 'Nixon's Cheshire Prophecy at Large', in *The Original Predictions of Robert Nixon, commonly called The Cheshire Prophet* (Chester, printed and sold by W. Minshull; also by G. Sael, London, ND), p. 10.

26 *The Prophesie of Mother Shipton in the raigne of King Henry the Eighth*, p. 4.

27 John Oldmixon, *Nixon's Cheshire Prophecy at Large Published from the Lady Cowper's Copy, with Historical and Political Remarks: and Several Instances wherein it is Fulfilled; The Sixth Edition; to which is added, The Life of Nixon* (London, J. Roberts, 1719), p. A1: 6d. A century later the price was the same: *Nixon's Original Cheshire Prophecy in Doggerel Verse* (Gainsborough, Henry Mozley, [1800?]), p. 1.

28 It is interesting that the MS of Nixon in CCRO appears to be deliberately using an antiquated and primitive style of script as well as language.

29 M.J. Bennett, 'Sir Gawain and the Green Knight and the Literary Achievement of the North

West Midlands: the Historical Background', *Journal of Medieval History*, 5 (1979), 63–88; M.J. Bennett, *Community, Class, and Careerism: Lancashire and Cheshire Society in the Age of Sir Gawain and the Green Knight* (Cambridge University Press, 1983), pp. 231–5; D.A. Lawton, 'Scottish Field: Alliterative Verse and Stanley Encomium in the Percy Folio', *Leeds Studies in English*, 10 (1978), 42–57, esp. pp.42–3; C.A. Luttrell, 'Three North-West Midlands MSS', *Neophilologus*, 42 (1958), 38–50 (Thomas Ireland of Hale and the Booths of Barton); John Rylands University Library, Manchester, Legh of Lyme MSS, MS of 'Scottish Field'.

30 Oldmixon refers to Camden's discussion of the prophetic swimming trees of Brereton that foretell the death of the heir to that house; and his reference to a comparable case from the abbey of St Maurice in Burgundy: 'Nixon's Cheshire Prophecy at Large', in *The Original Predicitons of Robert Nixon, commonly called The Cheshire Prophet* (Chester, printed and sold by W. Minshull; also by G. Sael, London, ND), p. 30.

31 J. Oldmixon, 'Nixon's Cheshire Prophecy at Large', p. 24; this is less true of the Shipton prophecy, but c.f. esp. *St. Stephen's Tripod: or, Mother Shipton in the Lower H**se. Comprising a Scheme of Prophecy Admonitory and Epigamatic* [sic], *formed on a Mystic and Denunciatory System of Revelation; and Delivered on the Ancient Principles of Sybilline Prescience and Oracular Inspriration* (London, G. Kearsley, 1782) (BL, 1600/1492).

32 Thomas, *Religion and the Decline of Magic*, p. 392, n. 19, notes links to *The Prophecies of Rymour, Beid and Marlyng*, and to a prophecy of 1553. For the former, see A. Fox, 'Prophecies and Politics in the Reign of Henry VIII', in A. Fox and J. Guy, *Reassessing the Henrician Age: Humanism, Politics and Reform, 1500–1550* (Oxford, Basil Blackwell, 1986), pp. 77–94, esp. pp. 81–7, dating the prophecy to some time shortly after the taking of Tournai in 1513. *The Romance and Prophecies of Thomas of Erceldoune*, ed. J.A.H. Murray, Early English Text Society, o.s., 61 (London, N. Trubner, 1875).

33 *The Prophesie of Mother Shipton in the raigne of King Henry the Eighth*, p. 5.

34 R. Head, *The Life and Death of Mother Shipton* (London, for Benjamin Harris, 1684), pp. 71–6 in GM edition. The prophecy of the White King had re-emerged in 1643 with the publication of *The Prophecy of a White King of Brittaine*; in the following year, William Lilly had produced his *The Prophecy of the White King and Dreadfull Dead-Man Explained*: Rusche, 'Prophecies and Propaganda', pp. 757–60; Friedman, *Miracles and the Pulp Press*, pp. 70–4.

35 CCRO, DDX 123, f. 23r.

36 *The Prophesie of Mother Shipton in the raigne of King Henry the Eighth*, pp. 1, 3; S.T. Bindoff, *The House of Commons, 1509–1558* (3 vols, London, Secker and Warburg for the History of Parliament Trust, 1982), vol. I, pp. 425–6.

37 *The Prophesie of Mother Shipton in the raigne of King Henry the Eighth*, p. 3.

38 CCRO, DDX 123, ff. 23r.–25r. *Victoria History of the Counties of England: The County of Chester* (3 vols and continuing, Oxford University Press, 1979) (hereafter *VCH Cheshire*), vol. III, pp. 162–4; G. Ormerod, *The History of the County Palatine and City of Chester*, second edition by T. Helsby (3 vols, London, George Routledge & Sons, 1882), vol. II, pp. 151–3.

39 *The Prophesie of Mother Shipton in the raigne of King Henry the Eighth*, pp. 1, 3; Bindoff, *House of Commons*, vol. I, pp. 425–6.

40 *Certaine Affirmations in Defence of the Pulling Down of Communion Rails* (Sept. 1641); *The Substance of Mr Pym's Speech to the Lords in Parliament* (noted by Thomason on 9 Nov. 1641).

41 Short Title Catalogue, 3448 (BL, 8610. d. 27.).

42 As Rusche points out, the prediction of wars beginning in the spring may have been a deliberate reference to the Bishops' Wars: 'Prophecies and Propaganda', p. 755.

43 '[T]he work of some sly Jacobite': *Chester Miscellany*, 1750; reprinted in T.W. Barlow, *The Lancashire and Cheshire Historical Collector* (Manchester, 1855): a letter dated 20 Nov. 1747 was sent to the press describing how in Cheshire a stone had been discovered with an inscription describing how the land would be crushed by taxation and overrun with scarlet dragons, a thinly disguised reference to soldiers; W.E.A. Axon, *Nixon's Cheshire Prophecies . . . With an Essay on Popular Prophecies* (1873), pp. 65–78. I. Sellers, 'Nixon, the Cheshire Prophet and his Interpreters', *Folklore*, 92(1) (1981), 34–5.

44 *DNB* (1909), XII, 790–2; G. Holmes, *British Politics in the Age of Anne* (London, Macmillan, 1967), pp. 191, 297.

45 On Oldmixon, *DNB* (1909), XIV, 1009–13; D.H. Stevens, *Party Politics and English Journalism, 1702–1742* (1916; reprinted New York, Russell and Russell, 1967), pp. 72, 102–3; J.A. Downie, *Robert Harley and the Press: Propaganda and Public Opinion in the Age of Swift and Defoe* (Cambridge University Press, 1979), pp. 122, 174, 182.

46 J. Oldmixon, *Memoirs of the Press, Historical and Political, For Thirty Years Past* (London, 1742); [J. Oldmixon] *The Life and Posthumous Works of Arthur Mainwaring, Esq.* (London, 1715), esp. p. 344.

47 *Diary of Mary, Countess Cowper, Lady of the Bedchamber to the Princess of Wales, 1714–1720*, ed. S. Cowper (London, John Murray, 1865), introduction and pp. 1–127; *DNB* (1887) XII, 386, 389–93.

48 'The Original Predictions of Robert Nixon, as delivered by himself' in *The Original Predicitons of Robert Nixon, commonly called The Cheshire Prophet* (Chester, printed and sold by W. Minshull; also by G. Sael, London, ND), pp. 9–16: 'Then rise up Richard, son of Richard, / And bless the happy reign. / Thrice happy he who sees this time to come, / When England shall know rest and peace together.' (p. 16). [from CCRO, DCC 37/3].

49 J. Oldmixon, 'Nixon's Cheshire Prophecy, at Large; from Lady Cowper's Correct Copy' in *The Original Predictions of Robert Nixon, commonly called The Cheshire Prophet* (Chester, printed and sold by W. Minshull; also by G. Sael, London, ND), pp. 21–31: p. 29. 'But that GEORGE, the SON of GEORGE, should put and to all. That afterwards the church should flourish, and England be the most glorious nation upon earth.' This edition notes the emendation in a footnote.

50 J. Morrill, 'The County Seats', in *VCH Cheshire*, vol. I, pp. 114–27; J.H. Hodson, *Cheshire, 1660–1780*, pp. 1–27.

51 D. and S. Lysons, *Magna Britannia: II(ii), Cheshire* (London, T. Cadell and W. Davies, 1810), pp. 814–16.

52 B. Tunstall, 'The Story of Vale Royal – II', *Cheshire Life*, 13 (3) (Mar. 1947), 24.

53 CCRO, note in list for DDX 123.

54 Tunstall, 'The Story of Vale Royal – II', 24.

55 Short Title Catalogue, 3445 (BL, E. 181. (15.)).

56 A. Fletcher, *The Outbreak of the English Civil War* (London, Edward Arnold, 1981), pp. 53, 160; on Charles's trip to Scotland, C. Russell, *The Fall of the British Monarchies, 1637–42* (Oxford, Clarendon Press, 1991), ch. 8.

57 Fletcher, *Outbreak of the English Civil War*, pp. 161–78; Russell, *Fall of the British Monarchies*, pp. 400–45.

58 Fletcher, *Outbreak of the English Civil War*, p. 231; Russell, *Fall of the British Monarchies*, pp. 477–524.

59 Short Title Catalogue, 3446.

60 'The second prophesie of Mother Shipton', in *Two Strange Prophesies, predicting wonderfull events to betide this yeere of danger; named Mother Shipton* (London, printed for G. Smith, 1642) (BL, E. 141. (2.)). Fletcher, *Outbreak of the English Civil War*, p. 244.

61 (London, 1642); Short Title Catalogue, 3443; BL, C. 40. f. 12. Musters at Oundle: Fletcher, *Outbreak of the English Civil War*, pp. 350, 362.

62 Formerly Short Title Catalogue, 3452.

63 Short Title Catalogue, 3454.

64 (London, H. Marsh, 1642): BL, E. 149. (16.); 718. g. 47.

65 Short Title Catalogue, 3455.

66 *Thirteen*: BL, E. 525. (14.); Short Title Catalogue, 3453. *Fourteene*: London, for Richard Harper. BL, E. 527. (7.) [Short Title Catalogue, 3444].

67 *Shiptons Prophesie* (London, by T.H. for Francis Coles and Richard Harper, 1651) (Short Title Catalogue, 3447); and *The Second Part of Mother Shipton's Prophecies* (London, for Joshua Coniers, 1651?) (Short Title Catalogue, 3451).

68 (London, by T.H. for Francis Coles and Richard Harper, 1651, new edition by A.B. for Francis Coles. 1659) (Short Title Catalogue, 3447A). Rusche claimed the reduction in publication of prophecies after 1651 was due to parliamentary control: 'Prophecies and Propaganda', p. 768.

69 (London, by T.P. for Francis Coles) (Short Title Catalogue, 3448).

70 (London, by P. Lillicrap for William Harris) (Short Title Catalogue, 3442).

71 (London, by T.P. for Francis Coles, 1663; new edition printed by A.P. and T.H. for Francis Coles) (Short Title Catalogue, 3448A).

72 BL, 8610. bb. 32.

73 (London, for Francis Coles; new edition, London, for W. Thackeray) (Short Title Catalogue, 3449). There was also an edition in 1685 produced in Edinburgh: Short Title Catalogue, 3456.

74 BL, 8631. aaa. 12. and 8610. d. 26. Finally at the start of the next century, another edition of *Mother Shipton's Prophesies* (London, previously for Francis Coles, for W. Thackeray, 1685, London, 1700) (Short Title Catalogue, 3450).

75 J. Morrill, *Cheshire 1630–1660: County Government and Administration during the English Revolution* (Oxford University Press, 1974), p. 3.

76 *VCH Cheshire*, vol. 2, pp. 9–35; D. Clayton, *The Administration of the County Palatine of Chester, 1442–1485*, Chetham Society, 3rd series, 35 (Manchester University Press, 1990).

77 R.B. Smith, *Land and Politics in the England of Henry VIII: the West Riding of Yorkshire, 1530–46* (Oxford, Clarendon Press, 1970); J.T. Cliffe, *The Yorkshire Gentry from the Reformation to the Civil War* (London, Athlone Press, 1969); M.E. James, *Family, Lineage and Civil Society: a Study of Society, Politics and Mentality in the Durham Region, 1500–1640* (Oxford, Clarendon Press, 1974); A.J. Pollard, *North-Eastern England during the Wars of the Roses: Lay Society, War, and Politics, 1450–1500* (Oxford, Clarendon Press, 1990), pp. 144–5.

Part 2

PROPHECIES IN THE AGE OF THE BEAST: REFORMING PROPHECY

The Reformation changed the parameters within which prophecy operated. Luther's challenge to tradition and authority released still further the power of inspired language in a multiplicity of contexts. All the papers gathered in this section deal with this new freedom of communication and its consequences.

Kenneth Gibson describes how Philip Ziegler and Ludwig Gifftheil, two 'lone prophets', were allowed to wander through Europe to preach Protestant unity and the fight against the beast. Gwilym Games's paper illustrates how prophecy, as the act of preaching, shaped a new society in New England, at once destroying the old and building up the new. It also shows how contested a territory prophecy was, waves of new religions contesting others and struggling to have their own prophets accepted. The last paper of this section reminds us how much science was tangled up with religious matters. Isaac Newton, the key figure of the age, played an important role in deciphering prophecies.

In many ways, Newton represented the culmination of this drive for prophetic interpretation set up during the English Reformation. After him, the momentum of biblical prophetic interpretation lost not only some of its political impetus but also its scientific rationale.

Part 2

PROPHECIES IN THE AGE OF THE BEAST: REFORMING PROPHECY

5

APOCALYPTIC AND MILLENARIAN PROPHECY IN EARLY STUART EUROPE: PHILIP ZIEGLER, LUDWIG FRIEDRICH GIFFTHEIL AND THE FIFTH MONARCHY

K. Gibson

During the early seventeenth century most of Europe witnessed a series of religious, political and social upheavals, which gave rise to a huge number of millenarian prophecies. This renewed interest in 'the latter days of the world' intensified the existing eschatological excitement, the anticipation of Judgement Day, inherited from the Middle Ages, and provoked a stream of prognostications ranging from astrological and astronomical calculations to the occult-based wisdom of the Rosicrucian movement with its call for universal reformation. This was buttressed by the appearance and frequent sightings of new stars and comets which signalled for most contemporaries the beginnings of the final acts of history and the culmination of a decisive battle between the forces of good and evil.[1] From this vast ocean of eschatological expectancy emerged a diversity of alchemists, prophets and other religious figures who challenged the political and religious order by proclaiming the dawn of a new golden age, among them two Germans, Philip Ziegler and Ludwig Friedrich Gifftheil. The travels of these two characters illustrate the physical movement of ideas and the dissemination of prophecies across Europe. In particular they illustrate the arrival of millenarian ideas in England that were to form an important part of the Biblically based 'Fifth Monarchy' movement. They also illustrate the liminal position of prophets in early modern European society, often rejected or reviled and yet always able to communicate to political classes well above their own.

The study of prophecy in Europe after the Lutheran reformation has received renewed academic attention in recent years. Robin Bruce Barnes among others offers a thorough analysis of the Lutheran apocalyptic literature and demonstrates the 'pervasiveness and persistence of eschatological but more especially apocalyptic views'.[2] More important, in the context of this chapter, is his comment on 'English scholars' who trace the development of these ideas through such figures as Thomas Brightman and Joseph Mede and identify the movement of ideas as being from England to Europe where millenarianism had a chance 'to take root in a climate favourable to further development'. Barnes suggests this assertion to be only partially true as 'Reformation prophecy developed later in England . . . and proved to be less intense than the prevailing Lutheran attitude'.[3] As will become apparent below, neither of these arguments can be fully supported because there existed an exchange of ideas between British and European eschatological and political commentators who all made significant contributions to the intensely expectant atmosphere of seventeenth-century Europe.

A starting point for the study of the two prophets is provided by Richard van Dülmen who, in the early 1970s, identified a small nucleus of religious reformers active in the town of Nuremberg between the years 1618 and 1648.[4] The tolerant attitude of the town's authorities allowed this group of disparate individuals to flourish. Although they were accused of being fanatics or enthusiasts, their ideas offered an educated and coherent challenge to accepted institutions within a framework of demands for a general Reformation. Their prime aim was to eliminate all political and religious conflicts and implement social reform in the interest of the underprivileged. This group, however, were not organized political radicals in the tradition found in the English sects of the 1640s and 1650s and never seriously threatened existing authority. Their demands were directed primarily to leading political, military and religious leaders who were perceived to possess the necessary powers to bring about the desired reforms. The members of this group, in particular the spiritual leader Nikolaus Pfaff, forged a wide range of contacts throughout Germany, and the town became a focal point for various forms of eschatological ideals. This is reflected in the varying demands for reform which were formulated from many individual and divergent viewpoints including millenarian, astrological and alchemistic predictions. It is therefore not surprising that both Ziegler and Gifftheil were attracted to this haven of eschatological speculation. Ziegler appeared there in 1619, causing an uproar by predicting the death of the Emperor Matthias for the following Monday, for which he was arrested, examined by a committee but subsequently released.[5] Gifftheil had much closer contact with this group and probably exchanged ideas with two other 'lone prophets', Wilhelm Eo and Johann Permeier. It was also here that Gifftheil met his life-long companion, Johann Friedrich Munster, who later accompanied him on his travels throughout Europe and later to England. Both Ziegler and Gifftheil fitted well within this community and formed part of the body of 'lone prophets' who appeared in Germany at this time.[6]

Tracking ideas is fraught with many difficulties. First, these prophets attracted much hostile criticism due, to a certain extent, to their prescriptive claims of God-given authority beyond accepted religious and political institutions. Second, their output is either lost because of the Second World War, or widely scattered throughout European archives.[7] Secondary material is equally difficult to locate and lies hidden in the journals of local history societies or in other specialist publications.[8] Examples of this are the articles by Ron Heisler on Ziegler and the publication by E. Eylenstein on Gifftheil. Heisler, whose article appeared in a journal devoted to occult history, sought to establish links between Ziegler and the Rosicrucian movement. This undoubtedly distorted his interpretation, which was also marred by historical inaccuracies and speculation concerning Ziegler's activities in Paris and London. Eylenstein, a German theologian who was sympathetic to Gifftheil's ideas, attempted to demonstrate that Gifftheil was a forerunner of the Pietist movement. This latter work is, however, very important as it contains a broad synthesis of Gifftheil's writings now lost to modern scholarship.[9]

Other accounts of these prophets, written in the late seventeenth and mid-eighteenth centuries by Gottfried Arnold and Heinrich Corrodi, relied heavily on the attacks published by contemporary confessional rivals, whose sole purpose was to discredit and undermine the prophets' credibility.[10] These one-sided accounts have made it convenient for more recent commentators to view the prophets as over-zealous radical Chiliasts who wandered around Europe with the naïve aim of erecting the New Jerusalem. In some instances, the choice of anecdotes provides evidence to question the mental stability of the prophets. A case in point is the oft-repeated incident in which Ziegler, in 1617, was thrown into an asylum in Frankfurt for ripping down the coat of arms from the town hall.[11] Arnold emphasized this act to make a political statement, that not only reflects his aversion to 'enthusiastic frenzy', but also suggests the insanity of anyone who violated the accepted social conventions or expressed religious or political dissent.[12] Arnold may be correct to question Ziegler's contact with reality, but his account was scarcely balanced.

Instances of a potential loss of mental stability can be found in Ziegler's account of his experience in a Zurich prison where he suffered repeated torture at the hands of his gaolers. His captors tied him with 'new bonds and chains and lacerated and tore me so much that I bit my tongue'. In his agony he began to sing and the spirit of fortitude returned to him so that the bonds and chains were broken. These 'severe trials' culminated in what he called 'miraculous interventions' when two people came into his cell 'whom I think to have been not men but angels' and released his bonds and applied a luxurious salve to his wounds. This divine experience appears to be a turning point in his life, as afterwards, when presenting himself as a key witness of the final age, he declared he was 'Origen the Great of Germany . . . the Herald of the Origenic Kingdom'. Ziegler further justified this by electing himself a prophet chosen by God who 'sends his prophets when some transformation of kingdoms, provinces and Empires is prepared'.[13] Ziegler closely associated political upheaval with a new age of prophecy. In spite of not having a clear political alternative in mind he knew himself to be part of tidal wave of change.

Later, in London, Ziegler was imprisoned once again, among other things for allegedly claiming to be an alchemist who could make gold.[14] He also attempted to win adherents to his cause at an earlier date at the University of Giessen by claiming 'students and teachers will no longer be required' in the future New Golden Age.[15] His prison experiences were not only turning points of his life but illustrated his unswerving commitment to universal reformation.

A glance at any of his extant writings reveals that he was a highly educated individual. A Philip Ziegler graduated from the University of Freiburg in 1597 who is probably to be identified with the prophet.[16] Moreover, his role in the production of a work published by the renowned Frankfurt publishing house of Theodore De Bry is a testimony to his versatile character and wide-ranging skills.[17] His own impressively illustrated textbook *Harmonia* is a scholarly and pedagogic work on the life of Christ compiled to introduce children to the scriptures.[18] Ziegler was accepted into the company of leading figures of the European intellectual élite. While in Holland he was on friendly terms with the leader of the Collegiant movement, the millenarian Adam Boreel, from whom he later received financial support.[19] On his visit to England he gained access to King Charles I through the influential clerk of the Chamber, Sir David Ramsey.[20]

Ziegler's ability to enter into reasoned academic debate and present clear and coherent arguments to defend his own ideas is reflected in his 'Reply and Cynosure'. This tract, originally written in Groningen in 1624 and later translated into Latin at Amsterdam, is a convincing and plausible defence against the attacks made by Matthias Ehinger, 'whose semi-learned, false and iniquitous censure I judge to be most hasty and precocious'. Ehinger, Ziegler tells us, was 'asked by many eminent people to make a judicial examination of the premises and arguments which inform the predictions of the new prophets in Germany including Wilhelm Eo, Paul Nagel and others'. Broadly speaking, Ehinger attempted to refute the ideas of these new prophets and to undermine the coming age of messianic peace. His attack was probably a response to the perceived political threat posed by the prophets and an attempt by the authorities to curb the appeal of their apocalyptic religious message. The main thrust of Ehinger's argument was that the new prophets were fortuitous and their predictions without foundation: 'they fill their bellies by means of splendid arguments' but are proved to be utterly false as Bible-based prophecies 'are to be interpreted spiritually' rather than as indicative of coming events.[21] Ziegler answered this by referring to the predictions of the Silesian furrier Christoph Kotter who prophesied the fate of Frederick V, the Elector Palatine, which, he argued, 'subsequent events have confirmed'.[22] He supported this by referring to his own prediction on the death of Matthias, which, he wrote, proved to be correct as the Emperor died 'on the day which I named'. The 'Reply and

Cynosure' also convincingly demonstrates Ziegler's wide knowledge of contemporary eschatological commentators and, moreover, his own complex vision of the coming messianic Kingdom.[23]

The roots of this vision are a fusion of Joachim de Fiore's Trinitarian interpretation of history, culminating in the third Age of the Spirit, and the Rosicrucian ideals of a Universal and General Reformation of the whole world.[24] The Rosicrucian ideas represent, as Frances Yates suggested,[25] not only an advancement of learning, but above all an illumination of a religious and spiritual nature. They are reflected in Ziegler's hopes for a 'future abundance and affluence of all things, an increase in good virtues and knowledge and a life of justice, honesty, purity and peace'.[26] The Joachimite scheme, as Marjorie Reeves has pointed out, develops through the three stages of Law and Grace to a future Age of Illumination in the Spirit, giving a progressive movement towards a further spiritual climax in history.[27] The preceding tribulations to this, such as religious strife and war, and the manifestation of multiple Antichrists, provided Ziegler with compelling evidence that the transition from the second to the third stage of history was imminent. To support this he gathered together many writings from the leading commentators of the day, including the Italian Joachimist, Joseph Brocado, and the English commentators Thomas Brightman and William Gouge, whom he mistook as the author of a work by Sir Henry Finch:[28]

> all prophets are of the opinion that the ruin of the Roman Empire is imminent, the destruction of the Spiritual Antichrist [the pope], the Universal Reformation of the world is rushing onward bringing with it the constitution of the Kingdom of Israel, both spiritual and corporeal in the most holy Third Age of the Holy Spirit, otherwise the time of Messianic Peace.[29]

Thus the key signs of the coming Age are about to be fulfilled, one of which, the conversion of the Jews and the physical restoration of the Kingdom of Israel, played a major role in Ziegler's eschatological scheme.[30] Using primarily the commentaries of Brightman and Finch/Gouge, he sought proof for Paul's promise in Romans 11: 25–31 'that all Israel shall be saved' and 'Jerusalem and the land of Canaan will be rebuilt and will never be destroyed. The calling of the Gentiles from all the lands of the world will follow the conversion of the Jews.'[31] The ultimate act to establish this messianic Kingdom is when 'the peoples of the world . . . join themselves with the Jews of David, to Elijah and others'.[32]

Further to Ziegler's vision of Christian unity and messianic peace, his 'Reply and Cynosure' reveals a political commitment to the Protestant rulers in Europe including Frederick the Elector Palatine, the King of Sweden, Gustavus Adolphus, and King James I and VI of Great Britain.[33] According to Heinrich Corrodi, Ziegler originally came to England to persuade James to admit

Protestant refugees of the Thirty Years War to this country (he came too late as James died before his arrival).[34] However, it seems more likely, given his political commitments, that he came for three reasons. First, he shared James's vision of a reunion of the Churches and a General Council on neutral ground attended by those who 'believe and profess all the ancient grounds of the true, ancient Catholic and apostolic faith'.[35] Ziegler built on this idea by drawing on Brocado's idea of a Council in Venice and proclaimed that the question for the whole Church 'concerns the Third Elijah in the future ecumenical Council of Constantinople to be confirmed, approved and announced by public voice'.[36] Second, Ziegler's refutation of the Pope's authority, which 'is not over human conscience and not over Emperors, Kings and Princes', and his reference to the precedents of Isaac Casaubon demonstrated his support for the king's position in his dispute with the Pope over the Oath of Allegiance and Papal claims to jurisdiction over kings.[37] Third, Ziegler probably sought backing for Frederick V among the circle of Palatine supporters in London who desired a more active English involvement in European affairs.[38] At the time that he wrote the 'Reply and Cynosure' many European Protestants still supported Frederick, despite his defeat at the battle of White Mountain, and hoped for a recovery of the Palatinate from the Habsburg powers. Ziegler gave Frederick a messianic role as the 'Lion from the North, the elected Emperor of the Golden Age who would destroy the Austrian Eagle' and usher in the new Millennium.[39] This clearly proved Ziegler's specific political aims on coming to England and that he supported them by the application of prophetic political propaganda. To dismiss him as a 'madman' or a 'charlatan', as Johann Rusdorf did during this visit, obscures the connections between high politics and prophetic agitation.[40]

At a later date, after the death of Frederick, Ziegler adapted this Paracelsian prophecy and applied it to Gustavus Adolphus 'who is that star in the North by whose birth the whole Roman Empire is to be destroyed'. He inserted Gustavus Adolphus in the tradition of the last world emperor who will arise and conquer many countries and clear the way for peace and prosperity when he stated 'Rex Succia [the king of Sweden] is Alexander the Great who will vanquish the whole world within the space of twelve years'. It is not known where Ziegler published this prophecy as he disappeared from the historical record after 1626, but it is possible that he left England and continued into the 1630s to travel around Europe.[41]

If we now turn our attention to Ludwig Friedrich Gifftheil, we find him, like Ziegler, gaining both sympathetic adherents to his cause and attracting the attention of an equal number of contemporaries who criticized him for his radical interpretation of the Last Days and his claims to be king David the Second.[42] The scholar Henry More adopted a reproachful attitude to Gifftheil's 'fancying himself that David the prophets foretell of who should be that peaceable Prince and Deliverer of the Jews'. With reference to a sighting of him in London, More said 'there have been several instances in History of those who have fancied themselves Monarchs, Popes and Emperors whereas they have been but Footboys, Grooms and Serving Men'.[43] Gifftheil's claims also provoked the anger of Paul Felgenhauer who reported that anyone refusing to 'serve him with writings and letters is perceived as being spiritually inert, lazy, lifeless, loveless and hypocritical'.[44] Earlier on in his career, he appeared before a Consistory Court in his home state of Württemberg accused of 'gross misunderstanding, irresponsible pride' and the undertaking of things for which he had no qualification. His response to this was a typical prophetic outburst warning the formidable group of gathered theologians that they had to 'retract publicly their own slanderous utterances . . . to forestall their imminent extinction[;] . . . as long as the world with its false prophets defies God, must you be subjected to temporal and eternal wrath, judgement and calamities'. Subsequently he was ordered to swear an oath of allegiance to the Church, which he refused to do, and this led to a prison sentence and a period of forced labour.[45] These examples were typical of the responses to Gifftheil's lifelong intense dissatisfaction with the ecclesiastical hierarchies and orthodox Church doctrines.

The early years of the Thirty Years War, which provided the context for the above incident, played a great part in the formation of Gifftheil's apocalyptic interpretation. He belonged to the loose grouping of Biblical interpreters who hoped to see the fulfilment of the prophecies contained in the Book of Daniel.[46] These visions predict the rise and fall of four successive and degenerating world monarchies which are followed by the eternal Fifth Monarchy. The 'woeful times and the desolate and destructive pit of depression' in which he lived was, for Gifftheil, the most specific sign of the fall of the Holy Roman Empire and the approaching end of the Fourth Monarchy.[47] With this message he bombarded the religious and political authorities with a multitude of tracts and letters, proclaiming the imminent return of Christ, the end of the Fourth Monarchy and the ultimate and final consummation of all things in the Last Judgement. This interpretation of history lay at the core of his beliefs. Moreover, he identified the common people as the elect or the chosen nation of God, who, with the coming of the Last Judgement, would enjoy fellowship with the Almighty, while the corrupt and degenerate élite, 'the uncharitable, predatory bloodhounds who persist with their tyranny and wickedness . . . will pay the price and do penance'.[48]

His writing is distinctive for its insistent and adamant denunciation of corruption in politics, ethics, morality and society. No one was immune from his multifarious attacks. He condemned the actions of many of the politicians and military leaders, accusing both Tilly and Wallenstein of promoting religious strife in their counter-reforming efforts.[49] He levelled severe criticism against judicial corruption, saying that, despite the growth of the legal profession, justice and fairness were non-existent. Moreover this rapid decline in morality and the pretended piety and reverence of the religious and professional classes perverted the values of true religion. He held all leaders of society, irrespective of religious or political commitment, responsible for the corruption of God's providential plan. As part of his repudiation of the political and religious élites, Gifftheil carried with him a life-long concern for his own country, ravaged by the Thirty Years War, and for those most affected: the common people. Friedrich Breckling, who met him in his later years at Amsterdam, wrote that 'Gifftheil's greatest desire in life was to save and protect the poor and persecuted' of Germany;[50] these remarks were supported by Henry More:

> he had a deep compassion of the sufferings of his country . . . [and] seemed to be very religious and a great hater of tyranny and oppression . . . a short writing of his which I had the opportunity of seeing . . . was full of Zeal and Scripture eloquence'.[51]

This implies not only a vast and erudite use of the Bible, but an underlying commitment to peace and religious harmony. Eylenstein emphasized Gifftheil's peacemaking efforts. On the death of Emperor Ferdinand, he thus made a concerted attempt to unite the conflicting parties in the war, pleading with them to find a peaceful settlement.[52] This lends weight to the suggestion that Gifftheil never contrived to influence any of the European leaders for his own personal advancement, or asked them to implement any specific religious or political policies. He persistently pleaded with them to examine their consciences and consider the results of their immoral and unethical behaviour. The wars in Europe were, according to Gifftheil, the results of their wrong actions, and it was their responsibility to assist in the building of the New Jerusalem. His deepest motives, Eylenstein suggests, were not political, but underpinned with an ethical and religious fervour to awaken the world to 'injustice, irreligion, miserliness and jealousy'. At the heart of his prophetic message the self had to be questioned and purified. Unlike in other cases of religious revival such as the Welsh revival of 1904–5 seen later in this volume, there was no denial of the self. Indeed, self-examination and the testing of conscience was, as Gifftheil postulated,

> necessary as everybody shares responsibility with God for his own ethical behaviour. The ones who pay attention to the inner part of their degenerate and irreligious character . . . they are the ones who are capable of delaying and avoiding the present ruin that stands before us.[53]

In 1648, during one of his many visits to England, Gifftheil was admitted to an audience with King Charles I where he 'pleaded with him to deliver the people of Germany out of their present miseries'.[54] An anonymous sympathizer tells us of an earlier visit where 'he desireth an army of three thousand men to dissipate the Pope, his cardinals, Bishops, Priests and all false leaders.' At this later meeting, however, he abandoned his war-like approach and attempted to persuade Charles and the Parliamentarian General Fairfax to abandon their divisive policies and pleaded with them to adopt new moral principles. It is not known how they responded to this plea, but Gifftheil tells us he was left with the vague promise that Fairfax would bring an end to the civil strife in England.[55] This was probably Gifftheil's final visit to England, as he later took a negative stance towards Cromwell's Protectorate, settling in Amsterdam where he continued to write and publish his tracts. In a particular address to the English people published in 1660, *Die Jetzige Regierung*, he condemned Cromwell's ungodly commonwealth and vigorously attacked General Monck for his part in restoring the Monarchy.[56]

It is never easy to trace or locate the beginnings of an idea or its pattern of diffusion. Within the context of eschatological thought in Europe, the tradition inherited from the Middle Ages had a decisive influence. The origin of the radical ideas of mid-seventeenth-century England remains a topic for further investigation. Gifftheil may have influenced the Fifth Monarchy movement, one of the radical religious sects of the late 1640s and early 1650s. As Eylenstein noted, the German origin of the Fifth Monarchy before its decisive development in England is worthy of further study. Moreover Gifftheil's writings were translated and published in England as early as 1643.[57] The 'great Intelligencer of Europe', Samuel Hartlib, was in possession of one of his tracts dating from 1640, although we do not know when he acquired it. It seems reasonable to speculate that the idea of the Fifth Monarchy emanated from continental Europe and was disseminated by prolific prophets like Gifftheil and thus became accessible before the great outburst of millenarian speculation in the 1640s and 1650s.[58]

Whether Philip Ziegler also influenced this spread of ideas in early Stuart England is perhaps more speculative. What Ziegler does demonstrate, however, is a movement of political and eschatological ideas from Britain to continental Europe in the writings of Thomas Brightman, Sir Henry Finch and King James and the existence of a network, including major intellectual figures like Adam Boreel. Prophecies were thus at the heart of transnational intellectual exchanges in seventeenth-century Europe.

I would like to thank the History Section, Department of International Studies and the Centre for Research into International Communication and Culture at the Nottingham Trent University for funding a visit to the Herzog August Library at Wolfenbüttel in the early stages of research for this article. I would also like to thank the staff of all the European archives who responded to my enquiries, but especially Dr Carlos Gilly, the librarian of the Bibliotheca Hermetica Philosophica, Amsterdam, for supplying me with important material on Philip Ziegler.

Notes

1 For the recent literature on apocalypse, prophecy and millenarianism in Europe see: N. Mout, 'Chiliastic Prophecy and Revolt in the Habsburg Monarchy' in M. Wilks (ed.), *Prophecy and Eschatology*, Studies in Church History, Subsidia 10 (Oxford, Blackwell, 1994), pp. 93–109; J. Theibault, 'Jeremiah in the Village: Prophecy, Preaching, Pamphlets, and Penance in the Thirty Years War', *Central European History*, 27 (4) (1994), 441–60; R.J.W. Evans, *The Making of the Habsburg Monarchy, 1550–1700: An Interpretation* (Oxford, Clarendon Press, 1979), pp. 396–9. For the development of millenarianism in Scandinavia see P. Laasonen, 'Die Anfänge des Chiliasmus im Norden', *Pietismus und Neuzeit*, 19 (1993), 19–45.

2 R.B. Barnes, *Prophecy and Gnosis: Apocalypticism in the Wake of the Lutheran Reformation* (Stanford University Press, 1988).

3 Barnes, *Prophecy and Gnosis*, p. 5, and, for British Apocalypticism and millenarianism, B. Ball, *A Great Expectation: Eschatological Thought in English Protestantism to 1660* (Leiden, E.J. Brill, 1975); P. Christianson, *Reformers and Babylon: English Apocalyptic Visions from the Reformation to the Eve of the Civil War* (Toronto University Press, 1978); P. Toon (ed.), *Puritans, the Millennium and the Future of Israel: Puritan Eschatology, 1600–1660* (Cambridge, James Clarke, 1970); E. Tuveson, *Millennium and Utopia: A Study in the Background of the Idea of Progress* (Berkeley, Harper Torchbooks, 1940); K. Firth, *The Apocalyptic Tradition in Reformation Britain, 1530–1645* (Oxford University Press, 1979); C.A. Patrides and J. Wittreich (eds), *The Apocalypse in Reniassance Thought and Literature* (Manchester University Press, 1984); B. Capp, *The Fifth Monarchy Men* (London and New Jersey, Rowman and Littlefield, 1972).

4 See the two articles by Richard van Dülmen, 'Prophetie und Politik: Johan Permeier und die Societas Regalis Christi (1631–1634)', *Zeitschrift für Bayerische Landesgeschichte*, 41 (1978), 416–73; and 'Schwärmer und Separatisten in Nürnberg (1618-1648)', *Archiv für Kulturgeschichte*, 55 (1973), 107–73.

5 W.E. Peuckert, *Das Rosenkreuz* (Jena, 1928), pp. 147–8. F.L. van Soden, *Kriegs und Sitten geschichte der Reichstadt Nürnberg* (3 vols, Erlangen, 1860), vol. 1, p. 561.

6 For the term 'lone prophets' (*Einzelgänger*) see van Dülmen, 'Prophetie und Politik', p. 418. Jürgen Beyer of Clare College, Cambridge, is presently undertaking a study of popular prophets in Europe. See his article 'A Prophet in Lübeck seen in the Local and the Lutheran Context' in R.W. Scribner and T. Johnson (eds), *Popular Religion in Germany and Europe 1400–1800* (London, Macmillan, 1996), pp. 166–82.

7 The original sources of Ziegler and Gifftheil used here are as follows: Bodleian Library, Oxford, Ashmole MS 1149 v and vi, Philip Ziegler, 'Responsio et Cynosura sive vera Prophetarum proba Philippi Ziegleri . . .', and 'Argumentum Origenicum de statu . . .' (1626); hereafter 'Reply and Cynosure' and 'Argumentum Origenicum', respectively. I would like to thank Dr Neil Franklin for help with these documents. P. Ziegler, *Anti-Arnoldus et Anti-Nagelus. Das ist Grundlicher Beweiss das weder die zehn Grunde . . .* (Frankfurt, 1622). I would like to thank the Royal Library, Copenhagen, for supplying me with a copy of this tract. L.F. Gifftheil, *Die Jetzige Regierung in England . . .* which is attached as an appendix to *Die ungehorsame verlogene Kinder . . .* (Amsterdam, 1660?), unpaginated. *Die Volcker dieser Vierten Monarchie* (no place of publication, no date), unpaginated. Th. Wotschke, 'Zwei Schwärmer am Niederrhein', *Monatshefte für Rheinische Kirchengeschichte*, 27 (1933), 144–78. Most of this article consists of letters between either the friends, patrons or enemies of Gifftheil. BL, Sloane MS 648, ff. 47, 57. The translations from the German are my own.

8 R. Heisler, 'Philip Ziegler the Rosicrucian King of Jerusalem', *The Hermetic Journal* (Oxford, 1990), 3–10; F. Fritz, 'Friedrich Gifftheil', *Blätter für Württembergische Kirchengeschichte*, 44 (1940), 90–105; E. Eylenstein, 'Ludwig Friedrich Gifftheil: Zum mystische Separatismus des 17. Jahrhundert in Deutschland', *Zeitschrift für Kirchengeschichte*, XLI (1922), 1–62.

9 I have relied heavily but cautiously on Eylenstein to analyse Gifftheil's religious and eschatological thought.

10 G. Arnold, *Unpartheyische Kirchen-und-Ketzer Geschichte* (Schaffhausen, 1722). In his interpretation of Ziegler, Arnold relied to some extent on Nicholas Baring, 'Treuherzige Warnung an alle fromme leute sich zü huten für den neuen propheten' (Hannover, 1646), p. 76 (Herzog August Bibliotek, Wolfenbüttel, Sig: 385.22 Theol 4° (25)). Heinrich Corrodi, *Kritische Geschichte des Chiliasmus* (Frankfurt and Leipzig, 1783), esp. section three, 'Von Einige propheten des Siebzehnten Jahrhunderts'. Corrodi relied to a certain extent on the theological dissertation (Leiden University) of Gisbertus Boetius, 'De signis und de Prophetie der Weissagungen' (date unknown).

11 The account of this incident is repeated in most German Encyclopaedias. See esp. C.G. Jöcher, *Allgemeines Gelehrten-Lexicon* (4 vols, Leipzig, Jöcher, 1750–1), vol. 4, entry 301.

12 For Gottfried Arnold see W. R. Ward, 'Is Martyrdom Mandatory? The Case of Gottfried Arnold' in D. Wood (ed.), *Martyrs and Martyrologies*, Studies in Church History, 30 (Oxford, Blackwell, 1993), pp. 311–18, and the literature cited there.

13 'Reply and Cynosure', pp. 84–5.

14 *Mémoires et négociations secrètes de Monsieur de Rusdorf*, ed. E.G. Cuhn (2 vols, Leipzig, 1789) vol. 2, pp. 785–7. I would like to thank Dr Bertrand Nairac for translating the revelant extracts concerning Ziegler.

15 I owe this information to Dr Carlos Gilly who kindly sent me a print-out of the database he is compiling for the Bibliotheca Philosophica Hermetica, Amsterdam. The claims by Ziegler are contained in a letter dated 22 Oct. 1622 from Balthasar Mentzer, Professor at Giessen University, to Graf Wolradt zu Waldeck. It is possible that Ziegler made contact in Giessen with the alchemical and hermetic writer Heinrich Nollius who was expelled from the university for his Rosicrucian views. For Nollius see H. Hotson, 'Johann Heinrich Alsted: Encyclopedism, millenarianism and the Second Reformation in Germany' (unpublished D.Phil. thesis, University of Oxford, 1994), p. 238.

16 H. Mayer, *Matrikel der Universitat Freiberg von 1460–1656* (Freiberg, H. Mayer, 1907), p. 683, entry 13.

17 The work referred to here is the publication of Theodore de Bry of Frankfurt, *America Das ist Erfindung und Offenbarung der Neuen Welt*, published by de Bry between the years 1590 and 1601 (Frankfurt, N. Hoffman, 1617). See Carlos Gilly, 'Iter Rosicrucianum auf der Suche nach Unbekannten Quellen der Frühen Rosenkreuzer', *Das Erbe des Christian Rosenkreutz* (Amsterdam, Pelikan, 1988), p. 88, n. 44.

18 *Harmonia und Harpffe Davids* (Frankfurt, 1620). Ziegler dedicates this work to the family of Johann Karl Rehlinger of Augsburg where he served as a private tutor to the three daughters Carin, Reginen and Euphemia.

19 E.G.E. Van der Wall, 'De Mystieke Chiliast Petrus Serrarius 1600–1689 en Zijn Wereld' (unpublished Ph.D. thesis, University of Leiden, 1987). A copy is available in the Warburg Institute, London.

20 Heisler, 'Philip Ziegler', p. 5; Cuhn, 'Rusdorf', p. 786.

21 'Reply and Cynosure', title-page and pp. 4, 29.

22 'Reply and Cynosure', p. 27. For Christoph Kotter and his connection to Frederick see Mout, 'Prophecy and Revolt', p. 100, and Corrodi, *Kritische*, section 6, pp. 81–2.

23 'Reply and Cynosure', p. 89, gives a list of prophets who were of the same opinion as him, which includes John Dee, Robert Fludd, Tycho de Brahe, Thomas Brightman, William Gouge, Rotmann of Poland and Szegedinius of Hungary.

24 For Joachim de Fiore see Lesley Coote in ch. 1 of this book and the literature cited there. Frances Yates, *The Rosicrucian Enlightenment* (London, Routledge & Kegan Paul, 1972).

25 Yates, *The Rosicrucian Enlightenment*, pp. 41–58.

26 'Reply and Cynosure', p. 25.

27 Marjorie Reeves, 'History and Eschatology: Medieval and Early Protestant Thought in some English and Scottish Writings', *Medievalia et Humanistica*, 4 (1973), 99–123.

28 For Brocado see M. Reeves, *The Influence of Prophecy in the Later Middle Ages* (Oxford, Clarendon Press, 1969), pp. 494–9. A good discussion of Brightman is contained in Firth, *Apocalyptic Tradition*, pp. 164–76. The work that Ziegler wrongly attributes to William Gouge is Sir Henry Finch's *The Worldes Great Restauration, or The Calling of the Jews* (London, 1621), although it is true that the preface was written by Gouge. For a fuller discussion of this tract see W.R. Prest, 'The Art of Law and the Law of God: Sir Henry Finch (1558–1625)' in D. Pennington and K. Thomas (eds), *Puritans and Revolutionaries: Essays in Seventeenth-Century History presented to Christopher Hill* (Oxford, Clarendon Press, 1978), pp. 94–117.

29 'Reply and Cynosure', p. 87.

30 For the idea of the conversion of the Jews see D.S. Katz, *Philosemitism and the Readmission of the Jews to England 1603–1655* (Oxford University Press, 1982).

31 'Reply and Cynosure', p. 1, and 'Argumentum Origenicum', p. 25.

32 'Argumentum Origenicum', p. 31.

33 For the Elector Palatine see Yates, *Rosicrucian Enlightenment*, pp. 1–29.

34 Corrodi, *Kritische*, pp. 22–3, and Capp, *Fifth Monarchy Men*, p. 234.

35 This sentence is based on P. White, 'The *via media* in the early Stuart Church' in K. Fincham (ed.), *The Early Stuart Church 1603–1642* (London, Macmillan, 1993), p. 222.

36 Reeves, *The Influence of Prophecy*, p. 498.

37 J.P. Somerville, 'James I and the Divine Right of Kings' in L.L. Peck (ed.), *The Mental World of the Jacobean Court* (Cambridge University Press, 1991), pp. 55–70; C. Russell, 'Divine Rights in the Early Seventeenth Century' in J. Morrill, P. Slack, and D. Woolf (eds), *Public Duty and Private Conscience in Seventeenth-Century England* (Oxford, Clarendon Press, 1993), pp. 101–20.

38 For the adherents to the Protestant Cause see esp. S. Adams, 'The Protestant Cause: Relations with the West European Calvinist Communities as a Political Issue in England 1585-1630' (unpublished D.Phil. thesis, University of Oxford, 1973), esp. chs 7 and 8. A. Milton, *Catholic and Reformed: The Roman and Protestant Churches in English Protestant Thought 1600–1640* (Cambridge University Press, 1995), pp. 503–15. K. Fincham, 'Prelacy and Politics: Archbishop Abbott's defence of Protestant Orthodoxy', *Historical Research*, 61 (1988), 36–64.

39 'Reply and Cynosure', pp. 20, 24.

40 *Mémoires . . . de Rusdorf,* vol. 2, p. 786. For other references to Ziegler in London see T. Birch, *The Court and Times of Charles I* (2 vols, London, Henry Colburn, 1848), vol. 1, pp. 175, 178 (John Pory to Joseph Mede, 27 Nov. 1626; Joseph Mede to Sir Martin Stuteville, 2 Dec. 1626).

41 BL, Additional MS 28,633, ff. 140–1 (the album of Dr Johann Gheselius). For Gustavus as the Lion of the North see M. Roberts, *Gustavus Adolphus* (2 vols, London, Longmans, Green, and Co., 1953), vol. I, pp. 407, 525–6.

42 Gifftheil signed himself as David the Second Warrior of God.

43 H. More, *Enthusiasmus Triumphatus, or a Brief Discourse on the Nature, Causes, Kinds and Cure of Enthusiasm* (London, 1656). This comment is found in 'A Brief Discourse of Enthusiasm, Several Examples of Political Enthusiasm', section 32, f. 22. See also K. Thomas, *Religion and the Decline of Magic* (Harmondsworth, Penguin, 1990), p. 164, n. 115, who mentions a German Prophet who can now be identified as Gifftheil.

44 Wotschke, 'Zwei Schwärmer', p. 172.

45 Fritz, 'Friedrich Gifftheil'.

46 Capp, *Fifth Monarchy Men*, introduction.

47 Eylenstein, 'Ludwig Friedrich Gifftheil', p. 22.

48 Wotschke, 'Zwei Schwärmer', p. 151.

49 For Tilly, the commander of the Catholic League army from 1610 until his death in 1632, see G. Parker, *The Thirty Years War* (London, Routledge, 1991), pp. 61, 75–9, 91–5, 125–9; and Wallenstein, commander of the Imperial army, pp. 100–1, 139, 196–7.

50 Wotschke, 'Zwei Schwärmer', p. 149.

51 More, *Enthusiasmus*.

52 Eylenstein, 'Ludwig Friedrich Gifftheil', p. 43.

53 For the quotation and the preceding paragraph see Eylenstein, 'Ludwig Friedrich Gifftheil', pp. 38–9.

54 BL, Sloane MS 648, f. 1.

55 BL, Thomason Tract E. 475 (16). An account of this audience is attached as an appendix to 'Votes in Parliament. A speech and some papers delivered to Lord General Fairfax'.

56 Gifftheil, *Die Jetzige Regierung.*

57 Eylenstein, 'Ludwig Friedrich Gifftheil', p. 61.

58 The Hartlib Papers on CD-ROM at the University of Sheffield, 59/3/1A, 'Den Untergang des Thieres und falschen Propheten betreffend' (1640). See also the comments by Capp on the existence of Fifth Monarchy ideas before 1640, *Fifth Monarchy Men*, p. 22.

6

'TO JUSTIFY THE WAYS OF GOD TO MEN': THE PROPHETIC ROLE OF MINISTERS IN EARLY NEW ENGLAND

G. Games

'God by a secret Providence is wont to move upon the hearts of his faifthul Servants, that they should speak according to what is in the Lords heart to do'.[1]

Discussions of prophecy in seventeenth-century English society often focus on the way prophecies could be used for political propaganda, even allowing disenfranchised groups such as the poor, women or radical sectarians to speak with increased authority. In this paper I want to deal with the issues raised by prophecy in a more complex manner. I will examine how New England ministers used prophetic roles in an attempt to buttress both their personal authority and the civil and religious institutions they had helped to establish. These roles evolved out of a unique interaction between English religious and social traditions, close reading of the scriptures, the personal character traits of the ministers and the needs of the local New England community, and yet they ended up following a pattern of prophetic leadership which has echoes in many other human societies. As the complex prophetic figures and symbols dealt with elsewhere in this volume indicate, in analysing prophecy we are dealing with a human tendency to try and anticipate and control not only the future, but the present and the past as well, through ideas supported by expert figures. The ministers' prophetic roles were based on a claim that the ministers possessed distinct knowledge unavailable to other people; knowledge that made them theoretically the best guides to understanding and controlling the spiritual lives of their flocks. However, the role of the prophet in New England, as elsewhere in human history, was dependent on the interaction between the larger-than-life figure of the prophet and the audience to whom he or she spoke. As a result, just like monarchs such as Elizabeth I, the ministers' autonomy in choosing their role was restricted by the expectations of their society. As we shall see, the most dangerous threat to a minister came from sources that questioned their prophetic and symbolic identity. Prophecy could not only empower people in New England; it could also prove the means of their destruction.

To understand the complexity of prophetic roles in New England there are perhaps no better figures to contrast against the New England ministers than the most successful radical group of the Civil War years, the Quakers. Although some recent writers have argued that it is not possible to trace an unbroken spectrum of Protestant belief from Puritan to Quaker, as had been previously thought, these spiritual differences only highlight the way both groupings fell into similar social patterns in the use of prophecy. The Quakers' belief in a spiritual 'inner light' present in everyone gave ordinary men and women a chance to prophesy, that is preach in their religious meetings. The Quaker concept of prophesying included elements from scripture, immediate inspiration and the trance-derived visions experienced mainly by female Quakers. The Quaker experience was not completely individualistic, as each Quaker's experience of the inner light fell into recognizable patterns derived from Quaker literature and the shared social medium of what became known as the Society of Friends. These ideas meant there was no need for learned ministers, 'hireling priests' as the Quakers called them, or in the case of some extreme Quakers, knowledge of scripture, to discover the path to salvation. Thus for Quakers it would appear there was no divide between prophet and audience, minister and flock, since any member could speak and talk of their spiritual experiences. However, as Quakerism developed, certain patterns emerged; all Quakers might have had a chance to prophesy within the society, but the prophesyings of some Quakers, like George Fox, Richard Farnworth and James Naylor, reached a larger audience than others.[2]

Even more significantly, the theoretical lack of division within Quaker ranks contrasted with their relationship with the outside world. There was a huge exterior audience that early Quaker prophets attempted to convert with great missionary zeal, and with surprising success considering the radical nature of their message. Nevertheless, these Quaker attempts at educating the wider world in true religion often met with hostility. One standard reaction of the Quakers was regularly to predict doom for those towns, churches, ministers and magistrates that refused to heed their message, an attitude seen in tracts like Humphrey Norton's *New England Judged by the Spirit of the Lord* (1661). An important part of prophetic denunciations of their opponents was the Quakers' use of symbolic gestures such as wearing sackcloth, and 'going naked for a sign'. By literally adopting Biblical imagery to castigate the outside world the Quakers established their prophetic credentials, to their own satisfaction at least. The persecution the Quakers faced was carefully recorded, at first in the stream of tracts Quakers issued and later in records of 'sufferings' at the local and national meetings. These sufferings had their stylistic origins in the martyrdoms of the early Church, the cults of medieval martyrs and, perhaps most importantly, John Foxe's influential *Actes and Monuments*. Just like in these earlier accounts of Christian suffering the Quakers were particularly keen to note judgements such as deaths and accidents that befell their persecutors. As a result of this they soon had an impressive catalogue of successful predictions of the wrath of God. Alongside these predictions the early Quakers recorded other favourable supernatural events and providences, such the miracle healings performed by George Fox and others. Part of the Quakers' success in creating a stable religious movement lies in the way they rapidly created a group identity with a self-referential prophetical history that served to strengthen internal cohesion.[3]

If we turn from the Quakers to the New England clergy we can see them attempt to fulfil similar prophetic roles, though generally in a less dramatic fashion. The New England ministers' position was difficult as they were moving from being non-conformist prophets at the edge of one society to patriarchs at the centre of another. For the ministerial prophet the search for an appropriate audience was all-important, and they managed to find one on a variety of levels. The most basic element of this was establishing the minister's social place in the local community, what we might term his role as a local patriarch. Ministers were well aware that, as Puritan divine Edward Calamy noted: 'The common people are more apt to enquire what ministers do, than what they say.' Thus the ministerial role evolved from a set of ideals defined in countless ministerial biographies: he had to show all the Christian virtues, be extremely learned, have an ordered household and of course be pre-eminent in piety. In their community they might also arbitrate disputes, champion local political causes, teach children, and often provide the only formal medical aid in the town. Of particular importance was the use of church discipline against members who were guilty of social or religious misbehaviour. In this process a minister took on a role similar to a magistrate in punishing sin directly, rather than simply castigating it. All these responsibilities, combined with the good social and family connections ministers often had, meant they were clearly high in the social hierarchy. This was particularly true in the early days of New England because ministers like Thomas Hooker and Ezekiel Rogers had a loyal nucleus of followers in their congregation who had followed them across the Atlantic. The shared experience of persecution and exile gave ministry and laity a joint sense of identity similar to that achieved by the Quakers. Essentially, a successful minister had to be at the heart of his community and yet had to retain a symbolic distance from his audience. His authority was very similar to the patriarchal head of a household or a monarch, intimate and distancing at the same time.[4]

This local prophetic role had its problems because of its idealistic quality and the demands it put on ministers. For example, ministers found it difficult to avoid becoming involved in the frequent disputes of New England towns, particularly if the question of wages arose. Once the minister took sides he was open to charges of sullying his ministerial position and he became a false prophet as far as his opponents were concerned. A good example is the troubles faced by Edmund Browne in the town of Sudbury where land and wage claims caused bitter argument. As New England got larger and new unknown ministers replaced the first generation the chance of such problems increased.[5]

Obviously a minister's patriarchal role in the community was linked to what was supposedly his prime role, tending to the spiritual concerns of his congregation. If he could establish authority in one area it tended to be firm in the other. Ministers saw their spiritual duty to their flock in prophetic terms: firstly, to preach the law of the Old Testament prophets and rebuke their congregation's sins, and secondly, and perhaps more importantly, to bring them to Christ by offering them grace in the manner of the apostles of the New Testament. The result of their work can be most easily examined in the conversion narratives that had to be given in most congregations to gain full admission to the church and access to the sacraments. The narratives of ordinary members of congregations show they tended to define their spiritual development in terms of the literature and the sermons of their ministers. A typical example, Nathaniel Sparrowhawk's conversion narrative, goes from one scriptural reference to another, explaining how particular sermons brought home the meaning of the word of God. When the laity articulated these narratives they too were prophesying, but did it in carefully defined and limited circumstances; in a sense ministerial prophesying resulted in a prophetic echo from their audience. Originally the New England churches allowed more frequent lay participation in preaching and in questions after sermons; this type of activity became restricted for reasons we shall explore later. It was particularly useful for ministers to be skilful in resolving individual cases of conscience, that is being able to respond to the personal spiritual difficulties of their congregations. Agonizing doubts and melancholy are frequently mentioned in contemporary spiritual autobiographies, and ministers were expected to help. Just as amongst the Quakers, all these spiritual feelings became enhanced by the social elements of religion. The laity discussed sermons and points of doctrine amongst friends and family. Given the powerful religious feelings of much of the New England laity it was often the ministers' success or failure in justifying the ways of God to men that determined their social influence.[6]

The ministers' success in their spiritual role was based on their ability to understand 'knotty' sections of scripture. Such expert understanding had more than merely spiritual implications, since for Puritans scripture was the sole source of understanding the divine will, and therefore the world as a whole. The implications of this can be seen in works of the influential Puritan theologian William Perkins, who insisted that ministers should use a plain style and stick close to the scriptures. If his advice was followed Perkins thought that it would be true to say that: 'When a true minister saith unto thee, on a true ground, I denounce thee a sinful man, and under the curse, or I declare thee to be righteous, and a child of grace, it is all one as though God from heaven had said so unto thee.' Here Perkins reflected the common assumption that people could expect some kind of fulfilment of the words of a true, that is a prophetic, ministry. The general belief in divine Providence, that God ordained all that came to pass in the world, helped support the belief that a true understanding of scripture could often indicate, if not directly predict, what would happen. Since the ministers were experts at understanding scripture, listening to them could be the equivalent of a weather forecast for us, they could make no certain predictions because of the absolute sovereignty of God, but they certainly could indicate general trends in the future. Thus when John Cotton asserted 'I speake as a poore prophet of the Lord according to the word of his grace in my text, which . . . is written for our example and our instruction: for God is the same yesterday, today, and for ever', he was making a potent claim for ministerial authority, even apart from the question of whether or not they held a special sacramental role. This sort of belief is reflected in the way ministers used sections of scripture to define themselves as ambassadors of Christ, watchmen, messengers of God, God's stewards, angels and of course prophets.[7]

All this meant ministerial expertise had a wide prophetic role to play outside their local community. Certain ministers had great political influence in defining the nature of New England's identity and institutions, particularly John Cotton in Massachusetts and Thomas Hooker in Connecticut. The New England magistrates consulted them in decisions of government and on what types of laws should be enacted to create a truly godly commonwealth. This was the secular counterpart to the drive to return the Church to its primitive purity that has been carefully explored by Dwight Bozeman. There seems to have been a general belief in the importance of instituting elements of Mosaic law into the government of the new colonies. However, like the divines of the Westminster Assembly the ministers of New England discovered that their role as prophetic councillors to the magistracy had serious drawbacks. Ministerial influence was limited by the fact that they were divided on how exactly government should be organized, paralleling the arguments between the magistrates of the General Court and the lower house of deputies in Massachusetts. John Cotton drew up a draft set of laws for Massachusetts called *Moses his Judicials* that were carefully based on scripture. In the code Cotton advocated that a magistrate should be selected for life and should have wide powers of discretion. Such ideas were opposed by ministers like Thomas Hooker and Nathaniel Ward who supported careful limitations on magisterial powers and more use of English law. Even worse was the dilemma faced when the needs of the commonwealth conflicted with the desires of the minister's congregation. For some ministers like Peter Hobart, who led his congregation in a serious dispute with the Massachusetts government, the local audience was of paramount importance.[8]

Some of the most important opportunities for ministers to exercise political influence were the occasional sermons delivered on election, thanksgiving and fast days. On such public occasions the ministers spoke not to their local communities but to the colony as a whole, just as the English sermons delivered to Parliament or at Assizes were aimed at a wider audience. These sermons examined the relationship of New England to God, the state of the public covenant, explaining the divine reasoning behind recent public achievements or disasters and advising the best course of action for the future, and almost inevitably asserted the importance of listening to God's messengers. These sermons, in both Englands, tended to involve castigation of sinful behaviour, whether amongst the court, local leaders, merchants, or the people in general. By the time of second-generation ministers, like Increase Mather, these sermons became an increasingly important opportunity to lament a decline in ministerial influence and in particular to castigate New Englanders for failing to live up to the ideals of the founders of the colonies. These sermons have been labelled by scholars as a particular genre, the Jeremiad, which seems to indicate that later ministers were unwillingly re-assuming the role on the periphery which suited prophetic discourse so well.[9]

The close stylistic connections of the evolving myth of New England's founding, seen in the ministerial sermons and the sort of history which John Foxe had written for England, are obvious. Thus it is no surprise that as early as 1636 one minister, Hugh Peters, should publicly advocate a continuation of the Book of Martyrs as a worthy scheme for someone in the colony to attempt. All contemporary histories of New England tend to follow Foxe's model, with a heavy biographical element focusing on ministers and magistrates and careful examinations of divine blessings and punishments. It reached a high point with Cotton Mather's *Magnalia Christi Americana*, which not only outlined New England's origin, place in the wider world reformation, and recounted the life-stories of its ministers, but towards the end had a section entitled 'Things to Come' in which Cotton recounted a contemporary millennial prophecy spoken by someone on their death bed. Just like Quakers, New England ministers were using their position to articulate perceptions of the future and the past to define their society's nature in the present.[10]

Ministerial prophets were not merely limited to the people of New England as an audience. The first generation of ministers spoke to their peers and the general public in England through letters and a stream of pamphlets. Many of these writings were concerned with justifying the New England or Congregational way of Church government, but others focused on practical questions of spiritual development or attacking heretical ideas. The ministers saw themselves as participating in an international movement that was attempting to return the Church to its original purity. By the 1640s revolutionary events in England made ministers, like many of their contemporaries, increasingly fascinated with the possibility that the Millennium was approaching. Probably the most consistent proponent of millennial ideas in New England was John Cotton whose interpretation of Revelation went into print in the 1640s, and his ideas and indeed his table of laws seem to have influenced some Fifth Monarchists. During these years some ministers returned to England and echoes of their cosmopoliton perspective can be seen in the fact that Cotton did not give New England a particularly special role in millennial events and saw the success of the Church there firmly within a wider framework of the Protestant reformation.[11]

The missionary efforts of John Eliot, the 'Apostle to the Indians', were also fuelled by millennial ideas as he and others thought that the Native Americans were of Jewish stock, and therefore success in converting them signalled the approach of the 'last times'. A series of tracts won Eliot's attempts much publicity and funds from Britain. Particularly fascinating is the strict biblical form of government Eliot created for converted Native Americans, a scheme which Eliot thought should be adopted in England putting the 'Crown of England upon the head of Christ'. For the converts, Eliot, according to contemporary statements, seems to have become almost a guru figure whose prayers were a good substitute for shamanic magic and, as a result, he wielded far greater power amongst them than amongst his own English congregation. Yet this wide perspective could cause difficulties for ministers when the laity did not share their concerns. John Norton was criticized by his congregation for spending more time writing polemic tracts than ministering to them. While Eliot's efforts at conversion won him fame in England King Philip's war showed that most New Englanders regarded his 'praying Indians' as little better than other savages despite their profession of Christianity.[12]

So New England ministers were far from parochial and had to juggle playing a prophetic role to their congregation, town, colony, nation and the world as a whole. The role they played on these different levels also could result in a popular belief that ministers could foretell the future. As we have seen, their audience was far from passive, and ministers had constantly to seek to justify their interpretation of God's will, so instances of what seemed to be supernatural support for their views were very important.[13]

As we saw earlier the doctrine of providence was a powerful support for the ministers. An event like the drowning of a young man after he had slighted his father was a providential happening which was indirectly connected to ministers because of their continuing attacks on sinful behaviour. Particularly important were the type of providences recorded with great glee by John Winthrop, first governor of Massachusetts, which seemed to prove that New England was under direct divine protection. An example is the explosion of the ship *Mary Rose* after its crew had slighted New England church services. These types of providences helped confirm people's faith in the divine order that the minister proclaimed and that New England really was under a watchful divine gaze.[14]

From these ideas it was easy to move on to the fully fledged predictions of the future that had always been associated with saint-like figures in the Christian tradition. Ironically, despite the Protestant hatred of 'idolatry', their own holy men and martyrs became credited with supernatural powers, particularly Martin

Luther. Luther became a folk-hero and his prophecies were a staple of the form throughout Protestant Europe. A common motif in such tales was martyrs predicting their own death or, as we saw with the Quakers, that their persecutors would suffer divine vengeance. This meant John Foxe could confidently say of Hugh Latimer that, 'if England ever had a prophet, he might seem to be one'. This reputation derived from a prediction of Queen Mary's reign and Latimer's famous remark to his fellow martyr Ridley, 'we shall this day light such a candle by God's grace in England as, I trust, shall never be put out'. John Knox also achieved a similar reputation from some stern warning advice he gave on his deathbed to the Earl of Morton and to the Earl of Grange. Both men later died in circumstances that seemed to confirm Knox had predicted their deaths, and Morton, as he faced execution, publicly lamented he had not listened to Knox's advice. In both these cases it is noticeable that the ministers concerned made some of their most notable prophecies just before they died. Death and prediction it seems were closely linked perhaps because part of the art of dying, portrayed in contemporary sermons and advice manuals, entailed giving advice and blessings for those left behind, and these 'famous last words' were particularly prone to becoming interpreted as predictive. John Foxe not only set many of these traditions in motion but he himself later gained a similar reputation as it was claimed: 'Many things did he fortell by occassion of comforting the afflicted, or terrifying those that were stubborn.' Thus even in resolving cases of conscience a minister's words could prove strangely predictive.[15]

In everyday life it was at the point when providential happenings occurred after a minister had recently spoken on the very topic that predictive reputations became established. In England, for example, Hugh Clark's sermons against Sabbath-breaking were followed by a string of disastrous accidents for those involved. As a result 'at least sixteen were brought to Christ' showing the very real effect predictive coincidences could have. Such coincidences were bound to happen in New England where the average person heard about 8,000 sermons in a lifetime and a minister was often at the centre of their community. The ministers' audience was all the more ready to believe such stories because it gave them a powerful sense of spiritual security as it meant their minister was all the more likely to be helping them on the thorny road to salvation. It was difficult to keep this sort of reputation under control once it had been earned, as shown by the biographer of Presbyterian divine John Ball, who was eager to show that Ball had needed no 'injections and impulses of spirit' to successfully predict in the 1640s the 'errors and hindrances of Reformation' which occurred in the 1650s. While ministers denounced attempts to predict the future by astrology, or by revelations, their self-portrayal as humble servants of God ironically served to increase the chance that predictive powers could become connected to them in retrospect; the better known a minister's sermons, the more holy he was perceived to be, and the more likely it was to happen. The result was that clergy of all shades of opinion, conformist and non-conformist, could become known as predictors of the future.[16]

Ministers were most likely to receive recognition for a prediction when people were searching for an explanation for a recent disaster; then condemnatory public sermons seemed all too true. An interesting example was the sermon delivered in 1627 to the Court by the most famous Puritan minister of his day, John Preston. Preston told the Court that current events indicated 'evil is intended against us' and that things 'were hastening to a period'. A few days later news arrived of the defeat of English forces by the French at the île de Ré that made 'many believe he was a Prophet'. Preston intended to handle the same text later in the month but opposition from the Church hierarchy prevented him; this interference only won Preston's sermon more attention. Compare this to events twenty years later in Boston in 1646 when John Cotton preached a sermon to a crowded lecture day in which he castigated critics of New England about to sail for London, and said they should toss their petition of grievances into the sea or suffer the consequences. When the boat experienced severe storms and a near-wreck, not surprisingly since it had sailed in winter, the result was that some on board insisted that the petition be thrown overboard, much to the jubilation of the New England authorities. Another example similar to Preston was Francis Higginson who, on leaving his lectureship in Leicester to go to New England in 1629, preached a fire-and-brimstone farewell sermon against the sinful nature of the town. Higginson died in 1630, but when Leicester was sacked during the Civil Wars someone remembered his sermon, labelled it as prophetic, and created a tradition that was eventually recorded by Cotton Mather. Thomas Hooker's farewell sermon was equally extreme, and built on a theme, seen throughout his English sermons and used by other Puritan divines, that God was leaving England, and therefore, like the Protestant countries suffering at that moment in the Thirty Years War, the country was threatened by destruction. One tradition indicates that while living in New England he retained a belief that England was likely to face future catastrophe, possibly explaining his noted unwillingness to return there.[17]

Possibly the most famous ministerial prophet of the first generation was the pastor of Boston, John Wilson, who seems to have predicted numerous deaths, recoveries from illness and even victory in the war against the Pequot tribe. Wilson also had predictive dreams, like the one he had before his arrival in New England, 'that, before he was resolved to come into this country, he dreamed he was here, and that he saw a church arise out of the earth, which grew up and become a marvellous godly church'. It seems that it was this dream and other coincidences, like the fact Wilson had often said he would go to the 'End of the World' to enjoy true religion while a student, which gave Wilson a commitment to the success of the colony of Massachusetts that was second to none. By the time of his death in 1667 Wilson clearly had an extremely powerful reputation, which is all the more unusual as unlike other leading divines he published virtually nothing. His one publication during his life was an epic poem, and it was Wilson's ability as a poetic wit that probably helped enhance his prophetic reputation since prophecies were often issued in verse form; at least one of his verses was later taken to be prophetic as it seemed to predict the death of three of Wilson's grandchildren. It is also notable that people travelled to gain a deathbed blessing from Wilson, and, like Knox and other divines, he used his death scene to exhort and warn his contemporaries. It seems likely that Wilson's long life-span enhanced his prophetic status, as it added to the aura of the saintly John Eliot, simply because it increased the opportunity for providential incidents. The many remarkable coincidences in Wilson's life must have left him facing, like many other ministers, the difficult task of reconciling humility with being a 'Son of Thunder' whose words resulted in divine action. Thus Hubbard could record after his death that Wilson had 'secret and strong persuasions . . . that no public judgement or calamity should come upon the country in his time; what hath fallen out since, is well known to the world'. Thus for Hubbard, although Cotton and Hooker created New England's Church system, it was Wilson's 'faith and prayers' which 'kept off the storm . . . as some have said of Luther concerning Germany'.[18]

One person who noted John Wilson's predictions in the Pequot War was the most powerful prophet of the second generation, Increase Mather. Mather's more openly documented life gives us a chance to examine the effects of ministerial prophecy more closely on an individual. Mather had first demonstrated his abilities while living in England. He had felt premonition of trouble, and preached in a sermon, 'that *futher suffering for the faithful witnesses of CHRIST* were to be looked for'; soon afterwards Charles II was restored to the throne. In 1673 Mather once again had a feeling of impeding doom and preached on a day of Humiliation a set of sermons which became a classic of the Jeremiad genre, *The Day of Trouble is Near*, castigating New England's sins, the lack of respect shown to the ministers and connecting them to troubles throughout the world. Increase saw the recent death of many ministers as one sign of adversity, since 'God hath called home many of his Ambassadors of late, and that's a sign that War is determined in Heaven against us'. Mather was convinced that the inspiration for the sermons came from a divine source when King Philip's War broke out a year later. His later predictions included a fire that destroyed part of Boston, including his own house, and a visitation of smallpox. As a result Increase was prone to a great belief in the power of his prayers and regard for the 'strange impressions' he felt warned him of future events. Perhaps this is why Increase was so interested in recording providential occurrences, as shown by *An Essay for the Recording of Illustrious Providences* (1684). The sense of power Increase felt could only have increased his obvious discontent with the provincial nature of New England.

Increase's predictions had a powerful influence on the young Cotton Mather, resulting in a conviction demonstrated in the *Magnalia* that the events surrounding ministers like his father, Eliot, and Wilson, showed that ministers might possess a special affinity to heavenly powers. His ideas can be seen when he said of his father's predictions that such impressions 'are often Produced in Minds, which by Piety and Purity and Contemplation, and a prayerful and Careful Walk with GOD, are made more Susceptible of them'. Cotton recorded 'particular faiths' in his diaries, possibly modelled on Increase's inspirations, which sometimes proved predictive, and sometimes felt he was inspired by angelic presences. In Cotton's case though, his particular faiths were often unreliable and his predictions were often unexpected, through a sermon or piece of conversation, but they still won public attention. Cotton told one impious man that he should expect God to 'speak unto you by a Blow!'; when the man later fell off a house he became a fervent church-goer. Cotton's fascination with these abilities probably has much to do with his feelings that in his time ministers had lost the status they had once held in the founding era.[19]

The importance of prophecy for ministers is underlined by the battle of providences and prophecies that broke out between them and the Quakers after they arrived in New England in 1657. The Quakers interrupted sermons, cursed the authorities, and followed their usual prophetic style. Even though it seems that Quakers won few converts outside Rhode Island the implicit threat they posed to the ministers meant they were met with a heavy response. Ministers like John Norton and John Wilson seem to have been very influential in advocating the death sentence against Quaker missionaries who refused to leave the colony. John Norton's *Heart of New England Rent* goes into great detail about the way of distinguishing a false from a true prophet and attacking the Quaker's position point by point. John Wilson's only published sermon from 1665 aimed at curbing people from listening to Quaker 'dreamers' telling them instead to 'hearken to the voice of the Lord spoken by his Ministers', those ministers who had done so much for them. When a bridge collapsed because it was overloaded with people returning from the execution of some Quakers in 1659, Quakers claimed it as a divine judgement against a female casualty who had been 'reviling' the Quaker martyrs. Meanwhile minister John Davenport said the bridge collapsed because there were Quaker sympathizers crossing it. Later when John Norton died of a stroke, Quakers exultantly announced it was a punishment from the Lord. Pressure from England made Massachusetts tone down their response after 1661, but the disaster of King Philip's War brought the issue into the limelight again for both sides. Quakers said the war was the long-predicted judgement against New England for the execution of Quaker innocents. The ministers, with Increase Mather at the forefront, argued the war was punishment for spiritual decline and tolerance of Quakers was one of the provoking sins that had brought divine judgement. As a result they managed to persuade a reluctant General Court to reinstate some anti-Quaker measures, although they were not enforced.[20]

The question of distinguishing false from true prophecy that was at the centre of the Quaker problem aroused such furore because it had also been at the centre of Antinomian controversy in 1636–8 and the case of Anne Hutchinson, called by her opponents the 'American Jesabel'. Anne is often grouped with the visionary prophetesses that proliferated in the Civil Wars. Instead it might make more sense to examine her in relation to the more conservative religion of godly women like Katherine Chidley or Dorothy Hazzard. She was certainly prophetic in the wider contemporary sense, of preaching and teaching the word of God, which she did in private religious meetings in which she established quite a large following. Just like the ministers her reputation in catering to spiritual needs was enhanced by her social position being known for exemplary piety, good birth, and as an active nurse and midwife. The controversy arose because she directly attacked the position of most of the New England ministers, especially John Wilson, by claiming they were failing to teach the word of God correctly. She seemed to advocate a more emotional, heartfelt religion, although certainly not going as far as the Quakers, since she continued to claim inspiration for her doctrines from John Cotton and John Wheelwright, and always emphasized scriptural warrant for her beliefs. Clearly one of the reasons that Hutchinson found support was because she could answer the spiritual needs and questions of her audience more effectively than some ministers. The group that surrounded her, mostly her Boston neighbours, interrupted ministers' sermons and questioned their doctrine, using the possibility of lay participation, not to echo the ministers' words but to oppose them.[21]

In the trial that led to her banishment, at a crucial moment Anne embarked on relating a kind of conversion narrative, explaining why she came to New England and why she disliked the words of so many ministers. She claimed that God had revealed to her the difference between a true and false ministry and guided her decisions. Moreover, citing scriptural references, she said that God would curse the General Court for any unjust punishment she might suffer, just as the Quakers did later. The problem was that her choice of language, the word 'revelation', enabled her ministerial and magisterial opponents to label her as the worst kind of radical Anabaptist mystic, who claimed revelations directly from God. The whole course of the trial from that point on centred on trying to define what she meant by a revelation, and it appears from Cotton's questions that she thought of it as a sort of 'Providence', but by then it was too late, and the damage had been done. Her exact beliefs remain difficult to define as many orthodox Puritans claimed that divine inspiration helped reveal and bring home the meaning of scriptural references and helped them in times of trouble. When we compare her words to the feeling of divine guidance we can find in conversion narratives and diaries there are many similarities. For instance, an ordinary church member William Hamlet said in his confession that the Lord 'showed him the difference between love of hypocrites and saints'. Just as Hamlet's words were partially inspired by a sermon by Thomas Goodwin, Anne Hutchinson's ideas owed their origins to John Cotton, but altered somewhat by her own private examination of scripture. Another parallel is to the minister Thomas Parker who said that 'the great Changes of his Life had been signified to him before hand by Dreams'.[22]

During the trial her opponents tried to connect further her to revelations, but the examples they used to support their case were weak, including that she had seemed to offer to predict when her ship would arrive in New England, that she was inquisitive after revelations and that she had said that England would be destroyed. Since fear of a judgement on England was a common source of motivation for emigrants, including Governor John Winthrop, she seems atypical only in the vehement way she expressed her beliefs. Although 'reports' of her 'revelations' were apparently common, at least according to her opponents, they produced few examples and there is no evidence to connect her to the dreams and visions of the typical female mystic. As there was an inherent tendency to inflate the prophetic credentials of spiritual guides, it could have been that Anne was gaining a reputation due to the over-enthusiasm of her supporters, but there is no way to be sure. It seems the problem was not so much what was said, but who said it; a minister could imply that God's judgement was imminent, that certain people were saved or damned, but a lay woman could not. What made the situation worse was that Anne Hutchinson suffered from the common Puritan affliction of being too eager to condemn other people, a dangerous thing to do in relation to ministers and magistrates. Because her opponents had already decided she was a dangerous heretic they also inclined to link her with the revelations that traditionally went with extreme heresy, just as they attempted to connect her with the sexual licentiousness associated with familist beliefs. By doing this the magistrates finally had a reason to banish an opponent who otherwise seems to have led a blameless life and who was well able to defend herself.[23]

Hutchinson's relative conservatism is further underlined by her later church trial. Since her banishment from the colony had already been ordered, she would seem to have had no reason to co-operate if she was a true radical. However, for Anne, like most Puritans, being rejected from church communion was something to be avoided at all costs. In the trial an accusation that she had claimed revelations against the General Court was one in a list of sixteen charges, moreover they were ones which were not really discussed and for which she apologized, saying the 'Scriptures that I used at the Court in Censuringe the Cuntrie I confes I did it rashly'. Because the revelations issue was sidelined in the church trial, despite its obviously extremely heretical nature, it seems all the more likely that her earlier words were misconstrued by a hostile General Court.

Despite these trials it seems that Anne Hutchinson was not really discredited within Boston until reports spread of what was labelled a 'loud speaking Providence from Heaven', when she and a female supporter gave birth to deformed foetuses. These so called 'monstrous births' branded Hutchinson guilty by a divine hand and succeeded in destroying her popular support where the combined efforts of the magistrates and ministry had failed. The female body could thus be used against women prophets. Ironically, after Anne's violent death at the hands of a native war-party in 1643, a tradition evolved that John Wilson, her most virulent enemy, had given a 'prediction or threatening' of her fate. As we have seen, Wilson by the end of his life had a reputation for making predictions, and it could be argued that if anyone was prophetic in the modern sense it was he, rather than Hutchinson. Whatever Anne Hutchinson's exact beliefs about revelations were, her case is interesting as an example of the way that allegations of revelations and predictions, far from supporting a women's spiritual authority, could serve to destroy it. Instead Hutchinson's threat arose from her willingness to assume the prophetic role of the ministers in applying scripture and resolving of cases of conscience.[24]

Prophetic roles then could lead to greatly increased authority for a minister but, as the examples we have examined show, their expertise was open to question from their audience. The most attentive audience to these New England prophets was other ministers, who built on their words to justify their own position. The diaries of ministers like Cotton Mather and Thomas Shepard reveal that the deep insecurities felt by ministers contrasted strongly with the bombastic claims of their sermons. This is particularly true from the second generation onwards as ministers' actual influence declined. As R.W. Scribner noted in the case of Luther in New England, it was the clergy who were most likely to record and spread tales of clerical wonder-working. Just like the Quakers, New England ministers were in a sense cut off from their audience by their sense of belonging to a special 'spiritual brotherhood' and had to justify their position to themselves and to others. Exactly the same is true of experts and scientists today. Even though they supposedly use more precise methods than scripture to understand the universe their position in our society remains far from secure because their very professionalism isolates them within it. It seems that human beings might need prophets, but the role is nowhere an easy one to fulfil.

Notes

1 I. Mather, *The Day of Trouble is Near* (Cambridge, Mass., Marmaduke Johnson, 1674), p. 11.

2 Due to limitations of space, I am in general concentrating on citing secondary sources as a guide to futher reading. B. Reay, *The Quakers and the English Revolution* (Hounslow, Temple Smith, 1985), ch. 1, pp. 32–7, 34. For the debate on the connection, or lack of it, between Quaker and Puritan spirituality see Carla Pestana, *Quakers and Baptists in Colonial Massachusetts* (London, Cambridge University Press, 1991), pp. 12–13; T. Bozeman, *To Live Ancient Lives* (London, North Carolina University Press, 1988), pp. 364–8.

3 Reay, *Quakers*, pp. 10–12, 37–45.

4 Edward Calamy's introduction to Samuel Clarke, *The Marrow of Ecclesiastical History* (3rd ed.,

London, Printed for W.B., 1675). D.D. Hall, *The Faithful Shepherd* (New York, North Carolina University Press, 1972), pp. 48–9, 67–70; G. Selement, *Keepers of the Vineyard* (New York, University Press of America, 1984), pp. 15–33.

5 Hall, *Shepherd*, pp. 145–9, 185–94; S. Powell, *Puritan Village* (Middletown, Conn., Wesleyan University Press, 1963), ch. 8.

6 For more see C. Cohen, *God's Caress: The Psychology of Puritan Religious Experience* (Oxford University Press, 1986); P. Caldwell, *The Puritan Conversion Narrative* (Cambridge University Press, 1983); D.D. Hall, *Worlds of Wonder, Days of Judgement: Popular Religious Belief in Early New England* (Cambridge, Massachusetts, Harvard University Press, 1990), pp. 119–39. G. Selement and B. Woolley, *Thomas Shepard's Confessions* (Boston, Colonial Society of Massachusetts, 1981), pp. 62–4.

7 W. Perkins, *Of the Calling of the Ministry* (London, Richard Faidel, 1607), p. 12. On Puritan ideas on the ministry see Hall, *Shepherd*, chs 1 and 2. On the concept of providence see Hall, *Worlds*, pp. 71–94; and K. Thomas, *Religion and the Decline of Magic* (Harmondsworth, Penguin, 1973), pp. 90–132. Cotton quoted in E. Winslow, 'New England's Salamander (1647)', *Massachusetts Historical Society Collections*, 3rd series, 2 (1830), 128.

8 Cotton's laws were printed in *An Abstract of the Laws of New England* (London, F. Coules and W. Ley, 1641). Hall, *Shepherd*, pp. 96–8, 121–54; Bozeman, *Ancient Lives*, pp. 151–92. On the political problems faced by Puritan ministers in England see T. Liu, *Discord in Zion: The Puritan Divines and the Puritan Revolution 1640–60* (The Hague, Nijhoff, 1973).

9 For these public sermons see H.S. Stout, *The New England Soul: Preaching and Religious Culture in Colonial New England* (Oxford University Press, 1986), pp. 27–31, Jeremiad, chs 4–6; T.H. Breen, *The Character of a Good Ruler* (New Haven, Yale University Press, 1970), ch. 1.

10 J. Winthrop, *Journal 'History of New England' 1630–1649*, ed. J. Hosmer (2 vols, New York, Barnes & Noble, 1946), vol. 1, p. 179. Early histories included E. Johnson, *Johnson's Wonder-Working Providence, 1628–1651* (New York, Barnes & Noble, 1910); N. Morton, *New England's Memorial* (Cambridge, Massachusetts, 1669). C. Mather, *Magnalia Christi Americana* (London, T. Parkhurst, 1702), book 7, pp. 101–4.

11 On this international perspective see Francis Bremer, *Congregational Communion* (Cambridge, Mass., Harvard University Press, 1994). J.F. Maclear, 'New England and the Fifth Monarchy', *William and Mary Quarterly*, 3rd series, 32 (1975), 223–60. For the dangers of over-emphasizing millennial thinking, Bozeman, *Ancient Lives*, pp. 193–226.

12 Bozeman, *Ancient Lives*, pp. 263–86; J. Eliot, 'The Christian Commonwealth (1659)', *Massachusetts Historical Society Collections*, 3rd series, 9 (1846), 139–40; N. Salisbury, 'Red Puritans: The Praying Indians of Massachusetts Bay and John Eliot', *William and Mary Quarterly*, 3rd series, 31 (1974), 27–54; Mather, *Magnalia*, book 3, p. 34.

13 A fuller analysis would also have to consider other supernatural capabilities such as healing and prayer; see Thomas, *Religion and the Decline of Magic*, pp. 133–51; the equivalent for New England is the excellent Hall, *Worlds*, pp. 86–91, 94–110, 196–204.

14 Winthrop, *Journal*, vol. 2, pp. 9, 62.

15 Thomas, *Religion and the Decline of Magic*, pp. 154–6, 465–6. On Luther see R.W. Scribner, *Popular Culture and Popular Movements in Reformation Culture* (London, Hambledon, 1987), pp. 301–53. J. Ridley, *John Knox* (Oxford University Press, 1968), pp. 515–20. J. Foxe, *The Actes and Monuments* (8 vols,

London, Seeley, 1847), vol. 7, pp. 463–4; S. Clarke, *Marrow*, pp. 237–8, 342–3, 382–4; predictions of death, pp. 222, 230–1, 256, 387, 392; the restoration of Protestantism, pp. 217, 226, 329.

16 S. Clarke, *The Lives of Thirty-Two English Divines* (London, printed for William Birch, 1675), pp. 127–8, 153, 136. Estimated sermons in introduction to Stout, *New England Soul*.

17 Clarke, *The Lives*, pp. 110–11; Mather, *Magnalia*, book 3, pp. 74, 62–3, more prophecies on pp. 117, 147, 182–3, and in book 4, pp. 142–3, 155. For Cotton's sermon see n. 7. G. Williams *et al.* (eds), *Thomas Hooker: Writings in England and Holland* (Cambridge, Massachusetts, Harvard University Press, 1975), pp. 49–52, 60–88, 228–52. For the threat to England see C. Hill, *The English Bible and the Seventeenth-Century Revolution* (London, Allen Lane, 1993), pp. 70–2, 284–97.

18 Winthrop, *Journal*, vol. 1, p. 84. Mather, *Magnalia*, book 3, pp. 41–51, 42, 44, 48. Other Jacobean poets with a prophetic reputation included George Herbert and George Wither. Only Hall seems to have noticed the significance of Wilson's prophetic reputation, *Worlds*, pp. 109–10. W. Hubbard, *A General History of New England* (New York, Arno Press, 1972), p. 601.

19 Cotton Mather, 'Parentator' in W. Scheick (ed.), *Two Mather Biographies* (Lehigh University Press, 1989), pp. 95, 127; M.G. Hall, *The Last American Puritan: The Life of Increase Mather* (Middletown, Conn., Wesleyan University Press, 1988), pp. 98–102, 127–8; Mather, *Day*, p. 21, also see the opening quotation above. D. Levin, *Cotton Mather* (Cambridge, Massachusetts, Harvard University Press, 1978), pp. 51–3; W. Ford (ed.), *Diary of Cotton Mather* (2 vols, New York, Fungar, 1954), vol. 1, pp. 12, 204, 372–3, 422.

20 Hall, *Shepherd*, pp. 237–41; J. Wilson, *A Seasonable Watchword* (Cambridge, Massachusetts, 1677), pp. 7–8; Mather, *Magnalia*, book 3, p. 38, book 5, p. 89; A.J. Worral, *Quakers in the Colonial Northeast* (Boston, University Press of New England, 1980), pp. 10–12, 27–9, 38–40; Pestana, *Quakers and Baptists*, pp. 29–31, 35.

21 There is much scholarship on the controversy. See the bibliography and documents in D.D. Hall (ed.), *The Antinomian Controversy 1636–8* (London, Duke University Press, 1990), pp. 310, 204–7, 371. Also, for an opposing view, Hall, *Worlds*, pp. 96–8, and also pp. 140–1, 101–2. For an English perspective see P. Crawford, *Women and Religion in England 1500–1700* (London, Routledge, 1993), pp. 75–83, 140–59.

22 Hall, *Controversy*, pp. 336–8, 340–1; Selement & Woolley, *Confessions*, pp. 126–7, also c.f. pp. 177, 107. Mather, *Magnalia*, book 3, p. 147. Patricia Caldwell's ideas support my interpretation, see 'The Antinomian Language Controversy', *Harvard Theological Review*, 69 (1976), 345–67.

23 Hall, *Controversy*, pp. 338–9, 340, 362–3. Also see sources in n. 17. There are more hostile reports of revelations in Johnson, *Wonder-Working*, pp. 127–9. Stephen Foster makes a similar point about accusations in the controversy in 'New England and the Challenge of Heresy, 1630–60', *William and Mary Quarterly*, 3rd series, 38 (1981), 646–50.

24 Hall, *Controversy*, pp. 352, 376, 215, 218; Hall, *Worlds*, p. 85; Scribner, *Popular Culture*, pp. 321–2.

7

THE PROPHETIC THOUGHT OF
SIR ISAAC NEWTON,
ITS ORIGIN AND CONTEXT

S.J. Barnett

Fundamental to the thought of medieval theologians such as Thomas Aquinas (*c.* 1225–74) was the belief that reason and faith were to be sharply distinguished. Yet, within the life-span of Sir Isaac Newton (1642–1727), there was an unprecedented fusion of scientific reasoning and religious thought, a greater integration of the physical and metaphysical than had been achieved in the several centuries since Aquinas.[1] That some aspects of that fusion, such as the discovery of shellfish fossils on a mountain, were seen as proof of the biblical Flood and Noah's Ark may seem naïve today. However, Newton was not the 'last of the Babylonians and Sumerians', as John Maynard Keynes put it in 1942.[2] One should not be tempted into peremptorily dismissing that integration as 'non-modern'. To do so would not only display a lack of historical sympathy; it would also underestimate the importance of the fusion of science and religion in the development of scientific thought in early modern Europe, the essential precondition to the emergence of 'modernity' itself. For Enlightenment thinkers such as Voltaire (1694–1778), Newton's main scientific publication, the *Principia* (1687), was a work of unusual genius and marked the beginning of the modern age. Voltaire understood Newton's religious studies as necessary light amusement after serious scientific studies; he thus failed to understand the relationship in Newton's mind between the study of science and the study of God.[3] For Newton, formulator of the law of gravity and founder of differential calculus, the study of nature was the attempt to unravel the intricate mechanics of God's creation and necessarily also a religious endeavour which complemented the study of Scripture.[4]

One of the problems faced by advocates of such research was how to avoid deistic or atheistic conclusions that removed God from the study of nature. That Newton and other scientists undertook their research from such a religious perspective was therefore of some importance: it helped ensure that religious barriers to scientific research were minimized. Some had still in mind the imprisonment in 1633 of Galileo (1564–1642) and the threat of torture used to force him to recant his anti-Ptolemaic views. Even in the relatively tolerant conditions of Protestant England, Newton did not feel able to proclaim his own

Unitarian heterodoxy. His work remained nevertheless a prominent example of the successful fusion of science and faith.[5] Indeed, the very success of that union prompted Newton to apply a quasi-scientific precision to his prophetic research of the Old Testament Book of Daniel and the New Testament Book of the Revelation of St John.[6] The aim of his attempt to comprehend the inscrutable message of the prophecies contained in these books was to discover the pattern of history leading to the future resurrection of Jesus Christ and the end of the world. The key events to be charted were the arrival of the Antichrist, the cause of the subsequent decline of medieval Christianity into Catholic 'corruption' and 'idolatry', and the eventual demise of the Antichrist that would usher in the approach of the Second Coming.

Historians' attitudes to Newton's thought on religion and prophecy have been very diverse. Before the 1963 work of Frank Manuel, *Isaac Newton, Historian*, writings on Newton were often virtually silent on his religious views. In the age of atom-splitting, the thought of one of the great British fathers of modern science as a Unitarian heretic and decoder of biblical prophecy that would enable Christians to predict the Second Coming was best left unexpressed or politely glossed over. On the contrary, it is now incontrovertible that our comprehension of the development of scientific thought in the seventeenth century is greatly enhanced by embracing the totality of the thought-world of scientists such as Newton, rather than censoring them and selecting those parts that suit our modern sensibilities.

Unfortunately, once accepted, the re-evaluation of the relationship between Newton's scientific and theological thought possessed its own dynamic. Historians, compensating for the past silence on Newton's religious and prophetic thought, began to probe more deeply, and often speculatively, into the relationship between Newton's childhood emotional experiences and the development of his religious thought. Despite the value of Frank Manuel's work upon Newton's non-scientific writings, it was Manuel himself who began the trend of Freudian speculation into Newton's childhood. This is a trend which has recently resulted in some interesting but intrinsically hypothetical insights into Newton's theological thought-world. Thus, since the 1950s, historians of Newton have moved from a virtually complete embarrassed silence on his religious studies to the now almost jubilant claim that Newton considered himself as a latter-day Moses, a messenger-prophet.[7] The object of this paper is to avoid such deductive and essentially putative analysis, and instead attempt to understand Newton and his prophetic thought-world in a much wider context than has normally been the case. Only by returning to the Reformation can one fully appreciate the Protestant prophetic tradition to which Newton belonged and therefore properly contextualize his theological outlook.

The German protagonist of the Reformation, Martin Luther (1483–1546), himself endeavoured to identify the Papacy with the Antichrist according to the prophecy contained in the Book of Daniel.[8] Luther's work quickly influenced English Protestants, and there developed a strong English tradition of prophetic thought focused on the advent and future decline of the Antichrist. Paradoxically, the Catholic Queen Mary (1553–8) unwittingly helped to develop the prophetic interpretation of history in England. Under her religious persecutions many leading Protestants were simultaneously forced into continental exile and into contemplation as to how God could permit such a weakening of the struggle against the Antichrist. In the minds of the exiles, the reason for the persecution was divine punishment for the apostasy of England, which was now worshipping the Beast – the Antichrist – as described in the Book of Revelation. For the Marian exiles, persecution was also a divine confirmation of their faith, just as it was for the suffering of the many pious medieval Christians who had opposed the 'idolatry' and corruption of the Roman Antichrist. Such persecution was thus to be considered the sign of the 'true' Church.[9] The exile was, therefore, also proof of God's Providential plan, leading to the Second Coming. The exact nature and course of divine Providence was still a matter for conjecture, because the key biblical texts accepted by most Protestants to relate to the future unfolding of God's will, the Book of Daniel and the Book of Revelation, lay shrouded in mysterious evocations and esoteric language.

Nevertheless, the Book of Revelation offered the possibility, via its progressive developmental framework of seven seals, trumpets and vials, of constructing a chronology of the historical development of the 'true' Church, by tying recorded events of Church history to its seven stages. Bishop John Bale (1495–1563) was one of the first to pursue this chronology, but it was in the work of the martyrologist John Foxe (1516–87) that these ideas found their most influential expression in England.[10] In the seventeenth century this prophetic interpretation of history was certainly not abandoned. On the contrary, the battle against the Antichrist and the unfolding of divine will leading to the Millennium was widely considered to be ongoing. Just as the defeat of the Spanish Armada of 1588 was commonly considered by Protestants to be a defeat of the Antichrist and proof of God's Providence towards the 'true' Church, seventeenth-century events such as the Thirty Years War (1618–48) were interpreted as further proof of the impending defeat of the Antichrist and the imminence of the Millennium. Set against the background of unprecedented revolt and civil war across mid-seventeenth-century Europe, the English Civil War helped to produce a quasi-apocalyptic atmosphere in the minds of many Protestants. In the struggle between parliament and King Charles, the king and his supporters were identified as the Antichrist, compounding the Protestant understanding that the divine plan was drawing to a close: the end of earthly history and the coming of the Millennium were imminent.[11]

It is in this political and religious context, and on the outbreak of the Civil War, that Isaac Newton was born in 1642. The modern mind can easily comprehend this turmoil in terms of war and revolt, but cannot empathize with the apocalyptic outlook of its Protestant participants. For a sincere seventeenth-century Protestant, born and raised in such times, to have had a cosmology entirely unaffected by the Protestant apocalyptic tradition would have been somewhat unlikely. That Newton was heir to this apocalyptic tradition is evident in his *Observations upon the Prophecies of Daniel and the Apocalypse of St John* (1733), published posthumously and representing just a fraction of his overall writings on biblical prophecy. He noted the coming resurrection of the flesh and the Millennium. The imminence of the end of history was indicated because of the growing revelation of God's word by interpreters of the prophecies, amongst whom 'there is scarce one of note who hath not made some discovery worth knowing; and thence I seem to gather that God is about opening these mysteries'. Thus God, in the last times, wished his divine historical scheme to be known to Christians.[12]

The interpretation of history, the present, and future times using prophecy was not, therefore, the preserve of isolated and overly 'enthusiastic' Protestant theologians, mystical thinkers or an intellectual élite, but rather a shared understanding of many Protestants. Even amongst seventeenth-century exponents of the use of reason in the investigation of religious truths, such as the Cambridge Platonist and Newton's first guide to prophecy, Henry More (1614–87), there was a continued belief in and investigation of prophecy.[13] Investigation was still needed because the Marian exiles had not solved the main barrier to the interpretation of biblical prophecy: its complex and esoteric nature. The Bible was the Word of God, but He had put his ineffable Word into figurative and sometimes obscure language. The veiled language of prophecy had to be systematically subjected to detailed and methodical analysis if divine truths were to be extracted with any degree of certainty as to their real worldly meaning. It was thus in a '*scientific* spirit that Protestant scholars, approached biblical prophecy', perhaps especially so Isaac Newton.[14]

Newton was the son of moderately wealthy Lincolnshire landowners; his father died before he was born. His stepfather did not wish Isaac to live with his mother, and Isaac was consequently raised by his grandparents. His childhood was spent in the anti-Catholic and millennialist climate described above, an outlook that determined much of Protestant thought and his own thought-world.[15] One should probably not dwell too heavily on the claim that Newton's theological outlook was 'invested, with implicit comparison between true and false Gods', and 'a true father and a false father'.[16] Similarly, Manuel's notion that Newton's anti-Catholic 'vehemence was only equalled by the anti-religious *philosophes* of eighteenth-century France' cannot be sustained. Many English Protestant works of the seventeenth century were equally, if not more, rabidly anti-Catholic than the anti-clerical writings of the European Enlightenment.[17] Confusion still exists over the nature of Newton's religious upbringing. By some, Newton has been described as having been raised with a Puritanical stamp,[18] yet by others, as having received a Church of England, High Church upbringing.[19] As we shall see below, Newton's beliefs and outlook certainly do not at all favour the latter interpretation of staunch Anglicanism. We know, from his unpublished works, that Newton became a Unitarian; and he was certainly not, as some have suggested, a deist.[20] Like some other heterodox Protestants, however, Newton did not wish to publicly expose his dissenting beliefs. In an age when religion was still considered a public duty rather than solely a private good, and when Unitarians could still not worship freely and were denied public offices, a reluctance to advertise one's heterodoxy might be considered to be more a sign of prudence than a lack of religious conviction.

Newton has been described, with some justification, as a tortured personality, a neurotic man who was continually on the verge of nervous exhaustion throughout his middle age.[21] Outstanding scientist, mathematician, historian, head of the Royal Mint, and alchemist, Isaac was a solitary, unmarried man, totally absorbed in his various studies, sometimes to the point of not feeding himself. A considerable portion of his time was spent analysing biblical prophetic writings – most of which manuscripts remain unpublished.[22] Among such men it was common to draw models of Noah's Ark, the Ark of the Covenant, and the Temple of Solomon, in order to establish what the physical properties of such divinely inspired architecture could reveal regarding the future paradise. Heated debates often ensued as to the correct interpretation. In the same sense that the Books of Daniel and Revelation were 'hieroglyphs' for the facts of past and future times, such constructions as Solomon's Temple were blueprints of heaven, the truth of God's kingdoms expressed in physical terms. Divinely inspired buildings and objects also had a prophetic dimension. Thus Newton also spent time constructing and reconstructing the alleged form and dimensions of the Temple of Solomon.[23]

Here we shall concern ourselves only with Newton's study of the written prophecies of Daniel and St John. This provides the opportunity in this book to examine more closely the techniques and practices of hermeneutics. Newton brought consistency to the art of translating visionary language in concrete historical or mathematical facts. Despite the large quantity of Newton's writings and re-writings on biblical prophecy that remains unpublished, one can still examine the main elements of his prophetic thought in his one published work on prophecy, his *Observations upon the Prophecies of Daniel and the Apocalypse of St John* (1733). In this work, Newton tells us of the method of analysis he applied to the prophecies. He thought that to understand biblical prophecy, we have to acquaint ourselves with the 'figurative language' of the prophets. 'This language is taken from the analogy between the world natural, and an empire or kingdom considered as a world politic.' That is to say, Newton equated elements of the natural world depicted in the prophecies with earthly kingdoms and peoples.

Thus, 'the heavens, and the things therein, signify thrones and dignities . . . and the earth . . . [the] inferior people. . . . Whence ascending towards heaven, and descending to the earth, are put for rising and falling in power and honour.'[24]

Newton's whole point was to be accurate, to develop a methodical system for the interpretation of the figurative prophetic language that would allow a greater degree of precision in the understanding and prediction of the divine plan – although his interpretative method seems less than accurate to the modern mind. His analogies between the depictions contained in the prophecies and earthly realities therefore needed to be more specific, and he goes on to note that 'the Sun is put for the whole species and race of kings'; the stars signify the 'subordinate Princes and great men', whilst 'the moon [is] for the body of the common people' (although he also equated the Earth – as above – with the 'inferior people'). If the prophecies were to be considered on a purely theological rather than a worldly plane, then, the 'Sun is Christ', and the stars the 'Bishops and Rulers of the people of God'.

In terms of natural events in the prophecies, Newton advanced similar simple equations: 'burning anything with fire', for instance, 'is put for the consuming thereof by war' and the experience of 'being in a furnace for the being in slavery under another nation . . . the scorching heat of the sun, for vexatious wars, persecutions and troubles inflicted by the king'. Similarly, he considered 'riding on the clouds', to be 'for reigning over much people; covering the sun with a cloud, or with smoke, for oppression of the King by the armies of an enemy', and the 'beginning and end of the world' is signified by 'the rise and ruin of the body politic'.[25] Newton also made use of simple opposites in his interpretation of prophetic depiction. Thus 'rain . . . dew, and living water', are to be understood 'for the graces and doctrines of the Spirit; and the defect of rain, for spiritual barrenness'. Physical transformations such as 'turning things into blood', he understood as 'the mystical death of bodies politic'. Houses and ships, he took to denote 'families, assemblies, and towns, in the earth and sea politic'. Animals and vegetables 'are put for the people of several regions and conditions . . . a forest for a kingdom; and a wilderness for a desolate and thin people'. Depictions of animals were considered not just for their physical form, but also their supposed qualities, thus 'several animals, as a Lion, a Bear, a Leopard, a Goat, according to their qualities, are put for several kingdoms and bodies politic'.[26] In the Books of Daniel and Revelation, Newton notes that when 'a Beast or Man is put for a kingdom, his parts and qualities are put for the analogous parts and qualities of the kingdom'. Thus the 'head of a Beast' denotes the 'great men who precede and govern; the tail for the inferior people, who follow and are governed'. However, if there is more than one head, they denote 'the number of capital parts, or dynasties, or dominions in the kingdom, and the horns on any head correspond 'to the number of kingdoms . . . with respect to military power'. Other qualities are also considered, for instance, 'the loudness of the voice' is equated to the 'might and power of the beast'.

In bodily parts, Newton also identifies a hierarchy based partly on size of the organ, but also upon its character, as derived from the nature of the bird or animal in question. Thus the 'hairs of a beast, or man, and the feathers of a bird' signify people, while the 'feet, nails, and teeth of beasts of prey' stand for 'armies and squadrons of armies; [and] the bones, for strength, and for fortified places'. The 'death of a man or beast' Newton equates to the 'dissolution of a body politic or ecclesiastic', and the 'resurrection of the dead' tells the reader of the 'revival of a dissolved dominion'.[27] In his interpretation of prophecy Newton also made use of mathematical calculations standard among the techniques of the cabbalists. One such form of calculation, known as gematria, involved the translation of a name or a noun into its numerical equivalent (A being equal to 1, B to 2, and so forth) in order, for example, to prognosticate a future date for the coming of the Messiah. The number of the Beast, as in Revelation itself, was of course 666.[28]

Newton understood the prophecies to be apocalyptic in character: they told of the fall of Christendom into corruption and the later purification of it in the Millennium. He notes that, as foretold by the Prophets and Apostles, there was 'a falling away among the Christians, soon after the days of the Apostles', and later, in the 'latter days God would destroy the impenitent revolters, and make a new covenant with his people'.[29] The 'falling away' of course refers to the Protestant perception of the corruption of Christianity by Rome, and the foundation of such a prophecy in the Old Testament Book of Daniel is to be located in Daniel's image of four metals. For Newton, the metals represent the bodies of four great nations, which are said to reign over the earth successively. The metals are twinned with four beasts, which also represent the four great nations.

The first nation is Babylonia and Media, ancient kingdoms of the Middle East, signified by gold and a winged lion. The second nation is the empire of the Persians, represented by a bear and silver. The third beast, the four-winged and four-headed leopard, is the kingdom of the Greeks, linked to copper; while the fourth, ten-horned beast is 'exceeding dreadful and terrible and had great iron teeth . . . such was the *Roman* empire', signified by iron.[30] The ten horns of the Roman beast represent the ten European kingdoms into which the Roman Empire disintegrated. However, three of these horns, representing the two northern Italian kingdoms of Ravenna and the kingdom of the Lombards, and the dukedom of Rome, become plucked out by their roots and are in turn replaced by one horn. This replacement or usurping horn represented, in Newton's scheme, what would come to be 'St Peter's Patrimony', what came to be the medieval Papal States of the Italian peninsula.

For Newton and most Protestants, the foundation of the secular rule of the popes in the early medieval period, after the failure of the Roman Emperor, then based in Constantinople, to retain the western Roman Empire, was the beginning of the great apostasy. In early modern Protestant thought the

Antichrist's rule at Rome dated to the time when Christianity lost its spiritual
purity and became venal, corrupted by worldly concerns. Antichristian Rome
then ruled the Church despotically, erected a massive European ecclesiastical
empire, and grew so powerful, rich and arrogant that it stamped on the rights of
kings and emperors, electing and deposing them according to its own secular
needs. It is from this historical vantage-point that Newton described the new
horn that supplanted the other three by noting that in

> this horn were eyes like the eyes of a man . . . and the same horn made war
> with the saints, and prevailed against them. . . . By its eyes it was a Seer; and
> by its mouth speaking great things and changing times and laws, it was a
> Prophet as well as a King. And such a Seer, a Prophet and a King, is the
> Church of Rome. . . . With his mouth he gives laws to kings and nations as an
> Oracle; and pretends to Infallibility, and that his dictates are binding to the
> whole world.[31]

Although Newton notes that the beginning of the corruption of the Church
into Roman idolatry and its dominion over the western Church is found in the
reigns of the Emperors Gratian and Valentinian II, in the year AD 378–9, the
pope had then not yet risen up 'as a horn of the Beast'. The supplanting of the
other three horns was only accomplished by the acquisition of 'temporal
dominion which made him one of the horns', fully achieved only 'in the latter
half of the eighth century' (with the donation of territories by the Frankish king
Pepin III [714–68]). The final fall of the ecclesiastical and temporal kingdom of
Rome represented by the new usurping horn would signify the 'latter days'. Then
'God would destroy the impenitent revolters, and make a new covenant with his
people', that is to say the end of earthly history and the advent of the
Millennium, the thousand year reign of the saints preceding the Second Coming
of Christ. Relying on the interpretation of biblical scholar Joseph Mede
(1586–1638), Newton translated the obscure formula in the Book of Daniel (Dan.
12: 6–8) for the duration of this antichristian kingdom. He arrived at a figure of
1,260 years duration, after which the kingdom would fall, by degrees, and be
'given unto the people of the Saints of the most High'.[32]

Before dealing with the issue of the date predicted for the Millennium, one
needs to briefly analyse the main features of part two of Newton's work, which
deals with the Apocalypse of St John, otherwise known as the Book of Revelation.
This dual study is necessary because, for Newton, '[t]he *Apocalypse* of John is
written in the same style and language with the prophecies of Daniel[;] . . . all of
them together make but one complete Prophecy'.[33]

The Book of Revelation proceeds via the progressive opening of the seven seals
of a book that can only be opened by Jesus Christ. As the seals are opened the
approach of the end is revealed and the redeemed are seen in heaven.[34] The

opening of the seventh seal begins a series of seven trumpet-calls. The seventh trumpet-call is followed by the proclamation of the Kingdom of God and of Christ. In terms of the general outline of Christian history and Newton's perception of the rise of the Antichrist and his downfall in the Millennium, it is the visions that follow the depiction of the last trumpet-call that are of most concern to us. The second vision is of a woman in the temple of heaven, who represents the Primitive Church. She is persecuted by another ten-horned dragon, which has seven diadem-crowned heads, and she consequently flees into the wilderness (Rev. 12). This marks, according to the Newtonian schema, the beginning of the division and degeneration of the Christian Church.[35] Later the woman, now bejewelled and resplendent, is found sitting on the dragon – otherwise referred to as the Beast. Revelation informs us that the seven heads of the dragon are in fact seven hills that the woman is sitting upon, and the ten horns ten kings, who will briefly share with the Beast the exercise of royal authority, before giving all authority to the Beast (Rev. 17: 3–14). Applying the geographical analogy between the seven hills upon which Rome was built and the seven hills upon which the woman was sitting, Newton, amongst other Protestants, identified the Beast with the papacy, signifying that the papacy was the Antichrist. Thus the ten horns of the Beast represent the same ten post-Roman-Empire European kingdoms Newton identified in the ten horns of the beast in the Book of Daniel.

The woman, identified in Revelation as the Whore of Babylon (Rev. 17: 4–6), and the Beast jointly represent Rome and the papacy, 'which reigneth over the kings of the Earth'. This portrayal fitted hand-in-glove with the common Protestant critique of the medieval and Catholic Church, accusing the Church of meddling in state affairs, of tyrannical rule inside the Church, and of spiritual corruption in order to amass great wealth. Thus the beast-mounted woman committed fornication with the ten kings and 'she was drunken with the blood of the saints'. Newton notes that Revelation predicts the coming of the *'false Prophets, or false teachers*, expressed collectively in the *Apocalypse* by the name of the false Prophet'. This false prophet would have the 'character of *Antichrist: And many*, saith he, *shall follow their lusts* [and] . . . be made drunk with the wine of the Whore's fornication'. Indeed, 'the kingdoms of the beast live deliciously with the great Whore, and the nations are made drunk with the wine of her fornication'. The duration of the despotic and antichristian rule of the dragon-mounted woman over Church and kings Newton gives as 1,260 years, the same figure he gives in his analysis of the Book of Daniel.[36]

This leads to the problem of dating the onset of the Millennium. The most common Protestant date for the onset of the Antichrist was the year 607 when, in the pontificate of Pope Boniface III, the pope was awarded supremacy within the Church and given the title of *episcopus universalis* by the Byzantine Emperor Phocas.[37] When one adds the 1,260 years of the reign of the Beast or Great

Whore to that figure, the resultant date is 1867. However, Newton did not consider it proper to attempt to predict the Second Coming with any degree of accuracy, although he considered that the end was approaching, judging 'by the great successes of late Interpreters' of biblical prophecy, such as More and Mede. This was because God had intended

> that these prophecies should not be understood till the time of the end. . . . 'Tis therefore a part of this Prophecy, that it should not be understood before the last age of the world; and therefore it makes credit of the Prophecy, that it is not yet understood.[38]

Nevertheless, the possible date for such a momentous event for the human race as the commencement of the Millennium could hardly be completely ignored by interpreters of prophecy. It would be surprising if Newton did not at least attempt some provisional calculations. He made many calculations of the likely date of the Second Coming but, given his understanding of the inscrutable design of the prophecies, which were deliberately created to conceal the date of the Millennium until 'the time of the end', he did not commit himself to any one of them. Another reason has been advanced as to why Newton refrained from committing himself to some dates at which he arrived, such as that of 1641. Matania Kochavi argued that Newton did not promulgate this particular date because it was too close to Newton's own birth date. The result, according to Kochavi, would have been an embarrassingly close correlation between the Second Coming and Newton's ability to interpret the prophecies.[39] Such an explanation does not account for the reason why Newton did not commit himself to other likely dates, such as 1867. Another problem with this hypothesis, and rather more fundamental, is that of the possibility that the Second Coming had commenced in 1641, but Christianity had not noticed the fact!

Newton's views of his role as scientist and religious thinker are here very important. The late seventeenth century was a period in which many still revered the civilization of ancient Greece as a past golden age of knowledge and wisdom. Newton extended this reverence to the point that he thought he was only recovering the knowledge – his scientific discoveries included – that had been known to ancients such as Pythagoras and Plato.[40] In the same way that he was discovering ancient truths from biblical prophecy, he was rediscovering ancient scientific knowledge. But this did not mean he undervalued his rediscoveries: it was precisely the recovery of ancient knowledge that was a sign of his ability. Similarly, disagreeing with Henry More, who thought biblical prophecy was potentially comprehensible to all, Newton considered that his own ability and that of a few others to comprehend the Holy Ghost's intention via biblical prophecy showed that they comprised a privileged group of Christians. He thought that certain religious truths were beyond the capacity of the vulgar, and that it was the duty of such select individuals to provide guides for their edification. Thus Newton and others were not real biblical prophets, but held the minor role of guides to the truth of biblical prophecy.[41]

This position is at odds with Kochavi's attempts to qualify Newton's prophetic thought as either religious eccentricity or 'enthusiasm'. Kochavi argues 'that Newton's activity served as a metaphor for the construction of the Tabernacle by Moses'. Thus, as an exegete, Newton had a central role in saving true Christianity and he was therefore, as Moses, a 'messenger-prophet'.[42] As outlined above, Newton was in very good and numerous company, and many other eminent men amongst his contemporaries had similar ideas and preoccupations. In spite of being versed in hermeneutics, there is no evidence that they generally thought of themselves as latter-day Moses! Indeed, although Newton considered that he was rediscovering the knowledge of the ancients, the general depiction of the medieval Church he drew from biblical prophecy was hardly original. The general outline of Newton's account was common amongst Protestant thinkers; John Calvin himself (1509–64) identified the papacy with the Beast in the Book of Revelation, and therefore with the Antichrist, noting it in the marginalia to the Geneva Bible (1560). One of the remaining issues is to identify why Newton thought himself a member of a privileged group. There is certainly one clue, and it is to be found in the 'Puritanical stamp' of his religious upbringing. Puritans were Calvinists and, in terms of their religious self-conceptions, they were either of the elect or the reprobate. The reprobate were predestined by God to hell and the elect to heaven. Only He knew if a person had been destined reprobate or elect, although it was commonly accepted that if one was elect, one would lead a godly life, and strive to excel in one's calling (natural abilities) which God had endowed one with. We know that Newton had strayed from the Trinitarianism of Calvinism to Unitarianism, but Unitarianism was a broad movement with significant variations in belief from one Unitarian to the next. It is therefore possible that Newton never fully abandoned the Calvinist notion of predestination and still considered himself to be one of the elect.

In attempting to understand the station Newton had assigned himself in his religious outlook, the religious climate of his youth should not be overlooked, strange as some of the prevalent conceptions might seem to some modern minds. For example, we should remind ourselves that virtually all seventeenth-century English Protestants agreed on the importance of the Fall in the development of world history. The sin of Adam and Eve had condemned the human race to sin, because they transmitted their sin physiologically, as noted in the Westminster Confession (1643).[43] Religious affliction, therefore, could be hereditary, and the most common affliction was considered to be idolatry. Indeed, Henry More, in his *Antidote against Idolatry* (1669) noted that the souls of men 'in this lapsed state, are naturally prone to so mischievous a Disease [idolatry], as both History and daily Experience do abundantly witness'.[44]

It was precisely the 'career' of idolatry that Newton traced in his exegesis of biblical prophecy: worship had been given to the Beast, the papacy. Nevertheless, Unitarians are said to have rejected the determinism of original sin, believing instead in the goodness of human nature. Newton's views on Scripture were therefore not typical of Unitarian thought, and this serves to emphasize once again its heterogeneous nature.

There are comments in Newton's works to suggest that his distinction between the knowledgeable and the ignorant had been based on a wider and more fundamental theological foundation, perhaps akin to Calvinist thought, and certainly not typical of Unitarian thinking with its positive view of human nature. For example, he twice cites Daniel (Dan. 12: 9–10) that 'God has so ordered the prophecies that in the latter days *the wise may understand, but the wicked shall do wickedly, and none of the wicked shall understand*. If one equates the elect with the wise and the wicked with the reprobate, one has another indication that Newton may have still considered himself to be of the elect, and his endowments, proven by his scientific prowess, would have seemed further proof of election. But this is a very different conception to the astounding assumption that Newton considered himself to be a latter-day Moses; a conception such a pious man would surely have considered presumptuous or even blasphemous. Thus he scorns the 'rashness' and 'folly of Interpreters' who have tried 'to foretell times and things by this prophecy [Daniel], as if God designed to make them Prophets', and adds that until the 'signal revolutions predicted by the holy Prophets', we can only 'content ourselves with interpreting what hath already been fulfilled'.[45]

Seventeenth-century attempts to put the study of prophecy upon a scientific basis were doomed to failure, because the contents of the prophecies were themselves not amenable to scientific or quasi-scientific investigation. The fact that such an attempt seems eccentric or naïve today can mislead us in to attempting to explain it via defects of the personality or delusions of religious grandeur. Instead, we must remind ourselves that Newton lived in a period characterized by a unique combination of science and religion. It is true that, in the eighteenth century, the study of the prophecies and the prophetic outlook did slowly decline. However, the prophetic outlook was too deeply ingrained into the English Protestant psyche to be suddenly and completely snuffed out by any such short-lived phenomenon as the ultra-rationalist and anti-Christian English deist Enlightenment of the years 1695 to 1740, as some have claimed.[46]

The growing secularization of society in the eighteenth and nineteenth centuries was one of the main factors in the slow decline of Protestant reliance on biblical prophecy. It is true that the Millennium had failed to arrive as soon as some Protestants might have hoped, but equally as important was that a fully Protestant interpretation of past and future times had already been achieved. The result of the achievements of expositors such as More, Mede and Newton was that the biblical mine was exhausted. Given the nature of the subject matter, it was hardly possible to subject the books of Daniel and Revelation to any greater degree of analytical precision using scientific language; and besides, the historical account that such men had discerned and detected perfectly explained the Protestant view of Church history. The project initiated by the Marian exiles had been completed. After 1700 the expository tradition was in slow decline, but the historical and eschatological scheme of the exiles lived on in Protestant thought. In the second half of the eighteenth century, the same prophetic framework was still used by Protestants to understand the development of history,[47] and the name of Isaac Newton was used by some to legitimate the predictive power of such prophecies.[48] Even amongst the scientific community of the late eighteenth century, there were those who looked to biblical prophecy, including the scientist who discovered oxygen, Joseph Priestley (1733–1804).[49] Indeed, it is significant that one of the very few Catholic works written on prophecy was by an Englishman, Charles Walmesley (1722–97), scientist, priest, mathematician and astronomer. Walmesley wrote *The General History of the Christian Church . . . chiefly deduced from the Apocalypse of St John the Apostle* (1771).[50] Albeit slowly, the late eighteenth and the early nineteenth centuries saw a divorce between prophecy and science, and even the secularization of religious schemes of historical analysis, nevertheless the learned language of prophecy and hermeneutics still found its place in historical analysis, either of the mythological understanding of the past or in some teleological expectation of a new dawn.

Notes

1 On the unprecedented fusion of science and religion in the seventeenth century see A. Funkenstein, *Theology and the Scientific Imagination from the Middle Ages to the Seventeenth Century* (Princeton, Guildford, Princeton University Press, 1986); J. Gascoigne, 'From Bentley to the Victorians: The Rise and Fall of British Newtonian Theology', *Science in Context*, 2 (2), (1988), 219–56.

2 J.M. Keynes, 'Newton the Man', *Collected Works* (14 vols, London, Macmillan, 1972), vol. 4, pp. 363–4.

3 P. Rattansi, 'Newton and the Wisdom of the Ancients' in J. Fauvel, R. Flood, M. Shortland, R. Wilson (eds), *Let Newton Be!* (New York, Oxford University Press, 1989), pp. 186–201, at pp. 186, 191–2.

4 S. Mandlebrote, 'A Duty of the Greatest Moment: Isaac Newton and the Writing of Biblical Criticism', *British Journal for the History of Science*, 26 (1993), 281–302, at p. 300.

5 Newton made a public distinction between the 'Book of Nature' and the 'Book of Religion', but there is no evidence that in his private thought he made any such dichotomy. See F.E. Manuel, *Isaac Newton, Historian* (Cambridge University Press, 1963), p. 164.

6 F.E. Manuel, *The Religion of Isaac Newton* (Oxford, Clarendon Press, 1974), pp. 38, 48–9. There were, it seems, limits to the fusion of science and religion in Newton's work, as for example of the issue of gravity; see J. Brooke, 'The God of Isaac Newton' in Fauvel *et al.*, *Let Newton Be!*, pp. 169–85, p. 172.

7 M.Z. Kochavi, 'One Prophet Interprets Another: Sir Isaac Newton and Daniel' in J.E. Force and

R.H. Popkin (eds), *The Books of Nature and Scripture: Recent Essays on Natural Philosophy, Theology, and Biblical Criticism in the Netherlands of Spinoza's Time and the British Isles of Newton's Time* (Dordrecht, Kluwer, 1994), pp. 105–22, at pp. 116–17, 120.

8 J.M. Headley, *Luther's View of Church History* (New Haven and London, Yale University Press, 1963), pp. 32, 195–6.

9 On the thought of the Marian exiles see J.A. Dawson, 'The Apocalyptic Thinking of the Marian Exiles' in M. Wilks (ed.), *Prophecy and Eschatology*, Studies in Church History, Subsidia 10 (Oxford, Blackwell, 1994).

10 J. Foxe, *Acts and Monuments of Matters happening in the Church* (London, John Day, 1563).

11 J.E.C. Hill, *Antichrist in Seventeenth-Century England* (Oxford University Press, 1971).

12 I. Newton, *Observations upon the Prophecies of Daniel and the Apocalypse of St John* (London, J. Darby & T. Browne, 1733), pp. 247–8, 253. See also Manuel, *Isaac Newton Historian*, p. 165; Kochavi, 'One Prophet Interprets Another', p. 116.

13 S. Hutton, 'Henry More and the Apocalypse' in Wilks, *Prophecy and Eschatology*, pp. 131–40; Mandlebrote, 'A Duty of the Greatest Moment', p. 291. Newton was also profoundly influenced by the work of the biblical scholar Joseph Mede (1586–1638). On the widespread application of Protestant scholars to biblical exegesis see also Manuel, *Isaac Newton, Historian*, p. 11.

14 J.E.C. Hill, *The World Turned Upside Down: Radical Ideas during the English Revolution* (Harmondsworth, Penguin, 1975), pp. 92–3, 287–93.

15 On the power of anti-Catholicism in shaping Protestant thought see such works as A. Milton, *Catholic and Reformed: The Roman and Protestant Churches in English Protestant Thought, 1600–1640* (Cambridge University Press, 1995).

16 Manuel, *The Religion of Isaac Newton*, p. 19.

17 Manuel, *Isaac Newton Historian*, p. 154. On the rabidly anti-Catholic nature of much of English Protestant thought see, for example, H. Care (ed.), *A Pacquet of Advice from Rome* (5 vols, London, Langley Curtis, 1678–83, from 1679 entitled the *Weekly Pacquet of Advice from Rome*).

18 R.S. Westfall, *The Life of Isaac Newton* (Cambridge University Press, 1994), pp. 23–4; Mandlebrote, 'A Duty of the Greatest Moment', pp. 285–6, 301 concurs with the idea of a 'provincial Puritanism'.

19 Manuel, *The Religion of Isaac Newton*, p. 5.

20 On the history of the deist charge see Mandlebrote, 'A Duty of the Greatest Moment', pp. 281–2.

21 Westfall, *Life of Isaac Newton*, p. 10. Newton suffered a temporary breakdown in 1693; see Manuel, *Isaac Newton Historian*, p. 11. On the life of Newton see also Manuel's *Portrait of Isaac Newton* (Cambridge [Mass.], Harvard University Press, 1968).

22 For some notes on the whereabouts of Newton's unpublished manuscripts see Manuel, *The Religion of Isaac Newton*, pp. 10–13; *Isaac Newton Historian*, p. 2. On Newton and alchemy see Westfall, *Life of Isaac Newton*, pp. 111–19; and J. Golinski, 'The Secret Life of an Alchemist', in Fauvel *et al.*, *Let Newton Be!*, pp. 147–67.

23 Manuel, *Isaac Newton Historian*, p. 161.

24 Newton, *Observations upon the Prophecies*, p. 16.

25 Newton, *Observations upon the Prophecies*, pp. 17–18.

26 Newton, *Observations upon the Prophecies*, pp. 19–20.

27 Newton, *Observations upon the Prophecies*, pp. 21–3.

28 See Rev. 13: 18; Newton, *Observations upon the Prophecies*, p. 248; Manuel, *Isaac Newton Historian*, p. 153.

29 Newton, *Observations upon the Prophecies*, pp. 13–14.

30 Newton, *Observations upon the Prophecies*, pp. 25, 28–30.

31 Newton, *Observations upon the Prophecies*, pp. 74–5, the italics are Newton's.

32 Newton, *Observations upon the Prophecies*, pp. 13–14, 90–1, 113–14. On the corruption of the Church see also pp. 208–9, 211, 215, 217; also R. Iliffe, '"Making a Shew": Apocalyptic Hermeneutics and the Sociology of Christian Idolatry in the work of Isaac Newton and Henry More' in *The Books of Nature and Scripture*, pp. 65–7. The formula for the time-span of the rule of this kingdom is given in the prophecy of Daniel (Daniel 12: 6–8) as 'for a time times and half a time'. The word 'time' translated into a prophetic year, which is 360 years; 'times' is translated into two prophetic years, or 720 years; 'half a time' into 180 years – all of which totals 1,260 years; see Kochavi, 'One Prophet Interprets Another', pp. 114–15.

33 Newton, *Observations upon the Prophecies*, pp. 254, 276; see also Iliffe, 'Making a Shew', p. 68.

34 Newton was a Unitarian and in the Newtonian Chronology, the opening of the sixth seal signals the onset of the 'corruption' of Christianity by the doctrine of Trinitarianism; see Iliffe, 'Making a Shew', p. 65.

35 Division into the eastern and western Christian Churches.

36 Newton, *Observations upon the Prophecies*, pp. 241-2, 279-80, 282-3, 313, 316, 318-20.

37 Iliffe, '"Making a Shew"', p. 72. Westfall, *Life of Isaac Newton*, p. 129.

38 Newton, *Observations upon the Prophecies*, pp. 250–1.

39 Kochavi, 'One Prophet Interprets Another', pp. 115–16.

40 Rattansi, 'Newton and the Wisdom of the Ancients' in Fauvel *et al.*, *Let Newton Be!*, pp. 186–201.

41 Iliffe, '"Making a Shew"', pp. 75–6, 80; see also S.Hutton, 'More, Newton, and the Language of Biblical Prophecy', pp. 39–53, p. 48.

42 Kochavi, 'One Prophet Interprets Another' in *The Books of Nature and Scripture*, pp. 116–17, 120. This trend was already present in Manuel, see *The Religion of Isaac Newton*, p. 23.

43 *Westminster Confession of Faith, 1643* (Glasgow, Free Presbyterian Publications, 1985), pp. 39–40.

44 H. More, *The Antidote Against Idolatry* (lst edn, 1669), in *A Brief Reply to a Late Answer to Dr. Henry More and his Antidote against Idolatry* (London, J. Redmayne, for Walter Kettilby, 1672), p. 48.

45 Newton, *Observations upon the Prophecies*, pp. 13–14, 250–3.

46 Manuel, *The Religion of Isaac Newton*, pp. 89–90

47 For example J. Brown, *A General History of the Christian Church from the Birth of our Saviour to the Present Time* (2 vols, Edinburgh, Gray and Alston, 1771), vol. I, p. 4.

48 See, for example, P. Nisbet, *An Abridgement of Ecclesiastical History, from the Commencement of Christianity, to the Beginning of the Present Century; Constructed on a New Plan, and Divided into Four Grand Periods* (Edinburgh, John Bell, 1776), p. 104.

49 See, for example, J. Priestley, *A General History of the Christian Church from the Fall of the Western Empire to the Present Time* (4 vols, Northumberland, USA, Andrew Kennedy, 1802), vol. I, preface pp. 28–9; also *An Answer to Mr. Paine's Age of Reason, being a Continuation of Letters to the Philosophers and*

Politicians of France on the Subject of Religion (London, reprinted for J. Johnson, 1795 but originally Northumberland USA 1794), letter six, 'On Prophecy'.

50 See [Charles Walmesley] Signor Pastorini, *The General History of the Christian Church, from her Birth to Her Final Triumphant State in Heaven; Chiefly Deduced from the Apocalypse of St John* (London?, 1771). Walmesley's work was reprinted in Dublin 1790; London 1798; Dublin 1806, 1812 and 1815; Belfast 1816; Cork 1820 and 1821; it was also translated into French (1777 and 1790) and reprinted in English in 1846. Various extracts of Walmesley's work were also printed in England in the nineteenth century; and it was translated into German, Italian and Latin, even with five editions in the USA.

Part 3

PROPHECY AND SYSTEMS OF BELIEF

This section stands separate from the previous one because, while scientific discourse was increasingly autonomous from prophecy, this did not mean that the Georgian age saw less interest in prophecy. Neil Hitchin shows that respectable theologians still saw prophecy as central to their biblical culture and to the truth of the revealed book. Nevertheless it was in the moral message of prophecy rather than its concrete predictive qualities that they increasingly found the truth of prophecy.

8

THE EVIDENCE OF THINGS SEEN: GEORGIAN CHURCHMEN AND BIBLICAL PROPHECY

N. Hitchin

Prophecy, it might be said, is the province of hysterical or deluded groups and people addicted to the morbid or the eccentric. There is much evidence to support this belief. But what are we to make of the interest shown in prophecy by highly educated churchmen in the age of reason?[1]

The Bible was believed by virtually all people to be the revelation of God to mankind. Of all the kinds of writings which appear in the Bible, prophecy makes the most immediate claim to being a revelation. Living prophets might claim to be inspired, but to most clergy and scholars the study of biblical prophecies was not at all the same thing as attending to contemporary utterances. Modern prophets were often thought to be knaves, fools or madmen, and a danger to society.[2] Since the age was one in which the grounds of human knowledge were being explored, it was natural to inquire into the nature of revealed knowledge. Because prophecy was the most overtly revelatory in nature an assessment of the attitudes of churchmen toward it is one of the clearest ways for us to make sense of their views on revelation.

While in the seventeenth century the Bible's authority as the chief source of divine knowledge was not seriously challenged, by the eighteenth century the Bible itself was under fire. Prophecy was used as one of the Evidences, or proofs, of Christianity, an evidence that the books of the Bible were a revelation from God. The appeal to the 'Christian Evidences' governed most Anglican apologetics in the eighteenth century.

The ways in which various writers organized the material might differ widely, but there were essentially two kinds of Christian Evidences: internal and external. The internal evidences arose from the meaning of the contents of the canonical writings, and were primarily moral and literary in character. The external evidences were divided into direct and collateral proofs. These were documentary historical proofs that the collection of writings which were said to be Christian revelation were the same writings as those the Church accepted as canonical from the earliest age, and that their textual content was well preserved.

Ideas differed on how the prophecies fitted into the scheme of evidence. Joseph Addison believed that the 'learned pagans' of the ancient world, who 'were . . .

guided [only] by the common rules of Historical Faith', were 'bound' by those rules 'and of right reason' to credit the gospel history. They were supposed to be especially persuaded by the prophecies of the coming Messiah, which Jesus fulfilled.[3] Thomas Sherlock, Master of the Middle Temple, considered prophecies to be 'an evidence subsidiary to miracles, though still necessary, as they provided an external evidence in support of the biblical record as a revelation'.[4] Thomas Newton, Bishop of Bristol, believed that 'the consequence is so plain and necessary, from the believing of prophecies to the believing of revelation, that an infidel hath no way of evading the conclusion but by denying the premises'.[5]

William Paley, likewise, acknowledged that some sought 'one single proof to turn to, which, like a demonstration in Euclid, makes an end of the question at once', but argued that the Evidences were an 'aggregate of many circumstances'.[6] For Paley only one prophecy had to be substantiated to help prove the Bible to be revealed by God. Paley distinguished different kinds of proofs, building up the case from each kind, rather than from each particular example. He included prophecy as the first of his auxiliary evidences.[7] Whatever ways apologists differed over the weight prophecy was to have, all agreed that prophecy was a significant evidence of the revelatory character of the Bible. What was prophecy? It took two forms. One was predictive, and was the more obvious form because the more overtly miraculous. The other was prescriptive, the moral message of the prophets.

Predictive prophecy was a miraculous foretelling of future events. If it could be demonstrated from historical evidence that a biblical prediction had been fulfilled, then apologists had a clear proof of the truth of Christian revelation. The trouble was that historical fulfilment of such predictions was susceptible to alternative interpretations. Looking at the differing interpretations of the fulfilment of prophecy provides insights into some cultural assumptions of the commentators.

The story of Israel and the Jews is the centre of all biblical ideas about time and history, but Christian interpretation defined the story according to the coming of the Messiah. Because they believed Jesus was the Messiah, Christian apologists writing about the relationship of the Jews to the prophecies inevitably promoted the view that the Jewish religion was redundant under the Christian dispensation. Nevertheless, apologists still saw the Jewish 'nation' as a living testimony to the revealed character of biblical prophecy.

Thomas Newton's *Dissertations on the Prophecies* was the most widely read treatise on the subject from the 1750s to the 1840s. His aim was to trace the historical fulfilments of the prophecies dating from the patriarchs, and of the Gentile nations which had oppressed Israel, identifying the respective contemporary nations to which they applied. His method was to present the textual material and relevant historical matter and then to show both that the prophecies had been fulfilled, and what was their contemporary significance.

Newton thought the Jewish nation in global exile was like Moses' bush, always burning but never consumed.[8] He proceeded to discuss the prophecy of Deuteronomy (28: 37): 'They should become an astonishment, a proverb, and a bye-word among all nations.'

> Is not the avarice, usury and hardheartedness of the Jew grown proverbial? and are not their persons generally odious among all sorts of people? Mahommedans, heathens, and Christians, however they may disagree in other points, yet generally agree in persecuting the Jews. . . . Their very countenances commonly distinguish them from the rest of mankind.[9]

Newton's words seem to express a common anti-semitism. On closer reading it clearly refers to the proverbial character, not to his own opinion of Jews. The use of the word 'persecution' to describe the treatment meted out to Jews by all peoples is a telling usage, for in Newton's mind, to persecute was to behave in an antichristian (read: popish) manner.

Beilby Porteous, bishop of London, was less cautious when he argued that the Old Testament prophecies which confirm the truth of Christianity would have been changed by the Jews if possible.

> We prove Jesus to be the Messiah from many of those very prophecies which [the Jews] themselves preserved; and which (if their invincible fidelity to their sacred books had not restrained them) their hatred to Christianity would have led them to alter or to suppress.[10]

He went on to offer a backhanded compliment, saying that they were backward in everything, except their conception of God, morality and religion. Followers of John Hutchinson, largely High Churchmen, believed that the Jews had changed the text by adding vowel pointing to the original, divinely given, consonants. His theological system depended upon 'faith in the Old Testament as the continuing revelation of God, and in the Hebrew language as the medium of its expression'. It was a literalist view of scripture, but with the quirk that the original text [of the Hebrew scriptures]

> must be consulted, simply as it stands, divested of those points or pricks for vowels which the modern Jew contrived. . . . These points are a heap of almost imperceptible dots, placed under the Hebrew letters, to give the same word different sounds, and, by virtue thereof, a variety of different, nay opposite significations, whereby the whole language is rendered vague and uncertain.

The 'misleading' vowel signs were invented only after the New Testament was written, *once the Jews realized that the prophecies of the Old had been fulfilled.*[11]

It was sometimes possible to address important and immediate political situations when writing about prophecy. Newton had been writing on the subject of the persecution and survival of the Jews throughout the centuries, when the Jew Bill crisis of 1753 arose. He found himself with a very timely sermon ready to preach.[12] The Jews had not yet been converted, he said

> but neither the prophecies concerning the Gentiles, nor those concerning the Jews, have yet received their full and entire completion. . . . The Jews will in God's good time be converted to Christianity, and upon their conversion be restored to their native city and country.

The promise was a futurity made easier to accomplish by their lack of a fixed nation. He went on:

> [The Jews] are blamable no doubt for persisting in their infidelity, after so many means of conviction; but this is no warrant or authority for us to proscribe, to abuse, injure, and oppress them, as Christians of more zeal than either knowledge or charity have in all ages been apt to do. . . . Compassion to this unhappy people is not to defeat the prophecies; for only wicked nations were to harass and oppress them; . . . and we should choose rather to be the dispensers of God's mercy than the executioners of his judgments.[13]

He reminded his listeners of the 'Prayer for the conversion of Jews, Turks and infidels', in the *Book of Common Prayer*, and that it was the duty of the Church to pray for the Jews.[14] These criticisms of English bigotry in an age of growing national pride are striking, but not unique. He had previously described the persecution of Jews throughout Europe, and did not forget to include their expulsion from England in the late thirteenth century. It was right, in recompense, that they should be readmitted during Cromwell's time. He noted also the improper theft of Jewish money and goods,[15] and compared the siege and mass suicide at York in the time of Richard I with Masada, in fulfilment of the words of Deuteronomy (28: 34).[16] The plight of the Jews was an ongoing fulfilment.

Newton's view that the Jews would be restored, possibly not long in the future, was part of a transition which was taking place during the century. In Addison's day it could be said 'we find by a long experience of 1500 years, that [Origen] was not mistaken, nay that his opinion gathers strength daily, since the Jews are now at a greater distance from any probability of . . . reestablishment [in Jerusalem] than they were when Origen wrote'.[17] Nathaniel Lardner also followed the standard view in writing that the '[t]he present [dispersed] state of the Jews was foretold by our Lord', and was therefore an 'argument for the divine authority of the gospel'.[18] By 1747 Samuel Collet MD could publish a tract pressing the argument that restoration and conversion would come, and possibly soon.[19] Charles Hawtrey, a vicar and controversial writer, thought that if the Muscovites or some northern power united with Persia against the Turk, it might be the time of the Jewish restoration.[20] In 1794 Paley related the opinion of the modern Jewish commentators that the prophecy in Isaiah (52: 13–end and 53) described the restoration of Israel, rather than the coming of the Messiah, though he doubted their interpretation.[21] The idea of a Jewish restoration to Palestine continued to gain momentum with Richard Graves, dean of Ardagh who observed in 1810 that a large work of missions and dialogue with Jews was taking place both through official missionary societies and privately.[22] Addison did not seem aware of the Jewish presence in Palestine when he wrote, and yet Graves could quote a traveller who had visited them there. Had the prophecy, in some part, already been fulfilled? Not yet, but a degree of fulfilment could still support belief in the prophecy.[23]

An unusual problem was raised by the study of some prophecies which seemed already to have been fulfilled, and yet also to refer to time to come. Such, for example, was the prophecy of the abomination of desolation being set up in the Temple.[24] It was generally thought that this part of Daniel had seen fulfilment in the person of Antiochus Epiphanes, who sacrificed swine flesh in the Temple, and, as his name suggests, set himself up as a god. Could a prophecy be fulfilled more than once? Joseph Butler thought so, arguing that merely to prove that another interpretation is possible is not proof against the first interpretation.[25] Elizabeth Carter, translator of the stoic philosopher Epictetus and a close friend of archbishop Secker, in her commonplace book wrote of Isaiah (7: 14: 'A virgin shall bear a child'), '[t]his prophecy, which had its full completion in the birth of our blessed Saviour, seems, in this primary signification, to relate to the son of Isaiah'.[26]

Thomas Newton provided several other examples, of multiple fulfilments, which was one of his keys of interpretation. He thought that the Jews had been brought into captivity more than once. 'At so many different times and different periods [from Moses' time] hath this prophecy been fulfilled.'[27] The prophet Jeremiah gave seventy years as the time of their captivity in Babylon. Commentators disagreed about how this prophecy had been fulfilled. Newton argued that there were 'various ways of fixing the fulfilment of 70 years. Taking it which way you will, and at what stage you please, the prophecy of Jeremiah . . . may be said to have been accomplished at three different times and in three different manners.'[28] On the other hand, there were some prophecies which could only really be fulfilled once, like the beginning of the Millennium, and the time of the Antichrist. But there might be more than one way of arriving at a solution to what might constitute a specific fulfilment. Newton's treatment of Daniel (7 and 9) was typical. 'We must compute the time according to the nature and genius of the prophetic language.' The time of tribulation was calculated based on the formulation 'time, times and half a time', which meant 'three and one half years'. The Jewish year was twelve months of thirty days. So three and one half years would equal 1,260 days. In prophetic language, one day equals one year. By adding 1,260 years to the date at which the trial seems to have started, one could arrive at a date for the second advent. Newton's view was that the beginning of these last times was when the papacy truly became a temporal power, in the eighth century (AD 737), which leads 'to about the year . . . 2000, or about the 6000th year of the world: and there is an old tradition . . . that at the end of 6000 years the Messiah shall come . . . and the reign of the saints on the earth shall begin.' But as Irenaeus says, 'it is surer and safer to wait for the completion of the prophecy than to conjecture and to divine about it. When the end shall come then we shall know better where to date the beginning.'[29] Only when it came to the subject of the Roman Church could Newton be drawn into making overt statements and predictions about prophetic applications to the contemporary scene, of the identity of times, seasons and the Antichrist.

The prophecy of the Destruction of Jerusalem was a centrepiece in prophetic debate. It was widely believed that the fulfilment of Jesus's prophecy of the destruction, and especially of the Temple, was essential to the credibility of the early Church.[30] But had Jesus intended the prophecies to refer to the end of the world, that is, to the Day of Judgement, or to the destruction of Jerusalem only, a sign of the end of the age of Israel, the coming of Messiah, and the beginning of the age of the Church?[31] N. Nisbett aligned himself with the great Caroline divine Dr Hammond in arguing the latter.[32] He rejected the possibility of a dual fulfilment, writing that 'neither Christ nor his Apostles, had any view in them, to the great day of judgment at the end of the world'.[33] Another writer, Dr Taylor, is noted as holding to the belief that the 'day of the Lord' was the day of each individual person's death, a view which Nisbett claimed was widely received.[34] Nisbett argued instead, that the phrase in Matthew translated as 'end of the world' (24: 3) ought to be translated 'end of the age' of the Jewish state, and the coming of Christ. Nisbett was supported by Isaac Newton's observation that the darkening, smiting or setting of sun, moon and stars were symbols of the cessation or desolation of a kingdom; likewise William Warburton thought their meanings referred to nations and empires.[35] Ralph Churton's Bampton lectures agreed with the relation between the coming of the Messiah and the destruction of Jerusalem. William Paley wrote:

It is objected, that the prophecy of the destruction of Jerusalem is mixed, or connected, with expressions which relate to the final judgment of the world; and so connected, as to lead an ordinary reader to expect, that these two events would not be far distant from each other. To which I answer, that . . . [i]f our Saviour actually foretold the destruction of Jerusalem, it is sufficient; even though we should allow that the narration of the prophecy had combined what had been said by him on kindred subjects, without accurately preserving the order, or always noticing the transition of the discourse.[36]

For Paley, it was only necessary to know whether Christ had foretold the destruction to prove his words prophetic.

The debate over the fulfilment of a prophecy could depend on quite detailed subsidiary arguments. Small comments in larger studies could take on significance. The prophecy of Haggai 2: 7–9 implies that the Messiah will come before the Second Temple is destroyed. This interpretation was undermined when it was pointed out that, according to Josephus, Herod had rebuilt the Second Temple. In defence of a non-messianic interpretation of the prophecy, Dr Heberden suggested that it had been fulfilled long before, when the riches of the nations were brought to the Temple and used for ornamentation. Cyrus had returned the vessels of Solomon's Temple, and Artaxerxes made presents. Expatriate Jews had sent 'all sorts of costly presents to Jerusalem . . . . [So that it was] probable, that the second Temple was in no respect inferior to the first, except in the want of the Ark [of the Covenant] and the Shechinah', or God's glory itself.[37] The crux of this argument was that the Hebrew word 'desire' had been mistranslated in the Authorised Version so as to read 'desire of nations'; whereas it had been translated as 'desirable' or 'precious' things in the Septuagint,[38] and in the Vulgate as *desideratus*.[39] But Charles Hawtrey, vicar of Bampton, Oxfordshire, maintained it was a messianic prophecy.

First, he explained, the ancient Church did not understand the passages as being messianic because they used the inferior Septuagint text, which had an additional word in Greek, which was 'destructive of the true meaning of the prophecy'.[40] Secondly, the key word could be translated as either *desire* or *riches* because of the particular idiom of the sentence construction.[41] Thirdly, Josephus contradicted himself about Herod's Temple building project.[42] Next, the question of what kind of glory is referred to was addressed. Heberden had made the error of understatement in calling the ornament of the Temple 'in no respect inferior'. The point, Hawtrey argued, was that Haggai said it would be superior. The first Temple had the glory of the Divine Presence. The second must not have less. How could the riches of the nations be more glorious than the Presence of their Creator?[43]

Finally, how was the promise of peace to be fulfilled? In the satisfaction of a good day's work spent ornamenting the building? Surely it was the peace and reconciliation with God through the true desire of nations, the Messiah. When he came to the Temple, the glory of God had returned.[44]

The defence of Haggai against the testimony of Josephus was a delicate matter. Thomas Burgess, an Oxford don, thought Hawtrey's case for Haggai did material damage to the defence of the faith. 'On the word of Josephus we are accustomed to build so much in proof of the Prophetic and Divine character of our Saviour.'[45] Hawtrey responded that 'Josephus *is* useful but not at all necessary towards our establishment in the Christian faith'. In any case, 'the passage in *Antiquities* which is relative to [Christ] is probably spurious'.[46]

The credibility of any interpretation of a major prophetic passage, such as Jesus's prediction of the destruction of Jerusalem and of the Temple, could be supported or undermined by the turn given to minor passages such as the one detailed above. Another question was whether Jesus fulfilled ancient prophecies of the Messiah. Did Isaiah (52: 13 to 53: end) refer to Israel which suffers destruction and dispersion, or to Jesus who suffers the Cross? Paley thought that both were possible, but only the second plausible.

> [T]he ancient Rabbins explained it of their expected Messiah: but their modern expositors concur, I think, in representing it as a description of the calamitous state, and intended restoration of the Jewish people, who are here, as they say, exhibited under the character of a single person. I have not discovered that their exposition rests upon any critical arguments. . . . [W]hat they allege in support of the alteration amounts only to this, that the Hebrew pronoun is capable of a plural as well as of a singular signification. . . . The probability therefore, of their exposition, is a subject which we are as capable of judging as themselves. This judgment is open indeed to the good sense of every attentive reader.[47]

Warburton thought that the images of destruction were so strong that they must seem like the last judgement to readers. But he was of the opinion that 'God's [theocratic] reign over the Jews, entirely ended with the abolition of the [T]emple, so the reign of Christ in spirit and in truth, had then its first beginning. . . .'[48]

The belief that 'the Messiah's kingdom should be erected on the ruins of the Jewish economy' after the 'destruction of old polities and constitutions' was common among Georgian churchmen, and the translation 'end of the *age*' fitted far better into the world they saw before them.[49] The destruction of the Temple was the necessary prelude to the fulfilment of Jesus's answer to the Samaritan woman when she asked where God was to be worshipped, that: 'the hour cometh, and now is, when the true worshippers shall worship the Father in spirit and in truth' (John 4: 19–26). John Jortin, archdeacon of London, friend to both Warburton and Thomas Newton, and Boyle lecturer in 1749, thought that the prophets were inspired by the Holy Spirit, but that the predictions 'have not yet received their entire completion; yet a great part of them [have] been remarkably & illustriously fulfilled'. He was writing of Isaiah (11: 9), which promises that 'the earth shall be filled with the knowledge of the Lord as the waters cover the sea.[50] Fine language which might describe the growth of the British Christian polity and its commercial empire.

Divines found that it could be argued in a new way that God was at work throughout the world, especially, it seemed, through the spread of the English constitution. The age of the Church, it could then be said, was in part expressed through the Christian nations, and the expansion of the gospel could take place through trade and development with unbelieving and backward nations.

Prophecy could also provide opportunities for commentary on political economy and social mores. This possibility was open not necessarily because the prophecies were thought to be fulfilled in the specific contemporary cases, but because such passages had a moral quality to them, rather like fables. For example Newton used prophetic scripture to address the moral state of Britain's 'polite and commercial people', drawing a comparison with the immorality of Tyre.[51]

> Trade is a fluctuating thing. . . . All nations almost are wisely applying themselves to trade: and it behoves those which are in possession of it to take the greatest care not to lose it. . . . Liberty is a friend to that, as that is a friend to Liberty. But the greatest enemy to both is licentiousness, which tramples upon all law and lawful authority, encourages riots and tumults, promotes drunkeness and debauchery, sticks at nothing to supply its extravagance, practices every art of illicit gain, ruins credit, ruins trade, and will in the end ruin liberty itself.

The suggestion that prophecy might reflect something of the preoccupations of national identity was hinted at in Newton's criticism of popular and political responses to the Jew Bill. The biblical Israel was an important landmark in the symbolic landscape of English national identity and virtue. Israel also held the central position in prophetic literature. Since definitions of Christian nationhood were necessarily developed within the context of the prophetic literature of the Bible, writers could not avoid confronting the relationship between Britain and ancient Israel, and the Church and the Jews. Some contemporary attitudes to the nation state and to its role in the fulfilment of the biblical eschatological scheme were also unveiled by their comments.

Prophecy was not only useful as proof that the Bible was a revelation from God. Many prophetic passages conveyed a moral message and truths about human and social nature.[52] Eighteenth-century divines turned these materials to a striking use. Prescriptive uses of biblical prophecy were the rational applications of the moral content of the prophetic message. Applying the message also required a writer to have worked out a biblical view of man, God and society, and biblical history, primarily the history of Israel as a nation, was the context of all understanding of God's self-disclosure in the world. Both defenders of the faith and opponents had to address this fact.

One oblique attack which antichristian writers used was to mock ancient Israel as an unfit vehicle for the divine blessing. If God was primarily moral, as the deists believed, then he would not have chosen such an immoral nation as Israel through whom to reveal himself. But the *ad hominem* attack was limited in effect.

More serious and ultimately constructive questions were posed as well. Since all mankind had reason, and the natural world showed signs of having been designed, God had surely revealed his character and moral truth to all through nature itself, and not merely to a small band of Israelites through their 'prophets'. The debate was between defenders of universal natural religion, on one side, and an historically revealed religion validated by particular events, on the other. Each position could be modified: natural religion could appeal to specific historical events, and revealed religion could reveal speculatively, through allegorical and figurative, or even strictly rational, means. But the question remained: 'Was the truth revealed only to, or through Israel?'

Christian apologists responded with a theory of the development of religious consciousness within the cultures of nations.[53] Thomas Sherlock tailored an argument to demonstrate how the history related in the Bible could have been a progressive revelation to a people. He wrote: 'The Prophecies of the several Periods . . . correspond to the State of Religion in the World, at the Time of giving the Prophecy. . . . I have gone thro' the several Periods of Prophecy and endeavoured to shew the main Design and Use of it. . . .'[54] In Sherlock's view it had been God's intention to draw humanity slowly onward into improved morals and understanding.

> The Blessings belonging to the special Covenant, given to Abraham and his Seed, were reserved to be revealed in God's appointed Time. The Prophets under the Law could not be commissioned to declare these Blessings openly and nakedly, without anticipating the Time of their Revelation. Hence it is that the Predictions concerning Christ and his Kingdom, are clothed in such Figures, as were proper to raise the Hope and Attention of the People without carrying them beyond the bounds of Knowledge.[55]

'The Light of Prophecy afforded to [Abraham's] Generation, corresponded to the State and Necessity of the Times.' God spoke the language of the time and place, guiding the evolution of a specific lineage of culture, with the great end of transforming all cultures. 'The Law of Moses, though a divine Revelation, and introduced to serve and advance the great ends of Providence with respect to Mankind, yet being given in the Age of the first Covenant, was in all Things made conformable to it' and was founded on the promises of happiness or misery in this life.[56]

The religion of Israel, then, 'did virtually contain the Hopes of the Gospel' and for this reason was itself a prophecy.[57] The point 'to be tryed on the Evidence of Prophecy' was: 'Is Christ that Person described and foretold under the Old Testament, or no?' When we believe that Christ was foretold, 'we may carry our Enquiries much further; we may contemplate the Steps of Providence relating to the Salvation and Redemption of Mankind' and discern that he is the 'end of the Law.'[58] Sherlock, a High Churchman, placed revelation over nature: thus his emphasis on the biblical history of religious development. Sherlock's case exemplifies the messianic teleology of writings on Old Testament prophecy. His lectures were an early exposition of the idea of development in religion. But the idea of a growing religious consciousness was one which could be found in John Locke's *Reasonableness of Christianity* in a more seminal form, and would be the source of further developments soon after Sherlock's exposition.

John Locke's religious thought was surprisingly bibliocentric, though his only criterion of faith was the belief that Jesus was the Messiah.[59] The coming of the kingdom of God was the teaching he brought into the world. This kingdom was a moral kingdom. Jesus preached the kingdom to inculcate repentance and baptism, and the laws of a good life, by the strictest rules of virtue and morality.[60] His kingdom might or might not be in conflict with human governments, but either way, Locke believed that God had providentially ordered the powers of the world.[61] Jesus was reticent to reveal himself as priest or as prophet, but he preached freely the kingdom of the Messiah, and the moral life, because it corresponded most to Jewish expectations.[62] God took culture into account in revealing himself to a society.

Normally, God used the natural course of the world to bring about knowledge of himself. However, though 'the works of nature everywhere evidence a Deity', the world generally makes little use of reason. Instead, sensuality, lust, carelessness and fear lead to false ideas, and ritual devotions which enshrine these ideas lead to priestcraft.[63] Faith derived from reason alone inevitably becomes customary. Each person is raised within a society of beliefs, and is presumptively inclined to think these his own, and to pass them on as self-evident. But revealed religion, as an implicit challenge to human custom, while also open to becoming customary, helps us to see that knowledge is, to some degree, artificial and incomplete – that reason can be 'constructive' rather than perceptive only.[64] While a person of great wisdom, might be able to produce an anthology of wise men's sayings from all nations, such a system (if such a system could be) would never be able to provide a binding moral code. Jesus, however, provided the fullness of morality with miracles to support his teaching as divine in origin. The evidence of the Saviour's miracles confirms his mission and oracles as true.[65]

Edmund Law, Cambridge professor of moral philosophy, was a devoted student of Locke's thought but he made greater use of the concept of natural society in working out a kind of sociology of revealed religion. He conceived that the natural inequalities of human life, arising from the inevitabilities of society and necessities of government, were a compelling analogy with the lack of universality in revealed religion.[66] The differences in societies were the source of diversity in natural religion.[67] The reception of Christianity depended upon 'men's natural and moral Dispositions'. It applied to both individuals and whole states. 'Each nation has its own Fitness of Time for receiving the revealed religion.'[68] The faith could only be propagated in a gradual and progressive manner.[69] Thus there was a need for a structure of civil government, and a principled society to help uphold religion. The individual would experience the religion within the stable context of the state. Christianity was a social faith.[70] The morality of the gospel would be congruent with the moral life of the nation which received it. The soul, individual or national, must do its part to be prepared to receive such a grace. Thus the role of human virtue could be defended on a secular level.

Stated simply, there were churchmen who did not assume that the literal reading was essential to orthodoxy. The figurative approach, advocated by Hutchinsonian and many other High Church apologists, did not eschew the literal veracity of the biblical text, but it did attend much more to the moral application of the scriptures to the individual soul.

Joseph Butler posed a defence of prophetic passages by appealing, in part, to the analogy of such writings with mythology, parables, fables and satirical writings.[71] Not that the scriptures were laced with myths and fables, but the hermeneutical hint was there. It was the moral teaching which really mattered, as the substance of what God had revealed. Butler's attitude to revelation was surprising, at least if we expect him to have held to literalism.

> The only valid objections against revelation are those directed against the evidences for it, since the human mind is incompetent of judging in advance what the contents of a revelation ought to be. No internal difficulties can lower the credibility of Scripture unless God had promised – which He did not – that the divine Revelation should be free from them.[72]

To emphasize the moral reading of scripture did not require belief in the inerrant character, the freedom from error of the scriptural text itself. Edmund Law repudiated the idea of the inerrancy of the text in the concluding pages of his *Considerations on the State of the World with regard to the Theory of Religion*.[73]

> Perhaps our very Reverence for these sacred writings misapply'd . . . may have contributed to cast a Cloud over the whole; which makes us look . . . afraid to look into them, and examine them with the same Freedom that we do . . . every other Book which we desire to understand: – I mean the Notion of an absolute, immediate Inspiration of each part and period; even where the Writers themselves, by the very manner of expressing themselves, most effectually disclaim it.[74]

From time to time, God gave revelations to his prophets, and they recorded these revelations, 'so far as was necessary, amidst the common . . . history of those times; and mix'd with various other Occurrences' with as much accuracy as human sufficiency required. Of the New Testament writers, he admitted the 'extraordinary assistance of the Spirit, which was to abide with them and lead them into all *necessary* Truth [italic mine]', but added that the Spirit's assistance is 'frequently suspended in the delivery of these fundamental truths', human reason being sufficient.[75] The apostles 'place the Evidence of Facts, on their own Senses only! declaring what they have seen and heard; which at all times, and which alone can be produced as proper Proof'. They 'add their private Sentiments; and in affairs of smaller moment, even their Conjectures, to what they had received from the Lord himself!'[76] No wonder William Paley could describe his patron Law as being 'refreshed last night by a large cargo of haeresy'.[77] But Paley himself believed that 'the truth of Christianity depends upon its leading facts, and upon them alone'. He declined to discuss the doctrine of biblical inspiration in detail.[78] Soame Jenyns, sometime MP and prominent convert from deism, took the same view, but put it more concisely. 'I readily acknowledge that the scriptures are not revelations from God, but the history of them: The revelation itself is derived from God, but the history of it is the production of men, and therefore the truth of it is not in the least affected by their fallibility, but depends on the internal evidence of its own supernatural excellence.'[79]

In 1776 Jenyns offered the opinion that the internal evidence of Christianity, 'which seems to carry with it the greatest degree of conviction, has never, I think, been considered with that attention, which it deserves'.[80] The 'excellence and clear marks of supernatural interposition' were the qualities to which he referred.[81] Though he was right, to a point, the congruence of the moral teaching of the gospels with the morality derived from nature and reason had been presented as the primary internal evidence of the divine origin of Christianity throughout the century. Revealed morality was simply the full expression of what man's unaided reason could discover; there might be mysteries, but they were consistent with the reasoning upon nature's laws. Jenyns was aware of the ideas relating the development of culture, society, religion and government. Yet he still felt that the internal evidences had yet to be properly attended to. His idea was that the New Testament contained a 'system of religion intirely [sic] new, both with regard to the object and the doctrines . . . unlike everything, which had ever before entered into the mind of man'. Nor did he believe that such a system could have been made up by any human, let alone a group of uneducated peasants from Galilee.[82] This point was sufficiently novel and compelling for Paley to incorporate it into the *Evidences*, but it did sit slightly uncomfortably with the main stream of thought relating the progress of the revealed religion in the world to compatible developments within a culture.[83] Jenyns did not consider the teaching of the Bible to be a polished system, such as an human one would probably have been. God never intended faith to be irresistible. 'He knew the imperfection of man was incapable of receiving such a system, and that we are more properly, and more safely conducted by the distant, and scattered rays, than by the too powerful sunshine of divine illumination.' Imperfect man was incapable of receiving a perfect system. It is with the difficult problem of how revealed truth must be mediated by language, symbols and figures that we shall conclude this discussion.

The complications of language which arise with the use of metaphor and symbolism are manifold, and prophetic language is unusually prone to the distorting effects of equivocal language. 'Speech', wrote John Locke, is 'the great Bond that holds Society together, and the common Conduit, whereby the Improvements of Knowledge are conveyed from one Man, and one Generation, to another.' But we do not all use our words 'constantly in the same sense', nor with 'determined and uniform *Ideas*'. Yet, we must try to communicate 'without Obscurity, Doubtfulness, or Equivocation'. To use words without 'any clear and steady meaning' is to lead into error.[84]

Sherlock addressed this problem directly, stating that plain language was plain and figurative language remained figurative, even when used for prophecy. But he admitted that 'whoever looks into the prophetical Writings will find that they are generally penned in a very exalted style . . . and oftentimes in such Images as cannot admit of a literal interpretation'.[85] We are left with general impressions, and no precise idea of how the words are to be fulfilled. 'But', he points out, in line with Locke, 'what is obscure to us may have been perfectly clear to those living at the same time in the past.' Words and meanings drift.[86] On the other hand, there was the view of George Berkeley, the philosopher and bishop, that 'the proper objects of vision constitute an universal language of the Author of Nature',[87] and that 'this language of nature doth not vary in different ages or nations'.[88] By appealing to an universal language of nature, Berkeley seems to have met the criterion which Locke posed for clear and distinct communication, at least so far as God's ability to communicate his revelation. Berkeley's ideas on universal language antedate the writings of John Hutchinson. But his philosophical exchange with Samuel Johnson, president of Yale, took place in 1729–30, not long before Hutchinson's ideas began to spread. There are some general similarities between their ideas of language and reality, and it might be with reason that both Berkeley's son and Johnson became adherents of the Hutchinsonian metaphysic.[89]

The close correspondence between the words in the Hebrew text and natural objects was the key to understanding the Hutchinsonian system. In the second half of the century, two writers who elaborated on the manner in which the system could be employed were George Horne, bishop of Norwich, and William Jones, his lifelong friend, biographer, and a priest in the parish of Nayland, Suffolk.

Jones explained why the system was so well-suited for scripture interpretation in his *Course of Lectures on the figurative language of the Holy Scripture, and the interpretation of it from Scripture itself* in 1787. The lectures were the fruit of many years of study, meditation and discussions with Horne.

God was the author of both nature and scripture. As nature is susceptible to the experimental philosopher, so is scripture to its students. In the same sense that we compare nature with itself to acquire knowledge of its workings, so we must compare scripture with itself; to look into its ways rather than upon its works. 'Every science has its own elements; it hath a sort of alphabet peculiar to itself; which must be learned in the first place.'[90] Admitting that 'there is a certain obscurity in the language of the Bible, which renders it difficult to be understood', he argued that there are 'elements or principles which must be known and allowed, before we can understand what the scriptures contain'. It is 'the heart and the understanding' which must be 'opened to admit the principles of the Christian Revelation. . . . This obscurity in the word of God doth not arise from the language or the grammar.' There has been much good textual work 'in clearing the scripture from the ambiguities to which all language is subject'. Furthermore, whatever difficulties remain in the original, 'are removed for all common readers by the translation of the Bible into their mother tongue'. The difficulties arise from the subject matter, and the various forms in which the matter is delivered.[91]

We have ideas of all sensual things stored in our minds and memories, but no ideas of 'invisible things till they are pointed out to us by revelation: and as we cannot know them immediately, such as they are in themselves', as we know sensible things:

> they must be communicated to us by mediation of such things as we already comprehend. For this reason, the scripture is found to have a language of its own, which doth not consist of words, but of signs or figures taken from visible things. . . . Words are the arbitrary signs of natural things; but the language of revelation goes a step farther, and uses some things as signs of other things; in consequence of which, the world which we now see becomes a sort of commentary on the mind of God, and explains the world in which we believe.[92]

For this reason, Jesus spoke in simple ways, to meet the universality of human experience, rather than 'be confined to the people of any particular nation or language'.[93] For Jones, the delight with pictures was the language with which children, and adults, might best be taught, 'being the life and soul of all the rest, and the best preparation of the mind for receiving the wisdom of God'.[94] Indeed, the attractiveness of the pagan myths was due to the fact that they were all degenerated from God's symbolic originals in the scriptures.[95] Jones included a number of supplementary sections, in which are discussions of the figural language of the constellations and zodiac,[96] poetical figures, which are virtues in symbolic form,[97] and a section on Christian ceremony and its degenerate form, idolatry.[98] He allowed that Christ's miracles, which he took to be historical events, are purposed as figures of spiritual life, which is an interesting gesture backward (or forward) toward the allegorical interpretation of scripture.

Whereas the literal reading of some prophetic biblical literature could be a liability, the application of a figurative scheme to the prophecies could be extensive, and in some books, such as the Apocalypse, the attractions are more than manifest.[99] Instead of reading the prophecies as evidences, they are to be used as a direct appeal to the spiritual sense of the hearer. The prophecy may indeed have been fulfilled, just as a miracle may have been a historical event; but the important thing for the present was how it was to meet the symbolic life of the individual.

George Horne's preaching was predicated on his extensive study of the 'language' of scripture symbols and figures.[100] At first, he held the view that preaching ought to address, in order, the literal sense of the scripture, then the interpretation or spirit of the passage, and finally the practical or moral use for the specific hearers. Later in life, he became convinced that it was better to take 'some narrative of the Scripture, and [raise] moral observations on the several circumstances of it in their order'. Best of all, he finally decided, was an opportunistic style, taking the objects around people to draw their attention to spiritual truths: at Brighton, he preached about the sea.[101]

The Hutchinsonian movement, although eccentric in some ways, deserves attention because their interest in the idea of a universal visual language, and its potential for later application in religious education, liturgy and apologetics was the essential background to the revival of liturgical thinking in the first decades of the nineteenth century. Also, they were not so far away from the common empiricist assumptions of their contemporaries as their fierce opposition to Isaac Newton's stance might imply.

Georgian churchmen's engagement with biblical prophecy, whether predictive or prescriptive, was clearly influenced by their national situation. The growing confidence of Georgian Britons was reinforcing a belief in secular progress, which in turn produced a greater willingness to interpret prophetic passages morally, in line with the spread of Christianity throughout the earth, more or less in conjunction with the spread of European empires. The evidence of fulfilled prophecy was before their eyes, thought some, especially so in the case of the Jewish nation. But the older, millenarian dimensions were not lost in the calm waters of the age of reason. The thought that dramatic fulfilments to come, like the restoration of the Jews to their land, grew throughout the century, and thoughts about the Antichrist were very much part of the mainstream of intellectual life. The ideas did not simply revive in the 1790s.

The apologetic task of the century was the defence and definition of revelation. Despite the redevelopment of the figurative tradition of interpretation, for the defence of revelation, evidence was needed. Proving each biblical prophecy in detail was the means to this end. But unlike the ages before, in the Georgian era the evidence had usually to be seen to be believed.

Notes

1 Studies of millenarian groups are more common than studies which take prophetic thought as part of the mainstream. J.F.C. Harrison's *The Second Coming: Popular Millenarianism, 1780–1850* (London, Routledge and Kegan Paul, 1979), and W.H. Oliver, *Prophets and Millennialists: the Uses of Biblical Prophecy in England from the 1790s to the 1840s* (Auckland, NZ, Oxford University Press, 1978) both begin late, and touch little on the mainstream. Also R.H. Popkin, 'Predicting, Prophesying, Divining and Foretelling from Nostradamus to Hume'in *The Third Force in Seventeenth-Century Thought* (Leiden, New York, Copenhagen and Cologne, E.J. Brill, 1992), pp. 285–307, esp. pp. 299–302 and 304. On eighteenth-century theology see G.R. Cragg, *Reason and Authority in the Eighteenth Century* (Cambridge University Press, 1964), pp. 54–6, 84–5, 110; J.M. Creed and J.S. Boys Smith, *Religious Thought in the Eighteenth Century* (Cambridge University Press, 1934); E.C. Mossner, *Joseph Butler and the Age of Reason. A Study in the History of Thought* (New York, Macmillan, 1936); and L. Stephen, *English Thought in the Eighteenth Century* (2 vols, London, 1876; 3rd edition, 1902; reprinted New York, Harcourt, Brace and World, 1962) esp. vol. 1, pp. 179–91.

2 H. Schwartz, *Knaves, Fools, Madmen, and that Subtle Effluvium: a Study of the Opposition to the French Prophets in England, 1706–1710* (Gainesville, Florida, University Press of Florida, 1978) on theological and medical explanations accounting for 'extravagant' religious behaviour (p. 1). Also *The French Prophets: A Study of a Millenarian Group in Eighteenth-Century England* (Berkeley and London, University of California Press, 1980).

3 J. Addison, 'Of the Christian Religion', *The Miscellaneous Works of Joseph Addison*, vol. 2, *Prose Works*, ed. A.C. Guthkelch (London, Tickell, reprint of 1721 edition of Addison's Works, reprinted G. Bell and Sons, 1907), pp. 419, 444.

4 T. Sherlock, *The Use and Intent of Prophecy, in the Several Ages of the World. In Six Discourses, delivered at the Temple Church, in April and May, 1724 . . .* (London, J. & J. Pemberton, 3rd edition, corrected and enlarged, 1735), Discourse ii, p. 30. Sherlock was latterly bishop of Salisbury, then of London.

5 T. Newton, *Dissertations on the Prophecies (1754)* (London, Thomas Tegg, 1837), p. 1.

6 In E. Paley, *An Account of the Life and Writings of William Paley, Works* (London 1823, reprinted Farnborough, Hants., Gregg International Publishers, 1970), p. 213. This corrects the suggestion that Paley's argument was such a Euclidian demonstration in N.W. Hitchin, 'Probability and the Word of God: William Paley's Anglican Method and the Defence of the Scriptures', *Anglican Theological Review*, 77: 3 (Summer, 1995), 394 note.

7 W. Paley, *A View of the Evidences of Christianity*, 2. i. He appeals to Isaiah (52: 13–53): the 'suffering servant' prophecy. We shall analyse eighteenth-century responses to this prophetic passage in more detail below. Unless otherwise noted, for all reference to the *Evidences* I have used *The Works of William Paley, D.D., . . . to which is Prefixed the Life of the Author* (Edinburgh, Thomas Nelson, 1845).

8 He admired Basnage's *History of the Jews*, from which he took this metaphor. Newton, *Dissertations*, vii, p. 100.

9 Newton, *Dissertations*, vii, p. 101.

10 Porteous, *A Summary of the principal Evidences of the Truth and Divine Origin of the Christian Religion*, in *Works of . . . Beilby Porteous . . .* (6 vols, London, T. Cadell & W. Davies, 1811), vol. 6, p. 456.

11 [Italics mine]. Porteous, *Evidences*, pp. 458–9. R. Spearman, *An Abstract from the Works of John Hutchinson* (London, E. Withers, 2nd edition, 1755), p. 42. See also D.S. Katz, *Sabbath and Sectarianism in Seventeenth-Century England* (Leiden and New York, E.J. Brill, 1988), pp. 181–97.

12 L. Twells (ed.), *The Lives of E. Pocock, by Dr Twells, of Z. Pearce, and of T. Newton, by themselves, and of P. Skelton, by Mr Burdy* (2 vols, London, F.C. & J.Rivington, 1816), p. 117.

13 Newton, *Dissertations*, viii, p. 122.

14 Newton, *Dissertations*, viii, p. 123.

15 Newton, *Dissertations*, vii, pp. 98–9.

16 Newton, *Dissertations*, vii.

17 Addison, 'Of the Christian Religion', *Works*, ii, p. 442.

18 Lardner, quoted in A. Kippis, 'The life of Nathaniel Lardner, DD . . . ', in vol. 1 of *The Works of Nathaniel Lardner, D.D.* (5 vols, London, printed by T. Bensley for Thomas Hamilton, 1816), p. xii. Kippis states that he is not the editor of the works, only the author of the 'Life', in the 'Advertisement'.

19 [S. Collet], *A Treatise of the Future Restoration of the Jews and Israelites to their Own Land. With some account of the goodness of the country and their happy condition . . .* (London, G. Freer, 1747). It was believed by some that 1749 might be the date

20 C. Hawtrey, *Evidence that the Relation of Josephus Concerning Herod's Having Newbuilt the Temple at Jerusalem is Either False or Misrepresented* (Oxford, J. Fletcher, 1786), p. 61.

21 Paley, *Evidences*, 2.i.

22 R. Graves, *Lectures on the Four last Books of the Pentateuch* (Dublin, William Curry, 5th edition, 1839), pp. 403–38.

23 J. Butler, *Analogy of Religion, Natural and Revealed*, ed. W.E. Gladstone (World's Classics Edition, cxxxvi, London, 1907), II. vii. 23, pp. 286–7.

24 See Daniel 8: 13 and Matthew 24: 15.

25 Butler, *Analogy*, II. vii. 28, pp. 290–2.

26 E. Carter, 'Notes on the Bible, and Answers to Objections concerning the Christian Religion' in M. Pennington (ed.), *Memoirs of the Life of Mrs. Elizabeth Carter, with a New Edition of her poems . . . together with her notes on the Bible . . .* (2 vols, London, F.C. & J. Rivington, 3rd edition, 1816), vol. ii, p. 212.

27 Newton, *Dissertations*, vii, p. 94.

28 Newton, *Dissertations*, viii, p. 103.

29 Newton, *Dissertations*, xiv, p. 247. He cites the Epistle of Barnabas ch. 15, and Burnet's *Sacred Theory of the Earth*, iii.5. Readers may be interested that the 1,260 years added to AD 737 give the date 1997. Alternately, one could use the 'one day is as a thousand years' formula (2 Peter 3: 8): six days of Creation, with a millennial sabbath. If, as Ussher had calculated, the Creation began in 4004 BC, the transitional year would be AD 1996.

30 N. Nisbett cited three eminent divines, John Jortin, and Thomas Newton for specific details, and Newcome's *Observations on our Lord's Conduct as a Divine Instructor*, in support of his position. Nisbett, *An Attempt to Illustrate Various Important Passages in the Epistles &c. of the New Testament, from Our Lord's Prophecies of the Destruction of Jerusalem, and from some Prophecies of the Old Testament* (Canterbury, by the Author, 1787), p. 3.

31 The prophecies in Matthew (24) and its parallels in Mark and Luke, are less parabolic than eschatological passages (for examples: Matthew 21: 33–46, Mark 12: 1–12, Mark 22: 1–7, Luke 13: 6–29, Luke 14: 17–24, Luke 19: 11–27, Luke 20: 9–19).

32 His identity remains somewhat obscure. He may be related to Charles Nisbett, a Scottish divine who emigrated to America.

33 Nisbett, *Attempt to Illustrate*, p. 11 and also pp. 44–6, where he challenged [Isaac] Newton over his view that Matthew (24: 29–31) may be interpreted as the end of the world as well as of Jerusalem. Nisbett accepted only the application to Jerusalem.

34 Nisbett, *Attempt to Illustrate*, p. 12.

35 Nisbett, *Attempt to Illustrate*, pp. 22–3 for Newton and Warburton (citing Warburton's *Divine Legation of Moses*, II. iv. 4). Zachary Pearce, bishop of Rochester and author of sermons on the prophecies, agreed the word ought to have been translated 'age', p.18.

36 Paley, *Evidences*, II.1. ii.5. In short Paley was noncommittal, noting the existence of both views. BL, Additional MS 12,080, f. 43v.

37 C. Hawtrey, *Relation of Josephus*, p. 3. Citing Dr Heberden, *The Bishop of Waterford's Book On the Prophets*, p. 71, which I have been unable to trace. Heberden may be the physician William Heberden mentioned in the *DNB* as attending William Warburton.

38 The ancient Greek version of the Hebrew scriptures.

39 Hawtrey, *Evidence* (1st edition), pp. 85–6.

40 Hawtrey, *Evidence* (2nd edition), ii–iii.

41 Hawtrey, *Evidence* (2nd edition), ix.

42 Between the *Jewish Wars* and the *Histories*. See Hawtrey, *Evidence*, pp. 1–36, where he lays out the argument.

43 Hawtrey, *Evidence* (1st edition), p. 76.

44 Hawtrey, *Evidence* (1st edition), p. 83.

45 Burgess, *Remarks on Josephus' account of Herod's temple at Jerusalem;. occasioned by a pamphlet . . . entitled Evidence . . . &c* (Oxford, D. Prince and J. Cooke & J.J. Fletcher, 1788), p. 8, cited by Hawtrey, *Evidence* (1st edition), p. 64.

46 Hawtrey, *Evidence* (1st edition), pp. 64–5. A point decided by the dissenting critic and patristics scholar Nathaniel Lardner in the 1760s, though it continued to be debated until many years later. A. Kippis, 'Life of . . . Lardner', *Works*, vol. 1, p. xxiii. Lardner's correspondence with Dr Samuel Chandler on the matter is in Appendix IX of this volume.

47 Paley, *Evidences*, 2.i.

48 Warburton, *Julian: or a Discourse Concerning the Earthquake and Firey [sic] Eruption, which Defeated that Emperor's Attempt to Rebuild the Temple of Jerusalem* (London, J & P. Knapton, 2nd edition, 1751), I. 1.

49 Nisbett, *Attempt to Illustrate*, p. 110.

50 In keeping with the tone of the whole chapter. Jortin's views are cited in Nisbett, *Attempt to Illustrate*, pp. 114–15.

51 Newton, *Dissertations*, xi, p. 177.

52 Which could be used in turn as additional moral evidences for revelation.

53 It has been argued that 'the decisive figure in the whole development was Edmund Law', and his *Considerations of the Theory of Religious Development* (1745). See R.S. Crane, 'Anglican Apologetic and the Idea of Progress, 1699–1745,' *Modern Philology* (Feb. 1934), 273–306, and (May 1934), 349–82. W.O. Chadwick, *From Bossuet to Newman* (Cambridge University Press, 2nd edition, 1987), pp. 79–86, 219–24. For Edmund Law see R. Brinkley, 'A Liberal Churchman: Edmund Law', *Enlightenment and Dissent*, 6 (1987), 3–18; T. Baker and J. Mayor, *A History of the College of St John the Evangelist* (2 vols, Cambridge, 1869), vol. 2, pp. 714–25; J. Gascoigne, *Cambridge in the Age of Enlightenment* (Cambridge University Press, 1989), esp. pp. 128–31, 192–8, 239–42, 245–7.

54 Sherlock, *Use and Intent*, Discourse vi, pp. 140, 171.

55 Sherlock, *Use and Intent*, Discourse v, p. 129.

56 Sherlock, *Use and Intent*, Discourse iv, pp. 106, 100–1.

57 Sherlock, *Use and Intent*, Discourse vi, p. 145.

58 Sherlock, *Use and Intent*, Discourse i, pp. 43, 44.

59 Best on Locke's religious thought are W. Spellman, *John Locke and the Problem of Depravity* (Oxford, Clarendon Press, 1988), and N. Wolterstorff, 'Locke's Philosophy of Religion' in V. Chappell (ed.), *The Cambridge Companion to John Locke* (Cambridge University Press, 1994), pp. 172–98.

60 J. Locke, *The Reasonableness of Christianity as Delivered in the Scriptures*, ed. G.W. Ewing ([1695]; Washington, DC, Regnery Gateway, 1965), p. 49.

61 Locke, *Reasonableness*, p. 46

62 Locke, *Reasonableness*, pp.137–8.

63 Locke, *Reasonableness*, p. 165.

64 Locke, *Reasonableness*, pp. 178–9.

65 Locke, *Reasonableness*, pp. 164, 172–5.

66 E. Law, *Considerations of the Theory of Religious Development* (Cambridge, J. Bentham for W. Thurlbourn, London, J. Beecroft, 2nd edition, 1749), p. 8.

67 Law, *Considerations*, p. 18.

68 Law, *Considerations*, p. 36. Also see Paley, *Caution Recommended in the Use and Application of Scripture Language: A Sermon preached July 17, 1777, in the Cathedral church of Carlisle at the visitation of the Right Reverend Lord Bishop of Carlisle* in *Works* . . . (Edinburgh, Thomas Nelson, 1845).

69 Law, *Considerations*, p. 33. 'Where there is no kind of good Order or Government established; no regular Forms of Education instituted, and observed where there is an universal want of Discipline; and a Dissoluteness of manners; there Christianity cannot subsist', p. 33. 'Ignorant, uncivilised brutish Nations are incapable of receiving and preserving the Faith', p. 35, note. Also Paley, *Evidences*, 3. vi.

70 Law, *Considerations*, p. 35.

71 Butler, *Analogy*, II. vii. 25, pp. 287–8.

72 Mossner, *Butler and the Age of Reason*, p. 94.

73 2nd edition, enlarged, 1749 (as cited above). Leslie Stephen failed to give an accurate description of Law's views on revelation. Stephen, *English Thought*, vol. 1, pp. 344–5.

74 Law, *Considerations*, pp. 278–9.

75 Law, *Considerations*, note on pp. 279–81.

76 Law, *Considerations*, note on p. 281.

77 W. Paley to [John] Law, [1775?] in *Transactions of the Cumberland and Westmorland Archaeological and Antiquarian Society*, n.s., 19 (1927), 149–51.

78 Paley, *Evidences*, 3. viii; see also M.L. Clarke, *Paley: Evidences for the Man* (London, SPCK, 1974), p. 108.

79 Soame Jenyns, *A View of the Internal Evidence of the Christian Religion* (London, J. Dodsley, 1776), p. 123.

80 Jenyns, *Internal Evidence*, p. 2.

81 Jenyns, *Internal Evidence*, p. 1.

82 Jenyns, *Internal Evidence*, p. 8

83 Clarke, *Paley*, p. 106.

84 Locke, *Essay concerning Human Understanding*, ed. P. Nidditch (Oxford, Clarendon Press, 1975, reprinted 1984), III. xi.1–6

85 Sherlock, *Use and Intent*, Discourse ii, pp. 29–31.

86 Sherlock, *Use and Intent*, Discourse ii, p. 38.

87 The first edition had 'universal language of Nature', G. Berkeley, *Philosophical Works*, ed. M.R. Ayers (London, J.M. Dent & Sons, and Rutland, VT, Charles E. Tuttle, Everyman edition, 1992), p. 51 note.

88 Berkeley, *Philosophical Works*, p. 49.

89 The recent volume of the *History of the University of Oxford* is dismissive of Hutchinsonianism: pp. 457, 465. But there were influential followers of the movement. See W. Jones, *Memoir of the Life of George Horne* . . . (London, F.C. & J. Rivington, 1818), and Stephen, *English Thought*, vol. 1, pp. 330–2. David Katz, on the other hand, insisted that it was especially in Oxford that Hutchinsonianism was adopted as a sort of High Church theological science. Katz, *Sabbath and Sectarianism*, pp. 181, 188. See Horace Walpole's letter to Richard Bentley, Horace Walpole, *Correspondence*, ed. W.S. Lewis, *et al.* (New Haven, Yale University Press, 1937–83), pp. xxxv, 156. For discussions of the later influence of Hutchinsonianism see F.C. Mather, *High Church Prophet: Bishop Samuel Horsley (1733–1806) and the Caroline Tradition in the later Georgian Church* (Oxford, Clarendon Press, 1992), pp. 10–15, 214 and 303; P.B. Nockles, *The Oxford Movement in Context: Anglican High Churchmanship, 1760–1857* (Cambridge University Press, 1994), and E.A. Varley, *The Last of the Prince Bishops: William van Mildert and the High Church Movement of the Early Nineteenth Century* (Cambridge University Press, 1992), pp. 40–3.

90 W. Jones, *A Course of Lectures on the Figurative Language of the Holy Scripture, and the Interpretation of it from Scripture itself* (London, for the author, 1787), p. 2.

91 Jones, *Course*, pp. 3–6.

92 Jones, *Course*, pp. 9–10.

93 Jones, *Course*, pp. 11, 293–4, 300. The second lecture described the various types of figures which the scriptures make use of. They were: 1. from the natural creation, or world of sensible objects; 2. from the institutions of the Mosaic Law; 3. from the persons of the prophets and holy men of ancient times; 4. from the actions of inspired men, which in many instances were not only miracles, but also signs of something beyond themselves.

94 Jones, *Course*, pp. 296, 297.

95 Jones, *Course*, p. 316.

96 Jones, *Course*, pp. 320–2.

97 Jones, *Course*, pp. 323–5; he mentions the anti-Hutchinsonian Robert Lowth's *On the Sacred Poetry of the Hebrews* approvingly.

98 Jones, *Course*, pp. 327–8.

99 Paley, for instance, who was rigorously factual in his approach, could find very little to say about the Apocalypse. His Greek Testament is quite full of references and reflections on all books, except for the last one, where they are scattered and few. On the number of the Beast (Rev. 13: 18), the only clear words are that someone 'is unsound to do this'. BL, Additional MS 12080, f. 372.

100 He had hoped to provide readers with a handbook to help them interpret the Bible correctly. His papers contain pages with numerous figurative headings and references to biblical passages in which the figures may be found. Cambridge University Library, Additional Ms 8134.

101 Jones, *Life of George Horne*, pp. 136–8.

Part 4

THE ENDS OF PROPHECY

By the nineteenth century, the centrality of prophecy in politics and religion became increasingly contested. Paradoxically this liminal position also unleashed the most violent instances of prophetic movements. The Taiping Rebellion demonstrated the amazing power of a transposed European prophetic language when associated with social unrest in China. Bill Roberts' paper emphasizes the extraordinary visions of political upheaval which the liminal position of the prophet still allowed.

One of the signs that prophecy in Europe has moved to the extreme margins of religious and political debates is the fact that those who participated in any inspired religious movement saw their activities become the object of science, in Rhodri Hayward's paper the object of early psychology. Another sign of this liminality is the marginalization of prophecy to the political extremes. Peter Davies's paper examines the current use by the French extreme right of Joan of Arc and millenarian nationalistic themes. While the sceptics are now better equipped to approach prophecy rationally, it remains an extremely powerful and religious language.

9

'GOLDEN BRICKS AND GOLDEN HOUSES AWAIT YOU': PROPHECY AND MILLENARIANISM IN THE TAIPING REBELLION[1]

J.A.G. Roberts

At a conference on millenarian movements held at The Hague in 1962, E.P. Boardman gave a paper on the Taiping Rebellion, which convulsed China between 1851 and 1864.[2] He measured some aspects of the rebellion against the definition of a millenarian movement given to the conference by Norman Cohn: that it was a religious movement guided by a 'phantasy of salvation' which was collective, terrestrial, imminent, total and accomplished by supernatural agencies.[3] Boardman considered that the Taiping Rebellion met some, but not all, of the criteria established by Cohn. The salvation promised by the Taipings was collective and terrestrial, but he argued that there was no sense of imminence and that the salvation they promised was not total. Boardman's acceptance of a millenarian element in the rebellion ran counter to the established view that the rebellion was the product of a social and economic crisis, compounded by the effects of western imperialism. Most modern writers have regarded the religious element as fortuitous and of superficial importance.[4]

There is much to commend that view, which provides a general explanation for the potentially rebellious or revolutionary situation which existed in Guangxi, the province where the rebellion began. But in the explanation of the origins and the rapid growth of the Taiping Rebellion, Hong's prophetic visions and encounter with radical Protestant Christianity are important and crucial to the creation of a prophetic leadership fostering a millenarian expectation which was essential to attract mass support. This paper sets out to review those experiences and then discusses what could be described as the prophetic and millenarian stage of the rebellion.

China has a long history of movements which have proclaimed the advent of an imminent millennium. In the late Qing period many of these were associated with the doctrines of Maitreyan Buddhism. One example was the Wang Lun uprising in Shandong in 1774.[5] Similar beliefs lay behind the great White Lotus Rebellion of the late eighteenth century and the Eight Trigrams uprising which occurred in the vicinity of Beijing in 1813.[6] Each of these events had as its inspiration the White Lotus religion which taught that history moved through great stages called kalpas and that the transition points between stages were accompanied by violent calamities and the arrival of the Maitreya Buddha. Another example of the prevalence, in the late Qing period, of millenarian expectations and of millenarian movements was that of the New Sect teachings of Islam, which gained support among Muslim groups which were culturally and religiously distinct from the majority population in a way which has been compared with the social discontents of the Hakka who played a leading role in the Taiping Rebellion. New Sect adherents in north-west China rebelled in 1781 and 1783, and when in 1862 the Taiping rebels invaded Shaanxi a major uprising under New Sect leadership took place.[7]

Hong Xiuquan (1814–64), the future leader of the Taiping Rebellion, was born in a village some twenty miles north of Guangzhou (Canton). He was a Hakka (Kejia) Chinese; the Hakka had moved to the south of China at a later date than the majority Cantonese, by whom they were generally despised. Hong competed in the official examinations held in Guangzhou, and in 1836, while in that city, he was given some Christian tracts. These had been written by Liang Afa, a Chinese catechist, and were entitled *Good Words to Admonish the Age*. Hong did not read the tracts at this stage. In the following year, after another examination failure, he suffered a nervous breakdown and had a visionary experience. In his visions he seemed to die, and was then transported to 'a beautiful and luminous place', where he was washed in a river and his heart and other organs were replaced. He was conducted into the presence of a venerable man with a golden beard who remonstrated with Hong that human beings, who were produced and sustained by him, did not have a heart to remember and venerate him. He then gave Hong a sword, a seal, and a yellow fruit to eat. Immediately Hong turned to exhort the others present to return to their duties, but they remained obdurate. The man with the golden beard then conducted Hong outside, and told him to look down from above, and said, 'Behold the people upon this earth! Hundredfold is the perverseness of their hearts.' Hong himself looked down, but could not endure the sight of depravity and vice. In a later vision, Hong heard the venerable man reprove Confucius for having failed to expound the true doctrine. Confucius was ashamed and confessed his guilt.[8]

Some years later – perhaps in 1843 – Hong read the tracts and had his first encounter with a version of Christianity. He identified his visions with what he read: the venerable man he now recognized as God, a middle-aged man he took to be Jesus, and he believed that he was Jesus's younger brother. He understood his given task to be to bring the world back to the proper worship of God.

Good Words contained millennial ideas connected with the Christian concept of Heaven. Liang had translated the term 'Heaven' as *Tianguo*, that is 'Heavenly Kingdom', which he said had two meanings, one denotes the everlasting happiness which the souls of good men enjoy after the death of their bodies in the *tiantang* or Paradise. The other denotes an area on Earth where there is a society or a commonwealth (*gonghui*) where all those who believe in Jesus Christ, the saviour of the world, gather together to worship. The Chinese expression for this is *Bai. . . Shangdi zhi gonghui* ('Worshipping God's Society') from which the *Baishangdi hui* ('Worshipping God Society') is obviously derived.[9]

The first meaning – the 'Kingdom of God', a non-material state in the process of realization – was not mentioned in the tracts of the insurgents. The second meaning – that of the Kingdom of Heaven – lost its character of futurity and was incorporated in the name of the new dynasty on earth, the Heavenly Kingdom of Great Peace.[10] Its millenary implications were confirmed by an annotation which Hong later made to Matthew (5: 19),

> Thus the Great Elder Brother formerly issued an edict foretelling the coming of the Heavenly Kingdom soon, meaning that the Heavenly Kingdom would come into being on earth. To-day the Heavenly Father and the Heavenly Elder Brother descend into the world to establish the Heavenly Kingdom.[11]

Liang Afa also used the term '*taiping*', that is 'great peace', the term adopted later to describe the rebellion itself. This was a reference to a past Golden Age, a recurrent idea in millennial thought. According to Teng Ssu-yü, Liang Afa

> envisages a situation in which the king of a nation is upright, its ministers loyal, its officials pure, and its people happy in the worship of God and the practice of His principles. If people could only attain such a goal, he says, 'they would permanently enjoy the good fortune of great peace (*taiping*)' and would live in a good, honest, and peaceful world where they need not close their doors at night, nor would they pick up things others had dropped on the road.[12]

The most striking indication that *Good Words to Admonish the Age* was a potential source of millennial ideas was that Liang Afa provided a series of quotations which emphasized the imminence of disaster and the urgent need for repentance. These included chapter 21 of *The Revelation of St John the Divine*, which begins 'And I saw a new Heaven and a new earth . . .', the chapter in the Bible which is most commonly taken as the source of millennial ideas within the Christian tradition. Other references were to Matthew (6: 31), 'Therefore take no thought, saying, What shall we eat?', James (5: 8), 'the coming of the Lord draweth nigh', and II Peter (3: 10), 'But the day of the Lord will come as a thief in the night.' The tracts often combined quotation from the Bible with Liang's own comments in a way which led Philip Kuhn to comment, 'the lack of a clearly specified time-frame leaves the unmistakable impression that he [Liang] is referring to China's present condition, at the end of a long process of moral degradation, with an apocalyptic redemption just around the corner'.[13]

After the visions Hong became a changed person. His cousin, Hong Ren'gan, recorded that,

> With the return of health, Xiuquan's whole person became gradually changed both in character and appearance. He was careful in his conduct, friendly and open in his demeanour, his body increased in height and size, his pace became firm and imposing, his views enlarged and liberal.[14]

Hong now communicated his beliefs to his family and converted them and a few friends. His activities brought him into conflict with the village elders and he then commenced a series of journeys to the inland province of Guangxi to 'travel throughout the realm and teach and instruct the people of the world about these matters'.[15] At this stage his mission was still to call men to true repentance. There was no claim that he himself personified the second coming. However Hong already exhibited many of the characteristics of those who have become the prophets of millenarian movements.[16] His educational background provided the skills necessary for a leadership role, while his examination failures ensured a sense of frustration within the existing social order. His visits to Guangzhou and his contacts with European society qualified him for the role of 'cultural broker'. His visions and belief in his mission were the essential ingredients for his assumption of the prophetic role.

Hong at first sought to reconcile the new revelation which he had received with China's historical and cultural tradition. In *The Taiping Imperial Declaration*, written by Hong in 1844–5, he declared that China had once been a monotheistic state, whose people worshipped the true god, but which later had strayed from the truth, a view which appeared in a number of other early Taiping publications including the *Trimetrical Classic*.

In 1847 Hong spent some time at the Guangzhou mission of the American Southern Baptist missionary Issachar J. Roberts. Roberts had been born in Tennessee in 1802, and had grown up in an atmosphere of fundamental Christianity typical of the Great Revival. The Reformed churches accepted a prophetic calendar which anticipated the arrival of the Millennium no later than the year 2000 and possibly as early as 1840.[17] Millennial ideas were interspersed with references to America's destiny, 'the whole of the American experience to that time was interpreted as a vital part of God's plan'. Following the injunction in Matthew (28: 19–20), 'Go ye therefore, and teach all nations . . . ,' a particular role for America was identified in the Great Commission, the conversion of most of the world to Jesus Christ, the necessary preliminary for the coming of the

Millennium. When the encounter between Hong and Roberts took place some missionaries in China anticipated that the prophecy concerning the land of Sinim, in Isaiah (49: 12), was about to be fulfilled and that this conversion would soon be accomplished.[18]

Until 1847 millenarian ideas were only a latent aspect of Hong's beliefs. He had formed a strong conviction that he had been appointed by God to restore the world, but there was no indication that he anticipated that the Millennium was imminent. This situation continued through Hong's first preaching mission to Guangxi, where he had made contact with the Hakka communities in the south-west of the province and obtained a number of conversions to his beliefs.

In the eighteenth century Guangxi had experienced a substantial migration of Hakka Chinese from eastern Guangdong, the province in which Guangzhou is situated. These new migrants had been forced to take up land which was poorer than that owned by the earlier Chinese arrivals, who were described as *Bendi* (Punti), or original inhabitants. As a consequence the newer Hakka communities lacked the corporate lineage structure of the richer indigenous population. As pressure on resources increased, feuding between the two communities became common, and the Hakka resorted to dialect group solidarity as a defence against wealthier lineages.[19] The area may also have suffered some indirect effects of the Opium War, in terms of the disruption of the tea trade. The insecurity of the Hakka communities in Guangxi, the more general threat to living standards and the rise of social tensions in south China at this time provided the 'disaster-prone environment' which has been associated with the rise of millenarian movements.[20]

Hong left Guangxi for nearly three years from September 1844. During his absence Feng Yunshan, one of Hong's first converts, established a congregation at Zijingshan (Thistle Mountain), a remote area in the south of the province. Many of his converts were miners and charcoal burners. The God Worshippers' Society, the name given to his converts, began to display a number of millenarian features. The religion which Feng preached was based on a new revelation of divine purpose, and he made frequent reference to Hong's ascent to heaven. It was described as a new and foreign doctrine. The ceremonies which the God Worshippers performed were not orthodox Protestant rituals, which were quite unknown to Feng. They included a form of purification. In *Good Words*, in a sermon referring to John (3: 5), Liang Afa had written, 'One repents of sin, receives the water of baptism, washing clean body and soul. . . . Then one can enter the kingdom of God and enjoy the blessing of everlasting joy.'[21]

Repentance and purification were essential preliminaries for membership of the God Worshippers. A prayer in *The Book of Heavenly Commandments* (*c.* 1847) entitled 'A form to be observed in repenting sins', said that the supplicant 'may use a written form of prayer, and when the prayer is over, he may either take a basin of water and wash his whole body clean, or he may perform his ablutions in the river, which will be still better'.[22] At the ceremony performed for admission to the God Worshippers a group of candidates repeated a written confession, and then had the words 'Purification from all former sins, putting off the old, and regeneration' addressed to them. They then had a drink of tea and generally each washed his chest and the region of the heart with water to signify the inner cleansing of their hearts.[23] The evidence of the baptismal service and of how the movement grew suggests that clans or lineages joined the movement collectively, and that a collective salvation was anticipated. Another millennial feature of the God Worshippers' religion was the application of puritanical prohibitions to various activities. Hong had already condemned opium and wine in *The Taiping Imperial Declaration*, written in 1844–5. *The Book of Heavenly Commandments*, which was probably written in 1847, contained an extended version of the Ten Commandments. The seventh Heavenly Commandment prohibited adultery and licentiousness. The comment on it contained an early reference to one of the most remarkable of the Taiping demands: the separation of the sexes among the elect:

> In the world there are many men, all brothers; in the world there are many women, all sisters. For the sons and daughters of Heaven, the men have men's quarters and the women have women's quarters; they are not allowed to intermix.

Other prohibitions included '[t]he casting of amorous glances, the harboring of lustful imaginings about others, the smoking of opium, and the singing of libidinous songs . . .'. The tenth commandment forbidding covetousness was interpreted as referring to coveting a man's wife or daughter, or another man's possessions, and included 'when a man engages in gambling and buys lottery tickets and bets on names'.[24]

These prohibitions were not social reforms. Sex between men and women, even husbands and wives, was not forbidden because it might weaken their resolve when the rebellion had started; opium was not prohibited because using it was an unpatriotic act and later a threat to military discipline, although the Taipings did voice these objections. These acts were prohibited because they were regarded as an offence against the Heavenly Commandments and only by strict compliance with these commandments could the God Worshippers hope to obtain salvation. The rewards for obedience, and the penalties for disobedience to these commandments was spelled out clearly in a poem which concluded *The Book of Heavenly Commandments*:

> Those who obey the Heavenly Commandments and worship the true God, when they part with the present, will forthwith ascend to heaven.
> Those who are mired in the world's customs and believe in the demons, when they come to their end, will find it hard to escape from hell.[25]

The separation of the sexes, which did not apply to the leadership, remained in force when the Taiping moved north. But the husbands and wives of the rank and file were segregated into separate camps. They were permitted to meet only once a week and that encounter had to be in public view. This prohibition may have become more necessary for an army on the march, for Taiping women were expected to take their share of the fighting. Sexual relations were to remain suspended until the Taiping kingdom had been established. At Yongan the leaders had promised the rebels that when they got to Nanjing it would be like ascending to paradise, where husbands and wives would be allowed to re-unite.[26]

After Hong returned to Guangxi in 1847 a number of other developments took place. The first was the clarification of Hong's role as a messianic leader and as the son of God and the younger brother of Jesus Christ. The earliest indication of such a claim appeared in the versions of Hong's visions recorded in *The Taiping Heavenly Chronicle*, dated 1848. In that document Christ was identified as the Heavenly Brother, and God's consort as the Heavenly Mother. Hong's experiences in heaven were described, and the task which he was to undertake on his return to earth was identified: he was 'to put the Father's affairs in order'.[27]

The second development was the manifestation of ecstatic behaviour. Hong Ren'gan recalled,

It sometimes happened that while they [the God Worshippers] were kneeling down engaged in prayer, the one or the other of those present was seized by a sudden fit, so that he fell down to the ground, and his whole body was covered with perspiration. In such a state of ecstasy, moved by the spirit, he uttered words of exhortation, reproof, prophecy, &c. Often the words were unintelligible, and generally delivered in rhythm.[28]

The culmination of this stage was the expression of claims that the Heavenly Father and the Heavenly Elder Brother had come down to earth and had spoken through the persons of two leaders of the God Worshippers, Yang Xiuqing, later the Eastern King, and Xiao Chaogui, later the Western King.[29] Claiming divine inspiration the two leaders had 'displayed innumerable miracles and powers', including the power of healing. A record of their instructions was compiled as *The Book of Heavenly Decrees and Proclamations*.

These claims have been regarded as deliberate deceptions.[30] Certainly in December 1851 there was a blatant piece of trickery alleging divine revelation – the unmasking of the 'traitor' Zhou Xineng. But this does not prove that from the beginning there was the systematic use of deceit. When discussing a movement which gained its original impetus from the visionary experiences of its leader, there is reason to suppose that the ecstatic utterances of Yang and Xiao were treated as genuine by the speakers themselves and by their audience.

The examples of divine intervention multiplied during this period. In 1849 a prophecy was given, 'A pestilence shall befall men; only those who believe shall be saved'. This prophecy proved true.[31] In the account given by Hong Ren'gan, there was reference to the performance of miracles, the dumb beginning to talk and the insane being cured. Yang Xiuqing in particular was said to possess the power to cure sickness through his intercession and it was suggested that he prayed to have the sickness conferred upon himself and that for a short time he himself bore the suffering of the sickness.[32] There can be little doubt but that the evidence of divine revelation, of prophecies fulfilled, and of miracles performed, played an important part in converting people to the movement.

The third way in which divine inspiration was identified lay in claims that the movement's remarkable success could only be explained by divine direction. An explicit statement of this claim was made in the *Taiping Songs on World Salvation*, first published in 1853 and attributed to Yang Xiuqing. In it Yang claimed,

> From the time when we five brothers, relying on the mercy of Heaven and our Sovereign, received investment as wangs [kings] and respectfully received the Heavenly Father's personal command to go down into the world and assist in the establishment of the true Sovereign, we have with united hearts and united efforts exterminated the hosts of demons and exhorted mankind to awake. . . . This in truth had long been pre-determined by our Heavenly Father; therefore, no battle was without success and no attack without victory.[33]

It is not easy to determine when the expectation emerged that the Taiping revelation would shortly be followed by the coming of the Millennium. This is partly because the concept can easily be confused with references to the heavenly paradise which is part of Christian eschatology. Certain passages in *Good Words* could be interpreted as meaning that divine retribution was imminent, and Hong's reaction after he had read or re-read the tracts emphasized the urgency of repentance. But this could still be regarded as a matter of personal salvation. However, early in 1850, after clashes between the God Worshippers and the *Bendi* had become increasingly severe, and it appeared that the authorities were siding with the latter, the God Worshippers began to mass at a village called Jintian. This development has been interpreted as the moment when a religious movement was transformed into an armed rebellion, the point when the God Worshipper's society changed 'from an amorphous religious following to a systematically functioning force of over twenty thousand poised for revolution . . .'.[34]

However, it can also be interpreted as the stage when the expectation that the Millennium was imminent was clearest and the millenarian character of the movement was most apparent. The massing at Jintian was explained as Hong's response to a prophecy given to him by God:

In the 30th year of Daoguang [1850], will I send down calamities; those of you who remain steadfast in faith, shall be saved, but the unbelievers shall be visited by pestilence. After the eighth month, fields will be left uncultivated, and houses without inhabitants; therefore call thou thy own family and relatives hither.[35]

In anticipation of this Hong had called upon members of his family to join him. A pestilence had broken out in Guangxi and this had led to a great increase in the number of the God Worshippers, for it was thought that by joining them people would escape the disease. A new message appeared in a poem written by Hong and included in *The Taiping Heavenly Chronicle*. It declared that salvation to be expected was communal, and it introduced an apocalyptic tone:

Having turned back from the road of deception, now spur yourself ever faster;
Stir up your courage and press ever forward.
Take all of your worldly passions and cast them away completely;
Only then will you be able to ascend directly to the nine levels of heaven.[36]

References to a terrestrial paradise were made principally in *The Book of Heavenly Decrees and Proclamations*, and in the proclamations issued by Hong in 1851-2, that is at the time when the Taipings had raised the standard of rebellion and were besieged at Yongan. Some of the expectations raised in these documents can be explained in terms of a rebellion aimed at the overthrow of the Manchus. But the terms in which the aspirations were expressed do not resemble those of normal political objectives. Two quotations illustrate this point:

When we arrive at the Heavenly Court [Nanjing], all those meritorious officials who together with us conquered the hills and rivers shall on the higher level be invested with the titles of chancellor, senior secretary, commander, general or imperial guard, or at the least with the title of corps general. These titles shall be handed down through successive generations, and, in dragon robe and horn-encrusted girdle, those [who bear the titles] will be permitted to attend the Heavenly Court. I sincerely inform you that since we are all fortunate in being sons and daughters of the Heavenly Father, and also fortunate in being brothers and sisters of the Heavenly Elder Brother, in this world we shall display majesty beyond compare and in heaven we shall enjoy interminable felicity.[37]

This proclamation was dated 4 December 1851. On 3 April 1852, two days before the battle which broke the siege of Yongan, Hong, the Heavenly King, issued a proclamation in verse which gave the most explicit statement yet made on the imminence of the Millennium:

Let men and women officers all grasp the sword.
As for your present clothing needs, one change will be sufficient.
With united hearts rouse your courage and together slay the demons.
Gold, valuables, and baggage shall be put aside.
Divest yourselves of worldly affections and uphold high Heaven;
Golden bricks and golden houses await you, all brilliant and flashing;
In high heaven shall you enjoy happiness, majesty in the highest.
The smallest and the lowest shall all wear silks and satins.
Men shall wear dragon robes and women shall be garlanded in flowers.
Let each be a faithful minister and exert his utmost energies. [38]

It has been argued that these proclamations did not necessarily refer to the millennial expectations of the movement. Of the second proclamation Franz Michael said that it was 'an exhortation and an order to be prepared' for the battle to break out of Yongan.[39] It did serve that purpose, but the evidence suggests that the expectation went far beyond the breaking out from a siege. When Franz Michael discussed why Nanjing was chosen as the capital of the rebel regime, he emphasized military and strategic considerations.[40] However, the identification of Nanjing with the Heavenly Capital and Hong's reference to it as the New Jerusalem, indicate that its capture was a key element in the millennial vision. Later in the rebellion it was noted that Hong's favourite reading consisted of the Bible and *The Pilgrim's Progress*. A version of the latter had appeared in Chinese in 1816 and was well known to Christian converts. Hong may have been familiar with its story at this time and may have identified Christian's journey to the New Jerusalem with his progress north to Nanjing. While *The Pilgrim's Progress* is taken as an allegory of the individual's path to spiritual salvation, for Hong it could refer to the movement which he headed and could confirm that the salvation which awaited the Taipings at Nanjing would be collective and terrestrial.[41]

Another aspect of the Taipings' expectation of an earthly and a heavenly paradise was their willingness to sacrifice their lives for the cause. This willingness may have been exaggerated, but it does accord with the expectation that total commitment to the Taiping cause would earn eternal bliss, whether on earth or elsewhere. In proclamation issued at Yongan and dated 14 September 1851, the Heavenly King stated,

All soldiers and officers, I earnestly beseech you to obey the heavenly commands, and not to offend again. I inform you of the truth that if at present you do not cling to life and fear death, you will afterwards ascend to heaven, and then will enjoy eternal life and immortality. If you cling to life, then you will not live; and if you fear death, then you will meet with death.[42]

Another development at Yongan was the introduction of the Taiping calendar, first used in late 1851 or early 1852. This step has been explained as either the traditional action of a rebellion about to establish a dynasty or as a revolutionary step to abolish the unpropitious days in the old calendar and so to sharpen the fighting spirit of the Taiping soldiers.[43] But it was also a declaration of the inauguration of a new era and the beginning of the Millennium, which was counted as having started in 1851, 'just as more than 1800 years ago a new age had started *post Christum natum* in the West'.[44]

The key feature of the rebellion which has yet to be discussed is the Taiping abandonment of the private ownership of earthly goods and the establishment of the sacred treasury. This feature became well known because of its inclusion in the most famous of the Taiping ordinances, *The Land System of the Heavenly Dynasty*. The system provided for all land to be divided into nine grades, and for it then to be distributed according to the number of individuals in a family, with men and women receiving equal shares and children a half share. Of the produce from this land, all surpluses should be deposited in the public granary. The document declared:

When all the people in the empire will not take anything as their own but submit all things to the Supreme Lord, then the Lord will make use of them, and in the universal family of the empire, every place will be equal and every individual well fed and well clothed. This is the intent of our Heavenly Father, the Supreme Lord and Great God, in specially commanding the true Sovereign of Taiping to save the world.[45]

The Taiping land system has usually been regarded as a response to the plight of poor peasants. The document which described it was probably written during the advance from Yongan to Nanjing[46] and in it two separate ideological strands may have become intertwined: on the one hand a practical strand which proposed a programme of revolutionary social and economic organization intended to offer security and comfort to those who joined the rebellion; on the other hand a millenarian strand, which literally took no thought for the morrow, which called upon peasants to surrender or destroy their meagre possessions and to rely on a supernatural agency rather than on the efforts of man to supply their needs. Of these two strands the earlier appears to be the millenarian one.

References to the common or sacred treasury had first appeared when the God Worshippers began to mass at Jintian. The account given by Hong Ren'gan recorded:

Xiuquan now sent messages to all the congregations in the different districts to assemble in one place. Already for some time previous to this, the worshippers of God had felt the necessity of uniting together for common defence against their enemies; they had commenced to convert their property of fields and houses into money; and to deliver the proceeds thereof into the general treasury, from which all shared alike, every one receiving his food and clothing from this fund. The circumstance that they shared all in common greatly added to their numbers, and thus they were prepared to abandon their homes at a moment's warning.[47]

Franz Michael related the common treasury to the Taiping belief that as children of God they all formed one large family, and that all property belonged to the head of that family, God, whose representative was the Heavenly King, the younger brother of Jesus Christ.

But there were also millennial features in this arrangement. In *Good Words* one of the texts used was Matthew 19: 21, 'go and sell that thou hast, and give to the poor, and thou shalt have treasure in heaven: and come and follow me'. In *The Book of Heavenly Decrees and Proclamations*, a series of proclamations referred to the establishment of the sacred treasury, and in those the idea of personal possession and the value of material goods were depreciated: 'When you have money, you must recognize that it is not an end in itself, and not consider it as belonging to "you" or "me"'.[48] Not much more can be said on this except to comment that it is surprising that the Taipings managed to persuade so many to abandon their land and their earthly goods, surprising that is unless many were like the family of Li Xiucheng, the Loyal King, which was so poor that its members had nothing to lose.

The Land System of the Heavenly Dynasty contained a plan for the collectivization of land. The ideas it contained can be traced back to a classical text, the *Zhouli*, but many historians have presented it as more than an utopian dream. Jen Yu-wen argued that although the scheme was not practical in the form in which it was enacted, nevertheless it was 'an expression of Taiping ideological principles'.[49] For Franz Michael, the land law 'envisaging a completely controlled economy integrated into a totalitarian administrative system', was an extraordinary plan, amounting in concept to a 'social revolution'.[50] They, and many other writers have assumed that it was the intention of the Taipings to implement a plan for land redistribution, but they were unable to do so because the rebellion never succeeded in establishing the stable conditions under which such a system could be introduced. But was the land law proposed as a practical measure? The legislation contained no reference to the establishment of any machinery to implement it, nor did it suggest how such a system might be sustained. About half the document did not even relate to the land law, but gave details of how in the new society disputes would be resolved and how matters of promotion and demotion would be arranged. It is more understandable if it is considered within the context of Taiping millennial expectations – as a description of the form of society which would come into being when the Taiping

Heavenly Kingdom had been established on earth. The principal beneficiaries in the new society would be 'those meritorious officials of the original following' who 'shall through successive generations enjoy heavenly emoluments'. However, those who had joined the movement later were guaranteed security. In the new society all would be brought into harmony,

> for the whole empire is the universal family of our Heavenly Father, the Supreme Lord and Great God. When all the people in the empire will not take anything as their own but submit all things to the Supreme Lord, then the Lord will make use of them, and in the universal family of the empire, every place will be equal and every individual well fed and clothed. This is the intent of our Heavenly Father, the Supreme Lord and Great God, in specially commanding the true Sovereign of Taiping to save the world.[51]

With the capture of Nanjing the Taipings were now in possession of their heavenly city, the confirmation of which was written by Hong in the margin of Revelations 3: 12, on the new Jerusalem, 'the name of the city of my God':

> Now the Elder Brother has come. The Heavenly Court has the temple of the Heavenly Father, God, the True Deity; it also has the Elder Brother Christ's temple, wherein are already inscribed the names of God and Christ. The new Jerusalem sent down from heaven by God the Heavenly Father is our present Heavenly Capital.[52]

And to Revelations (21: 1–27) he added, 'God's heaven now exists among men. It is fulfilled.'[53]

But it was at that very point that the millennial expectation began to fade. By choosing Nanjing as its capital the rebellion lost its impetus, its original membership was diluted by large numbers who had not abandoned their possessions to join it, and the mundane demands of administration forced its leaders to make a variety of compromises. Soon after the capture of Nanjing, Yang Xiuqing, the Eastern king, noting that Taiping discipline was beginning to flag, composed *The Book of the Principles of the Heavenly Nature*. In it he set out to urge followers to continue the struggle to destroy the 'remaining demons', the conventional Taiping description of the enemy, and in particular he sought to transmit to the 'new brothers and sisters', that is those who had joined the movement after the departure from Jintian, and who had not therefore participated in the fervour of the God Worshippers, the millenarian expectations of the original Taipings. To achieve this, he recapitulated the main tenets of Taiping religion, stressing that Hong, the Heavenly King, had been summoned to heaven in 1837 and that he had been given a divine commission 'to become the true Taiping Sovereign of the ten thousand nations of the world, and to save the people of the world'.[54] He explained how he himself had received a special commission to redeem mankind from sickness, and how, as a consequence, in 1850, he had become deaf and dumb, with pus pouring from his ears, and water flowing from his eyes. He represented the tribulations of the early period of the uprising as tests of the sincerity of the followers and the success to date of the movement as proof of divine guidance. The failure to achieve outright victory, the postponement of the Millennium, was explicable:

> the fact that our Heavenly Father refrains from immediately exterminating the remaining demons is perhaps due to his desire to make our younger brothers and sisters determined at heart, to make them double their efforts in purification that they may enjoy the Heavenly Father's great blessings.[55]

So the Eastern King insisted on the maintenance of discipline and the continuance of the puritanical life-style.

> Therefore, we brothers must be firm and patient in mind and must not, in the case of husband and wife, seek illicit union in disobedience of the Heavenly commands, nor should we violate the sisters in the camp and thereby greatly disobey the Heavenly Commandments.[56]

The rules of sexual segregation remained in force until 1855, but they did not apply to the leaders and their exemption has been seen as evidence of their hypocrisy. But Hong declared that the difference was a necessary one, which was connected with his expectation of the establishment of a millennial kingdom with himself at its head. In *The Book of Heavenly Decrees and Proclamations*, in a document dated 2 March 1853, he had described the special taboos applying to the Queen and added,

> I sincerely announce to you that the Queen's apartments are the source of good government and enlightenment, and the palace city the origin of morality. It is not that I am desirous of making severe restrictions; I only wish to embody the holy will of the Heavenly Father and Heavenly Elder Brother, in beheading the evil and sparing the good.[57]

This idea contained a strong echo of Hong's vision of heaven as described in *The Taiping Heavenly Chronicle*. It was perhaps in Hong's palace, and indeed in Hong's mind that millennial expectations survived longest. Elsewhere, as the movement became static, as new adherents with little commitment other than to material advantage joined and the puritanical prohibitions fell into disuse, above all as the millennial expectations were not fulfilled, the dream began to fade. When in 1856 the rebellion suffered the mortal blow of internecine strife, what remained was no longer a movement with a vision, only a disorganized rebellion which continued to threaten because of the military genius of a few leaders and the incompetence of the imperialist forces.

Before concluding, it is interesting to recall a comment made by the missionary W. H. Medhurst, whose translations of the Taiping books first brought Taiping beliefs to the notice of Europeans. Medhurst recorded a conversation he had had with a deserter from the Taipings who had related to him how severely the rebels dealt with infringements of the prohibitions on opium, tobacco, drinking and gambling, how the segregation of the sexes was enforced, how the soldiers neither received, nor expected to receive, any pay whatsoever. At the end of this account Medhurst exclaimed,

> What an extraordinary view does the above present, of the insurgent army! What a moral revolution! To induce 100,000 Chinamen, for months and years together, to give up tobacco, opium, lust and covetousness; to deny themselves in lawful gratifications, and, what is dearer to a Chinaman's heart than life itself, to consent to live without dollars, and all share and share alike, braving death in its worst form, and persevering therein without flinching. There may be defective teaching among them, there may be errors of a greater or lesser magnitude – but if what is above-detailed be true – or the half of it – it is confessedly a moral revolution – it is the wonder of the age.[58]

Although the millennial hopes faded, Hong continued to declare the Taiping kingdom to be the manifestation of the rule of God on earth. At some time after 1853, in the margin of his copy of the Taiping New Testament, beside Revelations 22: 10–21, Hong noted with some puzzlement,

> Now God and Christ have come; why are the saints not overjoyed? Moreover, this corroborates the gospel which you propagate; how can you not believe? This is exactly as the Elder Brother prophesied that I should come – like a thief, when no one knows. It is fulfilled. Respect this.[59]

Until the very end of the Taiping kingdom, Hong Xiuquan himself retained his belief that Nanjing was the Heavenly City and that the New Jerusalem was in sight. In May 1864, when the capture of the city was imminent, Li Xiucheng, the Loyal King, had suggested that the best strategy was to break out and capture the wealthy province of Jiangxi. But the Heavenly King had responded, 'Close the doors of the city! Eat Manna! This can feed you. You make Manna with grass. I have instructed the people to rely on the power of the Heavenly Father.'[60]

Millenarianism was not the only cause of the rebellion and was a transient stage in its course, but it was also a phenomenon of considerable importance, for it is difficult to explain why this movement grew so rapidly and gained such fanatical adherents if one relies mainly on the appeals of anti-Manchuism and land reform. The former was the rallying call of secret societies which had never elicited a mass uprising. With reference to land reform, the early history of the Chinese Communist Party shows how difficult it was to galvanize poor peasants into revolutionary action on that issue. In the case of the Taiping Rebellion, as in the case of many previous uprisings, the appeal which did work was that of millenary expectations. In the deposition which Li Xiucheng made before his execution, when he, the most valorous of the Taiping leaders, was asked to explain why his family had joined the movement, he made no mention of anti-Manchuism or land reform. He stated repeatedly that he had joined because they were poor and had nothing to eat.[61] But it was not possible that a group of rebels could have promised to obtain a secure supply of food by normal means. Some supernatural expectation must have been the source, not simply of a sufficiency, but of hitherto undreamt-of luxury, 'golden bricks and golden houses await you'. It is for this reason that it is suggested that at the heart of the movement, in its early years, there was a millennial dream raised by a prophetic leadership. The failure of their prophecies to materialize is part of the explanation of the movement's inevitable decline and ultimate disappearance. As a final point, one may mention the idea that it was the deeply subversive millenarian aspects of a movement such as this which contributed to the subsequent development of Marxist revolutionism. Henri Desroches suggested the concept of a 'socio-religious chain' that stretched from the Reformation to Marx. Putting the Taiping Rebellion into this context, the early prophetic and millenarian stage of the rebellion should be regarded as an essential preliminary to the later secular stage, because it introduced fundamental hopes of transformation. The key figure in this transformation was Hong's cousin, Hong Ren'gan, who had participated in the early religious stage and later rejoined the movement and formulated the new secular aspirations of a westernized Chinese state.[62]

Notes

1 Chinese names and Chinese terms are given in Pinyin, with surnames appearing first except in the endnotes where for the sake of consistency with western practice given names appear first. Chinese names and terms appearing in quotations have been amended to Pinyin.

2 E.P. Boardman, 'Millenary aspects of the Taiping Rebellion 1851–64' in S.L. Thrupp (ed.), *Millennial Dreams in Action: Essays in Comparative Study* (The Hague, Mouton, 1970), pp. 70–9.

3 N. Cohn, 'Medieval millenarism: Its bearing on the comparative study of millenarian movements' in Thrupp, *Millennial Dreams*, pp. 31–43.

4 Two notable exceptions to this are R.G. Wagner, *Re-enacting the Heavenly Vision: The Role of Religion in the Taiping Rebellion* (Berkeley, University of California Institute of East Asian Studies, 1982), and R.P. Weller, *Resistance, Chaos and Control in China: Taiping Rebels, Taiwanese Ghosts and Tiananmen* (Seattle, University of Washington Press, 1994). Rudolf Wagner showed how Hong Xiuquan systematically examined the proofs of the vision which he had experienced, and argued that that vision, once

proved, was responsible for both the success and the demise of the rebellion which he headed. Robert P. Weller used the example of the Taiping Rebellion, and in particular the characteristics of Taiping religion, to illustrate the theme of cultural resistance. He stressed in particular the importance of spirit possession in the formative stage of the movement.

5 S. Naquin, *Shantung Rebellion: The Wang Lun Uprising of 1774* (New Haven, Yale University Press, 1981).

6 S. Naquin, *Millenarian Rebellion in China: The Eight Trigrams Uprising of 1813* (New Haven, Yale University Press, 1976).

7 R. Israeli, *Muslims in China: A Study in Cultural Confrontation* (London, Scandinavian Institute of Asian Studies, 1980).

8 T. Hamberg, *The Visions of Hung-Siu-tshuen, and Origin of the Kwang-si Insurrection* (Hong Kong, China Mail Office, 1854; Peiping, Yenching University Library, 1935), pp. 9–12.

9 Quoted in Ssu-yü Teng, *Historiography of the Taiping Rebellion* (Cambridge, Massachusetts, Harvard University Press, 1962), p. 4.

10 E.P. Boardman, 'Christian influence upon the ideology of the Taiping Rebellion,' *Far Eastern Quarterly*, 10 (1951), 115–24.

11 J.C. Cheng, *Chinese Sources for the Taiping Rebellion 1850–1864* (Hong Kong University Press, 1963), p. 83.

12 Teng, *Historiography of the Taiping Rebellion*, pp. 4–5.

13 P.A. Kuhn, 'Origins of the Taiping vision. Cross-cultural dimensions of a Chinese rebellion,' *Comparative Studies in Society and History*, 19 (3) (July 1977), 350–66, at p. 354.

14 Hamberg, *The Visions of Hung-Siu-tshuen*, p. 14.

15 F. Michael and C. Chang (eds), *The Taiping Rebellion: History and Documents* (3 vols, Seattle, University of Washington Press, 1966–71), vol. II, p. 66.

16 M. Adas, *Prophets of Rebellion: Millenarian Protest Movements against the European Colonial Order* (Chapel Hill, University of Northern Carolina Press, 1969), pp. 112–21.

17 F.J. Hood, *Reformed America: The Middle and Southern States, 1783–1837* (University of Alabama Press, 1980), p. 69.

18 J.B. Littell, 'Missionaries and politics in China: The Taiping Rebellion', *Political Science Quarterly*, 43 (1928), 566–99.

19 M.L. Cohen, 'The Hakka or "Guest People": dialect as a sociocultural variable in south-eastern China', *Ethnohistory*, 15.3 (1968), 237–92.

20 M. Barkun, *Disaster and the Millennium* (New Haven, Yale University Press, 1974), pp. 62–90.

21 S.Y. Teng, *The Taiping Rebellion and the Western Powers* (Oxford, Clarendon Press, 1971), p. 39.

22 Michael and Chang, *The Taiping Rebellion*, vol. II, p. 115.

23 Hamberg, *The Visions of Hung-Siu-tshuen*, p. 35.

24 Michael and Chang, *The Taiping Rebellion*, vol. II, pp. 119–24.

25 Michael and Chang, *The Taiping Rebellion*, vol. II, p. 123.

26 Wen-lan Tu, *P'ing-ting Yüeh-fei chi-lüeh* (1871) quoted in V.Y.C. Shih, *The Taiping Ideology*, vol. II (Seattle, University of Washington Press, 1967), p. 69.

27 Michael and Chang, *The Taiping Rebellion*, vol. II, p. 61.

28 Hamberg, *The Visions of Hung-Siu-tshuen*, p. 45.

29 Michael and Chang, *The Taiping Rebellion*, vol. II, pp. 97–110.

30 Michael and Chang, *The Taiping Rebellion*, vol II, p. 97.

31 'Hung Hsiu-ch'üan's background', an essay written by Hong Ren'gan in 1852–3. See Michael and Chang, *The Taiping Rebellion*, vol. II, p. 5.

32 Hamberg, *The Visions of Hung-Siu-tshuen*, p. 46.

33 Michael and Chang, *The Taiping Rebellion*, vol. II, p. 241.

34 Yu-wen Jen, *The Taiping Revolutionary Movement* (New Haven, Yale University Press, 1973), p. 52.

35 Hamberg, *The Visions of Hung-Siu-tshuen*, pp. 47–8.

36 Michael and Chang, *The Taiping Rebellion*, vol. II, p. 76.

37 Michael and Chang, *The Taiping Rebellion*, vol. II, p. 107.

38 Michael and Chang, *The Taiping Rebellion*, vol. II, p. 109.

39 Michael and Chang, *The Taiping Rebellion*, vol. II, p. 109, note 32.

40 Michael and Chang, *The Taiping Rebellion*, vol. I, pp. 69–70 and note 44.

41 Wagner, *Re-enacting the Heavenly Vision*, pp. 59–60.

42 Michael and Chang, *The Taiping Rebellion*, vol. II, p. 105.

43 Teng, *The Taiping Rebellion and the Western Powers*, pp. 123–4.

44 Wagner, *Re-enacting the Heavenly Vision*, p. 99.

45 Michael and Chang, *The Taiping Rebellion*, vol. II, p. 314.

46 The earliest surviving editions of the *Land System* carry the date 1853, although it is probable that they were not published until 1854. See Michael and Chang, *The Taiping Rebellion*, vol. II, p. 309.

47 Hamberg, *The Visions of Hung-Siu-tshuen*, pp. 52–3.

48 Michael and Chang, *The Taiping Rebellion*, vol. II, p. 100.

49 Yu-wen Jen, *Taiping Revolutionary Movement*, p. 143.

50 Michael and Chang, *The Taiping Rebellion*, vol. I, p. 87.

51 Michael and Chang, *The Taiping Rebellion*, vol. II, p. 314.

52 Michael and Chang, *The Taiping Rebellion*, vol. II, p. 235.

53 Michael and Chang, *The Taiping Rebellion*, vol. II, p. 237.

54 Michael and Chang, *The Taiping Rebellion*, vol. II, p. 373.

55 Michael and Chang, *The Taiping Rebellion*, vol. II, p. 377.

56 Michael and Chang, *The Taiping Rebellion*, vol. II, p. 387.

57 Michael and Chang, *The Taiping Rebellion*, vol. II, p. 110.

58 *North China Herald*, 26 November 1853, quoted in P. Clarke and J.S. Gregory, *Western Reports on the Taiping: A Selection of Documents* (Honolulu, University Press of Hawaii, 1982), pp. 89–90.

59 Michael and Chang, *The Taiping Rebellion*, vol. II, p. 237.

60 Quoted in Wagner, *Re-enacting the Heavenly Vision*, pp. 113–14.

61 C.A. Curwen, *Taiping Rebel: The Deposition of Li Hsiu-ch'eng* (Cambridge University Press, 1977), p. 83.

62 C. Garrett, *Respectable Folly: Millenarians and the French Revolution in France and England* (Baltimore, The Johns Hopkins University Press, 1975), pp. 2–3, and H. Desroche, *The American Shakers: From Neo-Christianity to Presocialism* (Amherst, Massachusetts, University of Massachusetts Press, 1971).

10

From the Millennial Future to the Unconscious Past: The Transformation of Prophecy in Early Twentieth-Century Britain

R. Hayward

The Welsh Revival of 1904–5 was the last truly popular prophetic movement to surface in the British Isles, yet its history has been largely forgotten. Although it gains brief mentions in books on Welsh history or politics, its close study has for the most part been relegated to the works of wistful evangelicals or latter-day chroniclers of the supernatural.[1] The failure of this awakening to achieve any kind of major historical presence can be attributed to a number of causes.

At a most obvious level, the Welsh Revival lacked the millennial fervour and revolutionary impact associated with the other movements discussed in this book. Unlike the omens surrounding Elizabeth I or the Anabaptist groupings of interregnum England, the Welsh awakening failed to make any real impression on the social or political institutions of the United Kingdom. Although many of its leaders nurtured the hope that the awakening would transform the whole of Britain and eventually the world, most of its followers remained concerned with more limited and local aims, the conversions of friends and neighbours or the resolution of village disputes. It is this parochial history that has been recorded. The great majority of writings simply catalogue the miraculous conversions and divine marvels which accompanied the acknowledged leaders of the revival. They follow the inspired itinerary of Evan Roberts (1878–1954), the trainee minister and sometime collier who was seen as the movement's figurehead, detailing a succession of redeemed villages and transformed services across Wales and Merseyside.[2] Others have concentrated upon the role of organized evangelical groups such as the Free Church Council or the Keswick Conventions, arguing that it was their local missions which prepared the ground for the Revival.[3]

The anecdotal nature of these evangelical histories points to a far deeper

reason for the Revival's failure to achieve any kind of historical presence. For
many of the movement's supporters, the awakening itself was antithetical to
history. The introductions to their works are freighted with reservations and
disclaimers concerning the adequacy of historical narrative to this subject. The
Cwmavon minister, Howell Elvet Lewis, argued that no fixed history could be
attributed to the Welsh revival since 'dates, places and persons were only the
outward and visible symbols of a wave . . . that has no everyday name, no secular
explanation'.[4] Rhys Bevan Jones, a prominent Welsh evangelist, believed that:
'The very most that has been (or can be said) can only be glimpses after all, and
glimpses too of that which has come *within the ken of a finite human being*. God alone
can unfold what He has done.'[5] Perhaps the most important statement of this sort
came from the young revivalist, Evan Roberts. Roberts denied his own role in the
awakening, saying simply: 'We do not know how the revival originated; . . .
nobody knows how: nothing but the day of judgement will reveal it.'[6] This
rhetoric which located the history of the revival outside the compass of human
understanding replicates the political form of prophecy. In its assumption that
truth could only be accessed at the level of the divine, it provided the grounds for
a critique of mundane or conventional knowledge. It is the politics of this
critique, at the level of both social history and personal identity, that will be
explored in the remainder of this chapter.

Prophecy has developed a twofold meaning in modern culture. Both of its
meanings can be seen as somehow being opposed to history. Its original sense
was simply that of speaking or communicating the words of God. It was a sense
epitomized in the divine message to Jeremiah, when Jehovah told the prophet:
'Behold, I have put my words in thy mouth.'[7] The second and now more popular
connotation of prophecy, presents it as an activity akin to divination. It is seen as
an act whereby the future is revealed, either through omens, the direct word of
God or the interpretation of sacred texts. Both types of prophecy played a role in
the Welsh Revival though the latter form was much less common. The main
divinatory prophecies reported in contemporary newspapers or pamphlets were
simply predictions of the movement's inevitable success or indications of
imminent conversion. These divinatory omens and visions can be summarized as
follows.

The revival's figurehead, Evan Roberts, experienced at least fourteen visions in
the period leading up to the awakening and another seven whilst it progressed.[8]
These visions usually had an encouraging or consoling effect upon the young
evangelist, assuring him of his mission's coming triumph. Such consolation was
evident in Roberts's most widely reported vision, which occurred during a
moment of depression in Newcastle Emlyn. While in this 'Slough of Despond' he
walked in the garden. It was about four p.m. Suddenly, in the hedge on his left,
he saw a face full of scorn, hatred and derision and heard a laugh as of defiance.
It was the Prince of this World, who exulted in this despondency. Then there

suddenly appeared another figure gloriously arrayed in white, bearing in hand a flaming sword held aloft. The sword fell athwart the first figure and it suddenly disappeared. He could not see the face of the sword-bearer. 'Do you not see the moral?' queried the missioner, with face beaming with delight. 'Is it not that the Church of Christ is to be triumphant?'[9]

As the art historian, John Harvey, has noted, this vision appears to be rooted in biblical imagery. It parallels Christ's temptation in the wilderness (Matt. 4: 1–11), although its setting was more mundane. Other authorizing visions also drew upon Biblical references. In letters to friends, Roberts told of how he had witnessed the final defeat of the four horses of the Apocalypse, and later seen a misty figure, like the angel of Revelations, promising the redemption of 100,000 souls through his mission. More substantial visions were attached to the mission of Mrs Jones of Egryn, Meirionethshire. A farmer's wife, Mrs Jones had decided to dedicate her life to Christ after reading Sheldon's devotional work, *In His Steps*. When news of Evan Roberts's meeting reached her village in December 1904, she was moved to organize a series of local prayer meetings. Her mission was guided by a series of visions, which were remarkable in so far as they were witnessed by the general public. Neighbours reported fiery crosses and columns of fire hanging over the houses and villages where she was due to make her conversions.[10] These reports were soon taken up by the popular press, with the *Daily Mail* despatching a special team headed by Bernard Redwood to investigate the claims.[11] Although Redwood dismissed Mrs Jones as 'a religious maniac', others were more sympathetic. The Welsh publisher E.W. Evans reported how an elderly poet had been saved from a group of wild Meirionethshire animals when a vision of Christ appeared beside him.[12]

Other less visionary prophecies were also seen as authorizing and encouraging the Welsh Revival. The death-bed wish of Dean Howells that the Welsh people would enjoy a spiritual awakening was later reinterpreted as a prophecy of uncanny accuracy.[13] In a less religious vein were the reports of the talking baby of Bethesda. This infant was rumoured to have repeatedly forecast the revival's success during the one month of its brief life.[14]

These visionary prophecies were accompanied by justificatory examples of Biblical interpretation. Like Pentecost, the Revival was seen as a realization of the prophecy of Joel, that in the last days, the Lord would 'pour out his spirit upon all flesh; and your sons and daughters shall prophesy, your old men shall dream dreams and your young men shall see visions'.[15] Others saw it as fulfilment of the promise made in the Fourth Gospel that there would come a time when men would give up all thought of themselves and talk only of Christ.[16]

The political relevance of these prophecies is not immediately apparent. As noted before, the Welsh Revival seemed to be insulated from the wider political and social structure of the nation. Its prophecies were introspective, referring only to coming conversions or the movement's imminent success. However, if we follow the arguments of modern theorists such as Michel Foucault or Michel de Certeau, a more subtle politics comes into view.[17] Revivalism may have been superficially apolitical, yet it undermined the basic notions upon which politics, history and society depended. Prophecy, in its very act of articulation, cut through the ideas of authorship, selfhood and responsibility. Whatever the content of its message may have been, the form of prophecy was always subversive. The attribution of words and images to an external or divine agency, divided the body of the prophet. It cut off the individual's present speech or actions from their personal will and acknowledged past. Inspiration transformed the active and responsible agent into a passive instrument in the service of the divine. This point was clearly recognized by one of the English critics of the Welsh Revival:

> Our working conceptions of psychology and sociology are permeated with ideas of causation, of the self-identity of human beings, of the essentially gradual character of growth that is to be thought of as permanent or real. But if we attempt to understand what revivalism means to those actively engaged in it, we find that they set forth the possibility and the necessity of a sudden and fundamental change in human personality, and further, that they wholly repudiate the notion that personal influence can itself bring about such change.[18]

The distinctiveness of the Welsh Revival lay in its widespread adoption of this prophetic contestation of the self. Unlike previous movements which had centred around the inspired command of a prophetic leader, in the awakening of 1904–5, this inspiration became generalized. As had been predicted in those Biblical passages attached to the Revival, the vision of Joel and the promise of John, it was a great section of the population which entered this new relationship with God. This generality was stressed in the metaphors and images used to describe the awakening. They pictured the Holy Spirit descending, not so much on individuals but across the Principality as a whole. 'Wales' as one dramatic headline claimed, 'was in the grip of supernatural forces.'[19] It was the achievement of Evan Roberts and the other revival leaders, that they discovered the methods and techniques which would facilitate this mass uptake of prophecy.

Evan Roberts transformed prophecy from an individual to general phenomenon by developing a formula or practice which would enable his followers to recognize and obey the inner voice of the Holy Spirit. Roberts called his formula the 'amodau diwygiad' or four articles of faith. Modern commentators following Foucault would probably term it a 'technology of the self' for it involved a series of practical and intellectual techniques which would render the body prophetic.[20] In the version given below, it was widely publicized through sermons and newspaper reports.

First. The past must be cleared: every sin must be confessed to God
Second. Everything doubtful must be removed once and for all from out of
   our lives.
Third. Obedience prompt and implicit to the Holy Spirit.
Fourth. Public confession must be made of Christ.[21]

These four articles of faith could be seen as development from, or a practical application of, a division which was quite familiar in Calvinist Methodist theology. This was division between the eternal soul and the death-bound self. Following the model given by St Paul in epistles to Romans and Corinthians, Roberts had argued that the 'self' was rooted in sin.[22] Created through a mixture of carnal desire and everyday opinion it distracted man from his real relationship with God.[23] The autonomy and plenitude of this selfish ego was contrasted with the emptiness and dependence of the divine soul. As Roberts wrote in his first sermon:

> God, through Adam's transgression left his home in the soul, and that therefore left a depth of emptiness to be felt in us. . . . The feeling of emptiness is in our soul and it needs to be filled . . . it is impossible for anything visible to the senses, finite, carnal and temporal, to satiate the deep inward longing of an immortal soul.[24]

The soul lacked any real content or definition, it was simply the point of contact between the individual and God and as such it existed as the organ of prophecy. Within the framework of Roberts's theology, prophetic office could only be achieved if the earthly ego was destroyed in favour of the divine soul. This transformation could be accomplished through familiar means. Like previous evangelical authors, Roberts identified the ego with personal history, holding up the moment of conversion as the gateway to both the death of the self and the divine life. It was a model rooted in the theology of the crucifixion. As Roberts explained in one of his later writings:

> The Cross is the power of God, the power of God even to deliver us from self. It works death to the life of the self. . . . Face the Cross, and you will trample on sin, self, and all the powers of darkness. But before we realize this conquest we must do what God did. He gave his all to the Cross. We too, must yield all, that is give up your will to God.[25]

Roberts thus identified the moment of conversion with the achievement of prophecy. It was in the casting off of the old self, that one finally surrendered one's agency to God. For the revivalist, the gift of prophecy was not simply bestowed from above, rather it had to be prepared for from below, through the continual destruction of the carnal self. The struggle involved in this kind of inner preparation was vividly described by Roberts in a letter to the Tylorstown minister, D.M. Phillips:

> What a commotion there is in the tents! My soul is a kind of tabernacle, and self dwelling in innumerable tents around it, and what takes place is the slaughtering of the troublesome, howling, thankless rebellious inhabitants, and so on. . . . I see today that 'self' has its houses, palaces and dens. But how cunning this can be in his den! But away, after him! Behold he fleeth into his cave! Here cometh the divine searchlight on its strong wings. Satanic, Ha! Ha! Ha! Lo, self is made a corpse by the pointed arrow.[26]

Although self could be made a corpse if one followed the four articles of faith, selfhood would always return when the individual started to relax or take pride in their achievements. This point was brought out by Evan Roberts during a discussion with students at the Theological College, Bala: 'Do not think you will be entirely rid of sin in this life even after the baptism of the Spirit. Self will persist; you can never shake hands with self and bid it goodbye.'[27] Because of this risk, Evan Roberts urged a form of perpetual vigilance, in which one's actions and desires were continually scrutinized for signs of self. In a letter to his college friend Sidney Evans, Roberts explained how this continual process of inner scrutiny had allowed him to maintain his prophetic voice during a revival service:

> . . . Like Moses, may you be allowed . . . to speak the Words of God. The Evil One often tempts me to speak my own words: but, Praise Him! the Holy Spirit through His wisdom overcomes me, overcomes the world, and the Devil, in all his wiles: and so He gives me words and ideas to answer to the need of the crowd. . . .
> . . . Another way he has, is to try to get me to push myself to the front. But! Oh! that would be a curse to me, would spoil the work and rob God of glory. Really is it not important to keep ourselves in the background? I remember how in a meeting a voice said to me, Cry out the word, 'Judgement. Judgement!!' But, Praise be to the Spirit, I was prevented from doing so, else 'Mr Self' would have manifested himself at once.[28]

Such acts of scrutiny contributed towards Roberts's fourth article of faith, the practice of obedience. In his sermons, the evangelist had repeatedly stressed the need for 'total and implicit obedience to the Holy Spirit. . . . You must do anything and everything; anywhere and everywhere.'[29] As Foucault has noted, such advice provides a perfect strategy for self-transformation, since it removed the individual's autonomy and surrendered his body to an external agency.[30] It created a state similar to that of prophecy, in so far as it was the law or narrative of another which ran through the body and guided future action. As Foucault said, the practice of obedience leads to a situation in which, 'you will have become the *logos* or the *logos* will have become you'.[31] Evan Roberts had apparently achieved this state, as he noted in his diary: 'I carry not the Gospel, the Gospel carries me.'[32]

These various strategies for rendering the agent passive and prophetic were also aided by the kind of predictive or divinatory visions discussed earlier. On the level of personal experience, the mystical vision could be seen as indication of the prophet's submission to the external. As the Jesuit historiographer Michel de Certeau has argued, the religious vision reverses the priority of sight. Whereas normal vision (the gaze) demonstrates our dominance over the other (since it leads to the others objectification); the vision always escapes objectification and instead impresses its own meaning upon us.[33] It shows how the mystic has changed from one who acts upon others to one who is acted upon. Likewise, the more general divinations of the Revival's success could also be seen as reinforcing this idea of the bankruptcy of human agency. In their very Calvinist assertion that God's plan had already been laid out, they showed that there was nothing man could do to change his fate. He remained a passive instrument in the hands of the God, freed from the motivating forces of carnal desire and personal history.

As noted before, these techniques which encouraged the surrender of personal will and agency to the external command of the divine could have deeply political repercussions. Cutting through conventional notions of authorship, identity and responsibility they created a situation in which the prophet gained authority, yet remained immune from blame or criticism for their inspired words or actions.

Although Roberts himself vehemently denied that he had any special place within God's plan of the revival, his own life soon took up the political forms associated with the prophetic office. His delegation of his speech and will to the command of the divine rendered him a deeply unaccountable figure. Such unaccountability was evident in his conversations, dialogues which were often reprinted verbatim in the daily papers. The following exchange appeared in the *Western Mail*, concerning Roberts's refusal to attend a mission meeting in Cardiff:

Mr Jones asked the revivalist if he was coming to Cardiff on the morrow.

'No' replied Evan Roberts with considerable emphasis.

'Are you still too unwell to come?' questioned Mr Jones.

'No it isn't that' returned Mr Roberts, 'I am feeling quite well and strong.'

Obvious surprise was depicted on Mr Jones's face, and he again asked the revivalist why he was not coming to Cardiff.

'The Cardiff meetings have been on my mind for five days,' replied Mr Roberts, 'I have prayed constantly for guidance, and the answer of the Spirit is thou art not to go.'

Mr Jones observed that there was a close connection between the body and the mind. Was Mr Roberts sure that he did not mistake bodily weakness or reluctance for the answer of the Spirit?

'I am certain that the Spirit has spoken to me,' returned the revivalist still speaking in Welsh 'as I am of my own existence.'

Mr Jones wanted to know if Mr Roberts would come in the future.

'Yes, as soon as I get permission,' was the reply, 'and not before.'
'What about the girls? Shall they come?' asked Mr Jones.
'No!' with emphasis, 'they shall not, I have asked the Spirit about that too.'
. . . In the course of a conversation with a local ministerial friend, Mr Roberts declared that the voice said: 'If you go I shall not go with you' and on its being pointed out to him that his non-appearance would be a serious disappointment to many in Cardiff he said: 'I can't help it. I'm not going with this voice ringing in my ears.' He was then asked 'What about the crowds that will be expecting you' and he replied 'That is it. I want to be kept in the background,' 'Is it that you do not want to go to Cardiff?' 'Oh no, I will go anywhere he leads, but I will not go anywhere without him.'[34]

As the Revival progressed these spirit-led pronouncements became markedly more dramatic. In the February of 1905, the Paraclete ordered Roberts to retire from his mission for one week. Exiled to a bedroom in Neath, the young evangelist maintained a complete silence, simply being waited upon by his mission companion, Annie Davies. At the end of this interlude, which the national press had presented as an episode akin to Christ's forty days in the wilderness, Roberts became convinced of his closer communion with the Holy Spirit. In particular he was inspired by a divine message which had occurred around twenty past five one Thursday evening:

5.21 – Voice: Take thy pen and write: – Lo, I am the Lord, Who hath lifted thee up from the depth. . . . Open thine hand, and I will fill it with power. Open thy mouth, and I will fill it with wisdom. Open thy heart and I will fill it with love. . . . To kings turn thyself and say, 'Bend.' To knights, 'Submit ye.' To the priests, 'Deal out judgement, pity, forgiveness.' Ye islands, seas and kingdoms, give ear unto Me, I am Almighty.[35]

This message, which mimicked the Old Testament prophets in its style and intention, encouraged Roberts to take up a more punitive role in his relationship with both the churches and his audience. During his mission to Liverpool the young revivalist demonstrated a new series of supernatural gifts.[36] Through his deeper communion with God, Roberts had become endowed with a 'telepathic' power, a power which allowed him to scrutinize the inner consciences of his congregation. This newly bestowed ability did little to endear the missioner to his audience. His meetings degenerated into a series of personal confrontations as Roberts denounced laymen and ministers for their private doubts and secret lack of faith. These confrontations reached their height at the beginning of April, 1905. After a bitter confrontation with a vaudeville hypnotist and a Liverpool minister whose paralysis he had predicted, Roberts's prophetic critique began to strain public tolerance and credulity. This strain reached breaking-point when the young evangelist denounced the Free Church of Wales, claiming that the organization had fallen from the Rock, and thus no longer stood with Christ.[37] A few weeks later, Roberts, encouraged by friends and ministers, retired from his mission. The newspapers attributed this withdrawal to the onset of nervous strain.[38]

Had the Welsh revival been limited to Roberts's mission it would easy to write-off the awakening as simply the rise and disgrace of a charismatic preacher whose ideas seemed to rise above his situation. However as we have noted earlier the revival was a mass movement, and it was in the widespread imitation of Roberts's rhetoric and action that the awakening achieved its political effect. Throughout the cities, towns and villages that the movement touched, those who had been disenfranchised within their communities – women, youths and children – were able to cast off their restrictive and debilitating identities and assume instead an authoritative position based upon their new-found status as prophets acting under the command of God.

The most obvious examples of this reversal of authority brought about by the descent of the Holy Spirit occurred within the chapels themselves. Ministers and deacons, traditionally seen as figures of power and authority within the villages, were prevented from preaching or taking services. A familiar prayer compared the priests to rusty locomotives which needed shunting to the sidelines.[39] In the Rhondda, one congregation prayed that their minister would be prevented from ever speaking again, whilst an American evangelist declared that God, 'had told the ministers to stand on one side and let Him have a try'.[40] In the absence of ministerial control the meetings followed a Pentecostal pattern with members of the congregation singing, preaching or just interrupting as the Spirit led them. As the English spiritualist and social reformer, W. T. Stead reported:

> The most extraordinary thing about the meetings which I attended was the extent to which they were absolutely without any human direction or leadership. 'We must obey the Spirit,' is the watchword of Evan Roberts . . . it is go-as-you-please for two hours or more. . . . People pray and sing, give testimony; exhort as the spirit moves them. As a study in the psychology of crowds I have seen nothing like it.[41]

Within this new arrangement women quickly came to the forefront, taking over religious services and occasionally becoming leaders in their own communities.[42] This phenomena was widely commented upon by pressmen, many of whom saw the revival as part of the general historical process of female emancipation. Thus John Gibson, the pro-suffrage editor of the *Cambrian News*, employed a psychodynamic model to explain the revival and critique the establishment: 'Nothing', he argued, 'is more certain than that the Revival is the outcome of a general and widespread sense of religious repression exercised by organized religion which excludes women from all activity in the Churches.'[43] Likewise, the similarly sympathetic William Stead noted how, 'in the present Revival, women are everywhere to the fore, singing, testifying, praying and preaching.' He went on to hope that 'as the Revival of 1859 led to the enfranchisement of the male householder, the present Revival may be crowned by the recognition by the State of the full citizenship of women'.[44]

The most famous woman to rise to prominence in the Revival, Mary Jones of Egryn, has already been discussed in connection with the Meirionethshire lights. Other more exotic figures have attracted less press attention. In Carmarthenshire, a local housewife named Sarah Jones led a deeply millenarian awakening. Although poor and illiterate, she claimed miraculous powers and visionary gifts. Unlike Roberts, she did not receive her prophecies through the felt presence of the Holy Spirit; rather she claimed that she could fly to Heaven, receiving her instruction direct from Christ. These instructions were relayed by Sarah Jones, usually in a familiar verbal form but sometimes through secret patterns of stigmata which were examined and interpreted by her followers. Convinced of Christ's imminent return, her disciples engaged in a series of psychic battles against a growing demonic horde which they believed had already invaded parliament.[45]

While such events may be extreme, they do give some idea of how women were able to draw upon the logic of the revival in order to take up new and authoritative identities. Depicted within contemporary culture and their own communities as weak and passive, they were uniquely qualified for the prophetic role. Like Deborah in the book of Judges, they became one of the weak things which carried out the will of God.[46] This same logic extended down to the level of children. Like women, they drew upon their previous disenfranchisement to justify new prophetic roles, taking over revival services and interrupting the chief evangelists.[47] This connection to the Holy Spirit allowed them to subvert the traditional framework of parental and community control. The chapel became a forum in which children could safely criticize their parents and work for their conversion. In Kenfig Hill, a boy of eight prayed for the salvation of his father's soul: 'the meeting was electrified. The father sobbing, thanked God that his little son had led him to the Cross.'[48] This would seem to have been a general phenomenon. In Cwmbwrla, a meeting was devoted to recounting tales of children converting parents in Clydach Vale and Pontypridd.[49]

Children organized their own prayer meetings independently of any ministerial supervision. At Pen-y-Wern, a teacher testified that in her school, 'children . . . were filled with the Spirit, and when in school turned from their lessons to sing and pray the moment the backs of the teachers were turned'.[50] At Cefn in Glamorgan, children held clandestine prayer meetings on a nearby mountain-top.[51] J. Vyrynwy Morgan recorded how in Newcastle Emlyn children held a secret meeting in a pig-sty to ask the Spirit's advice (rather than their parents') on visiting a circus. The Spirit refused permission but later allowed them to go on a merry-go-round. 'When asked the reason why they had chosen such a place for their meeting, the answer was that their parents were not likely to look for them in an empty pig-sty, and they did not want the "old-folks" to intrude.'[52]

The idea of spirit guidance undid the responsibility of the child. Roberts's old tutor, Evan Phillips, related how his four-year-old nephew took up this doctrine, refusing to have supper with him since the Spirit had instructed him to visit his grandmother for tea instead.[53] Another child complained to God: 'O Lord, you know that mother is always after me, . . . and I am terribly bored. O Lord, make her understand that she can do nothing against me, since I belong to you.'[54] Those narrative chains of identity which bound the child to his or her family and responsibility were severed through the supernatural presence of Holy Spirit. While these examples may seem whimsical the same logic could have much more violent effects. In Rhosllanerchrugog in North Wales, police were called when revivalists bidden by the spirit picketed a ball held by local army volunteers. In Liverpool one revival march degenerated into a riot as inspired converts attacked passing Catholics.[55]

The widescale assumption of prophecy would thus seem to entail its form of small-scale millenarianism. In its disruption of familiar identities and hierarchies it revealed the contingency of the world and the emptiness of earthly authority. Confronted by the anti-nomianism and possible anarchism implicit within the logic of the revival, the traditional community leaders – the deacons and the ministers – turned to a much older rhetoric in order to both reassert their authority and demonstrate the need for academic expertise. This was the rhetoric of false prophecy.

There had always been a strong scriptural justification for the notion of false prophecy. In the Old Testament, Elijah's contest against the prophets of Baal and Jeremiah's denunciation of Hanniah's divine predictions had raised the idea that prophecy, however sincerely given, could be rooted in delusion. In the book of Ezekiel such delusional predictions were given their clearest definition. His writings rail against those 'foolish prophets of Israel' that 'prophesied out of their own heart' or 'followed their own spirit'.[56]

This form of attack had become prominent again in late nineteenth-century Britain. The dramatic growth of spiritualism – itself a minor prophetic practice –

whereby ordinary individuals became the mouthpieces of dead and departed spirits, had caused alarm in academic and professional circles across Europe and North America. In Germany, the psychologist, Eduard von Hartmann complained that spiritualism had become an epidemic, threatening the bases of justice and society.[57] In Britain a group of scholars and scientists gathered around the philosopher, Henry Sidgwick, had formed the Society for Psychical Research, to investigate the burgeoning number of prophetic claims.[58] In order to diminish the spiritualist threat they posited the existence of a subconscious or unconscious mind as the unacknowledged source of the spirit utterance.

The Society for Psychical Research (SPR) thus devoted itself to the analyses of hundreds of automatic scripts and trance speeches, searching for clues and traces which would demonstrate a connection between the spirit message and the known biography or memory of its recipient. One of their most famous investigations centred upon the possessed domestic servant of the London accountant, Morell Theobald. Messages in English, Hebrew and Raratongan were communicated through the servant, with their authorship being claimed by the Persian poet, Saadi. These inspired productions were soon dismissed, when the SPR investigators discovered that they had appeared in a copy of *Chambers' Magazine*, published some months before.[59] More famously, the Swiss psychologist Théodore Flournoy had obtained an international audience with his investigation into Hélène Smith, a shop girl possessed by a small host of spirits, ranging from Marie Antoinette through a Martian visitor to an Indian princess. Flournoy traced each of these exotic incarnations back onto forgotten aspects of Smith's self, aspects which ranged from childhood fantasies to books on history and science fiction once read in Genevan libraries.[60]

The implication of these investigative operations was clear. They revealed the persistence of the self and its unconscious memory within the many episodes of spirit or divine possession. They showed how prophecy may be rooted, as Ezekiel had warned, within that heart and spirit that the mystic believed they had left behind.

Towards the end of the 1880s the SPR turned its attention to cases of prediction and divination. It collected various reports of prophecies and visions gained in episodes of religious experience and crystal gazing and in 1889 it arranged its first field expedition to investigate stories of second sight amongst the Scottish Highlanders. The conclusion to all these investigations was largely the same.[61] They simply revealed that the future vision was in most cases little more than a fragmentary image of a badly-remembered past.

Ada Goodrich Freer, a practising spiritualist who helped with the SPR's investigation into Highland second sight, carried out her own experiments in crystal gazing.[62] In this study, visions of blood and warnings of the approaching death of friends turned out to be little more than mistaken memories of spilt red paint and newspaper obituaries. Such experiments had a very moral implication.

They emphasized the strength and permanence of that self which prophets and revivalists such as Evan Roberts had tried so hard to destroy. As the German psychical researcher, Max Dessoir, noted:

> they [crystal visions] often supply us with a deep view into the secrets of character, and inculcate with terrible emphasis the truth that nothing is lost in the realms of the soul. . . . Every thought that ever traversed our brain, every emotion that has ever thrilled our heart, every wish that has ever been animated for a fleeting moment in our breast — has all been entered in ineffaceable characters in the day book of our earthly existence. Would that this knowledge could strengthen our feeling of moral responsibility.[63]

The concept of the subconscious, articulated in these SPR investigations, thus undermined the idea of prophecy on two levels. On a very obvious level, it revealed that the source of inspiration lay within the individual's own memory rather than the mind of God. Secondly, and as a corollary to this, it demonstrated that the subversive vision of the future articulated within prophecy, was little more than a fabrication knitted out of desire and a badly remembered past.

For the Welsh clergy, threatened by the mass uptake of inspiration during the revival, this new notion of the subconscious had an immediate rhetorical value. It allowed them to reassert the need for an expert ministry – for a trained pastorate – which could discriminate between the false prophecy of the subconscious and the genuine inspiration of God. Moreover, as we have just noted, this argument had an important secondary effect. In its reconnection of the prophetic utterance with the personal history of the inspired individual, it restored the forensic responsibility of the agent.

This psychological critique was launched in Wales by one of Evan Roberts's fiercest critics, the Revd Peter Price of Dowlais. In a letter published in the *Western Mail*, Price claimed that there were 'two so-called Revivals going on. . . . The one, undoubtedly from above, Divine, Real, intense in its nature, and Cymric in its form . . . [and] another Revival – a sham Revival, a mockery, a blasphemy, a travesty of the real thing. The chief figure in this sham revival is Evan Roberts.'[64] Drawing upon the writings of William James, Price argued that all the supernatural manifestations associated with the revival had their origins in the subconscious. However, whereas he had written off most of Roberts's work as a form of hysterical neurosis, he was willing to recognize a healthier source for the Revival's more temperate results, such as the return to the churches or the conversions of sinners. Price believed that such episodes could be attributed to a divinely guided subconscious, a deeply non-conformist creation supplied by the uplifting and morally certain memories of chapel training and the Sunday schools.

This second part of Price's argument held considerable appeal for ministers and educated commentators on the Revival. Its reference to the subconscious as the hidden source of most of the Revival manifestations allowed them to redescribe the apparently divine and gratuitous events of the awakening, locating them within a human history that reflected their own positions and interests. As the English critic, W.F. Alexander claimed, 'the subconscious acquires great value because it enables us to perceive a thread of continuity which before was invisible'.[65] The clergy used this invisible tread to embroider their own narratives on the origins and sources of prophecy. Those non-conformist ministers who wrote histories of the Revival, such as D.M. Phillips or H.E. Lewis, partly replicated Price's argument. They claimed that the Sunday school lessons of the Welsh child had created 'a stock of buried knowledge and expression', or a 'spiritual and moral reservoir', which resurfaced during the soul's awakening.[66] This explained the inspired and eloquent speeches produced by a number of apparently uneducated people 'in the excitement of the moment and under the contagion of the crowd'.[67] French commentators, such as the Protestant theologian Henri Bois or the psychiatrist Jean Rouges de Fursac pursued an anti-English claim in their analyses. They emphasized phenomena such as the Welsh *hwyl* (an untranslated word that can signify enthusiasm or a particular rhythm of speech) and moments such as Roberts's refusal to speak English when under the influence of the spirit, arguing that these were indications of the awakening's deep racial origins. Within their schema the Revival appeared as the final uprush of a Celtic consciousness which for centuries had been repressed under the yoke of Saxon domination.[68] A different version of this racial model was given by the psychical researcher A.E. Fryer. Fryer believed that the visions of Mrs Jones and Evan Roberts could be explained if one recognized their common Cardiganshire ancestry. The population of this county had been ascribed an Iberian origin by Victorian anthropologists, thus the experiences of the revivalists could be seen as a recapitulation of their Spanish mystical heritage.[69] The similar but more partisan argument was put forward by the Catholic writer 'S.F.S.'. He suggested that the glowing crosses, witnessed by many of the movement's followers, could be seen as the 'revivification of types of consciousness' associated with pre-Reformation worship.[70]

These psychological accounts locate the motivation of the revivalist in a history he or she believed they had escaped. This irony was most obvious in the case of Evan Roberts, whose flight from selfhood was mediated through obedience to the voice of the Spirit. Within the terms of this psychological analysis, this 'voice' became a simple manifestation of his subconscious: a subconscious formed through Roberts's racial and individual history. Thus the psychiatrist Rouges de Fursac, having met Roberts after his seven days' silence in Neath, diagnosed intense automatism and psychic asthenia, brought about through his concentration on the idea of Christianity.[71] Likewise, his compatriot Henri Bois believed that Roberts's conversion had instilled an *idée fixe* of the revival which dominated his subconscious so completely that automatic discharges took place.

Those voices and visions which led him throughout his mission were fragments of forgotten memory, returning to haunt him.[72] Within these accounts the young revivalist, who had tried to sever his relation with the past, was seen as a neurotic figure dumbly playing out the stories of his childhood and his nation.

In conclusion, we can see that the Welsh Revival stood at a point of transition in the understanding of prophecy. Through the rhetoric and perspectives of the new psychology, the meaning of prophecy was reversed. It was no longer seen as a revelation of the future but was instead interpreted as the eruption of a forgotten past. It was an intellectual transformation which brought about a concomitant political change. Prophecy was no longer seen as a divine sign of the intervention of God, rather it was interpreted as a psychological symptom demanding the intervention of pastors and psychiatrists.

Notes

1 For some of the more wistful accounts see R. Ellis, *Living Echoes of the Welsh Revival* (London, The Delyn Press, [1954]); M. Bickerstaff, *Something Wonderful Happened* (Liverpool, Committee for the 1904–5 Revival Memorial Fund, 1954), and the more critical version by E. Evans, *The Welsh Revival of 1904* (Bala, Evangelical Movement of Wales, 1969). For references in the paranormal press see X. Phillips, 'Rolling in the Aisles', *Fortean Times*, 77 (Oct. 1994), 24–8. The one outstanding piece of scholarship on the awakening is only available in Welsh: R. Tudor Jones, *Ffydd ac Argyfwng Cenedl: Cristionogaeth a diwyllant yng Nghymru 1890–1914* (2 vols, Swansea, Ty John Penry, 1981), vol. 2. For shorter theoretically informed pieces see C.R. Williams, 'The Welsh Religious Revival of 1904–5', *British Journal of Sociology*, 13 (1962), 242–59; C.B. Turner, 'Revivals and Popular Religion in Victorian and Edwardian Wales' (unpublished Ph.D. thesis, University of Wales, 1979), ch. 5.

2 The books of D.M. Phillips remain the best sources for Roberts's early life and mission: see D.M. Phillips, *Evan Roberts: The Great Revivalist and his Work* (London, Marshall Bros., 1906); *Evan Roberts a'i waith* (Dolgellau, E.W. Evans, 1912).

3 Typical examples of this genre include J. Penn-Lewis, *The Awakening in Wales: and some of its Hidden Springs* (London, Marshall Bros., 1906); R.B. Jones, *Rent Heavens: The Revival of 1904* (London, Stanley Moulton & Co., 1931). On the role of the Keswick conventions in Victorian Britain see J. Kent, *Holding the Fort* (London, Epworth, 1986); J. C. Pollock, *The Keswick Story: The Authorised History of the Keswick Convention* (London, Hodder & Stoughton, 1964). On the Forward Movement see H. Williams, *The Romance of the Forward Movement* (Denbigh, Gee & Son, [1949]).

4 H.E. Lewis, *With Christ Among the Miners* (London, Hodder & Stoughton, 1906), p. 5. On Elvet ('Elfed') Lewis (1860–1953) see B. Jarvis, 'H. Elvet Lewis', *Bwletin Cymdeithas Emynau Cymru*, 3 (1990–91), 94–107.

5 Jones, *Rent Heavens*, p. 7. For Rhys Bevan Jones see B. Pierce Jones, *The King's Champions* (Newport, B.P. Jones, 1968).

6 Quoted in Lewis, *Miners*, p. 10.

7 Jeremiah 1: 9.

8 Jones, *Ffydd*, vol. 2, p. 131; T. Francis, *Yr Diwygiad a'r Diwygiwr* (Dolgellau, E.W. Evans, 1906), pp. 45–7; J. Harvey, 'Spiritual Emblems: The Visions of the Welsh Revival', *Llafur*, 6 (1993), 75–93.

9 W.T. Stead, *The Revival in the West*, p. 49; W.P. Hicks, *The Life of Evan Roberts* (London, Christian Herald, [1906]), pp. 17–18; H. Bois, *Le Réveil au Pays de Galles* (Toulouse, Société des Publications Morales et Religieuses, 1906), p. 404; *South Wales Daily News* (19/11/1904). It gained a passing mention in *The Lancet*, 2 (26/11/1904), 1514–15.

10 B.G. Evans, 'Merionethshire Mysteries', *Occult Review*, 1 (1905), 113–20, 179–87, 287–96; Bois, *Réveil*, ch. 8; Lewis, *Miners*, pp. 236–9; H.E. Lewis, 'A Mystic of the Revival', *British Weekly* (26/1/1905), p. 424; A.E. Fryer, 'Psychological Aspects', *Proceedings of the Society for Psychical Research*, 19 (1905), 97–100; E.V. Hall, 'Some Aspects of the Welsh Revival', *Annals of Psychical Science*, 1 (1905), 323–30; W.M. Jones, 'Ymweliad a Mrs Jones Egryn', *Cymro* (2/3/1905); K. McClure, 'The Fading Star', *The Unexplained*, 4 (1981), 798–800; T. Francis, *Diwygiad*, pp. 210–13; T. Davis, 'Mary Jones a Diwygiad yn Egryn', National Library of Wales, MS ex 1467.

11 His report was rejected by the *Daily Mail*, but was published in Fryer, 'Psychological Aspects', appendix, part 17.

12 *Y Goleuad* (6/1/1905).

13 Lewis, *Miners*, p. 38; Bois, *Réveil*, p. 18.

14 On the talking baby of Bethesda see the *Western Mail* (21/1/1905); [Anon], 'The Journalist at Large in Psychical Research', *Journal of the Society for Psychical Research*, 12 (1905), 66–7.

15 Joel 2: 28. For Roberts' claim that the revival was the fulfilment of this prophecy see the *South Wales Daily News* (14/11/1904).

16 John 16: 13–14. See Lewis, *Miners*, p. 38.

17 M. Foucault, 'The Subject and Power' in H. Dreyfus and P. Rabinow (eds), *Michel Foucault: Beyond Structuralism and Hermeneutics* (Brighton, Harvester Wheatsheaf, 1981), pp. 208–26; M. de Certeau, 'Discourse Disturbed' in *The Writing of History*, translated by T. Conley (New York, Columbia University Press, 1988).

18 W.F. Alexander, 'Revivalism and Mysticism', *Contemporary Review*, 89 (1906), 350.

19 *Liverpool Echo* (18/1/1905).

20 Foucault defined 'technologies of the self' as those practices 'which permit individuals to effect by their own means or with the help of others a certain number of operations on their bodies and souls, thoughts, conduct, and way of being, so as to transform themselves in order to achieve a certain state of happiness, purity, wisdom, perfection or immortality'.: 'Technologies of the Self' in L.H. Martin, H. Gutman, P. Hutton (eds), *Technologies of the Self* (Amherst, University of Massachusetts Press, 1988), p. 18. For a similar statement see 'About the Beginnings of the Hermeneutics of the Self,' *Political Theory*, 21 (1992), 203.

21 This is from a verbal account given by Roberts to W.T. Stead: *The Revival in the West* (London, Review of Reviews Office, 1905), p. 53; other accounts in Lewis, *Miners*, p. 70; Phillips, *Evan Roberts*, p. 195; Jones, *Rent Heavens*, p. 57; Jones, *Ffydd*, vol. 2, p. 134; L. Oehler, *Die Bewegung in Wales* (Stuttgart, Gundert, 1905), p. 37.

22 Romans 5: 12–14, 7: 7–25; 1 Corinthians 15: 21–3, 45–9. For nineteenth-century commentaries on this passage see W. Sanday and A.C. Headlam, *The Epistle to the Romans* (Edinburgh, T. & T. Clark, 1895, repr. 1911), pp. 131–47; G.B. Stevens, *The Theology of the New Testament* (Edinburgh, T. & T.

Clark, 1901, repr. 1911). For a modern exposition see L. Dumont, 'A Modified View of our Origins: the Christian Beginnings of Modern Individualism' in M. Carrithers, S. Collins, and S. Lukes (eds), *The Category of Person: Anthropology, Philosophy, History* (Cambridge University Press, 1985), pp. 93–123.

23 Written on 1 June 1904; reproduced in Phillips, *Evan Roberts*, p. 465.

24 Phillips, *Evan Roberts*, p. 469.

25 Address given in Bangor 24 April 1906; printed in Phillips, *Evan Roberts*, p. 478.

26 From a personal letter of 9 October 1905 to D.M. Phillips, reproduced in Phillips, *Evan Roberts*, p. 448. Compare the language of the one of the most popular revival hymns, 'R Hwn Sy'n Gyrru Mellt Hedeg': 'Send the arrow of conviction// To these hearts we Pray to Thee// Open wide our self-made prisons// Send the firebrand from the flame' in S.B. Shaw, *The Great Revival in Wales* (Chicago, S.B. Shaw Publishing, 1905), p. 2.

27 Lewis, *Miners*, p. 158; Phillips, *Evan Roberts*, p. 438.

28 Letter dated 27 January 1905, printed in Phillips, *Evan Roberts*, p. 353 (Roberts's emphasis).

29 Sermon at Siloh Chapel, Pentre (4/12/1905), 'Awstin', *Religious Revival in Wales*, no. 1, p. 25. For a clear statement of the doctrine of obedience see E. Roberts, 'A Message to the Church', *Homiletic Review*, 49 (March, 1905), 434–5.

30 Foucault, 'Technologies of the Self', pp. 43–9; 'Hermeneutics of the Self', pp. 215–23.

31 'The Ethic of the Care of the Self as Practice of Freedom' in J. Bernauer (ed.), *The Final Foucault* (Cambridge, Mass., M.I.T. Press, 1988), p. 6.

32 Phillips, *Evan Roberts*, p. 485. Cf. Margam Jones, *The Study of Nature* (Merthyr Tydfil, Joseph & Williams, 1905), pp. 143–4: 'Roberts did not start the Revival, the Revival started Evan Roberts.'

33 M. de Certeau, 'Surin's Melancholy' in *Heterologies*, translated by Brian Massumi (Minneapolis, University of Minnesota Press, 1986), p. 107.

34 'Awstin', *Religious Revival in Wales*, no. 4, p. 5; Bois, *Réveil*, pp. 432–3. The Holy Spirit frequently prevented Roberts from complying with requests. In many services he was forbidden to speak English: R.H. Brewer, 'Collier Revivalist', *Good Words*, 47 (1905), 416; W.G. Hall, 'More about the Revival in Wales', *The Friend*, 45 (1905), 27. The girls mentioned in the passage were Annie and Maggie Davies, the singing evangelists. On John Morgan Jones (1861–1935), Calvinist Minister at Merthyr Tydfil, see *Dictionary of Welsh Biography*, pp. 486–9.

35 'Awstin', *Religious Revival*, pp. 6–7.

36 On the Liverpool mission see G. Hughes, *Evan Robert's Revivalist: The Story of the Liverpool Mission* (Dolgellau, E. W. Evans, 1905); Jones, *Ffydd*, vol. 2, pp. 169–72; Lewis, *Miners*, pt. 3, ch. 2; Oehler, *Bewegung*, ch. 10.

37 'Awstin', *Religious Revival*, no. 6, p. 23; Hughes, *Liverpool Mission*, pp. 72–3.

38 See the interviews with W.O. Jones and Caradoc Rees in Hughes, *Liverpool Mission*, pp. 74–5, and the letter of Daniel R. Hughes, pp. 85–7; H.E. Lewis, 'The Welsh Revival: Mr Evan Roberts', *British Weekly* (23/3/1905), p. 616. More caustic pieces appeared in the *Cambrian News*: 'Revival Delusions' (24/2/1905); 'Revival Manifestations' (3/3/1905).

39 J.V. Morgan, *The Welsh Religious Revival: a retrospect and criticism* (London, Chapman and Hall, 1909), p. 42.

40 *Evening Express* (26/12/1904); *South Wales Daily News* (26/12/1904); 'Awstin', *Religious Revival*, no. 2, p. 6.

41 *Daily Chronicle* (13/12/1904), repr. in W.T. Stead, *The Revival in the West*, pp. 38–9. On William Stead (1849–1912) see *DNB*.

42 For examples of women taking over services see 'Awstin', *Religious Revival*, no. 1, pp. 4, 9, 11, 24; no. 2, pp. 5, 15, 21; no. 3, p. 22; no. 6, p. 17. For statements on the role of women see Lewis, *Miners*, pp. 184–5; Florence Booth, 'Ministry of Women', *South Wales Daily News* (15/12/1904); D. Adams, 'Y Diwygiad – Sut i Ddiogelu ei Ffrwyth', *Y Dysgedydd*, n.s., 29 (1905), 181–2.

43 'The Revival and Organised Religion', *Cambrian News* (3/2/1905); 'Elementary Religion', *Cambrian News* (17/2/1905). On Gibson and his proto-feminist views see W. Gareth Evans, 'Introduction' in Sir J. Gibson, *The Emancipation of Women* (Llandyssul, Gwasg Gomer, 1992).

44 Stead, *Revival*, p. 56.

45 On Sarah Jones see Jones, *Ffydd*, vol. 2, pp. 182–3; D.R. Davies, 'A Social History of Carmarthenshire' (unpublished Ph.D. thesis, University of Wales, 1989), pp. 275–7; *South Wales Daily News* (14/4/1906), p. 6; 'Revival Revived', *South Wales Daily News* (13/4/1906), p. 6. These two articles were reprinted in *Carmarthen Weekly Reporter* (20/4/1906). 'Wonderful or What?', *South Wales Daily News* (16/4/1906), p. 6; 'Carmel Revivalism,' *South Wales Daily News* (17/4/1906), p. 5; 'Revival Pandemonium', *South Wales Daily News* (18/4/1906), p. 6; 'Carmel Revivalist', *South Wales Daily News* (23/4/1906), p. 6; 'Letter from W.D. Griffith', *South Wales Daily News* (21/4/1906), p. 6; 'The New Revival', *South Wales Daily News* (25/4/1906), p. 6; 'The New Revival', *South Wales Daily News* (26/4/1906), p. 6.

46 For a contemporary exposition see Mrs Stephen Menzies, *The Christian Woman* (London, Samuel Bagster & Sons, 1905) ch. 1. For a parallel discussion on this subversion of the notion of female passivity by Victorian spiritualists see A. Owen, *The Darkened Room: Women, Power and Spiritualism in Late Victorian England* (London, Virago, 1990).

47 'Awstin', *Religious Revival*, no. 2, pp. 1, 11, 15; no. 3, pp. 6, 24, 26, 29. Morgan, *Religious Revival*, describes 'young girls, naturally timid and shy, who had not previously spoken or prayed in public, moved by the Holy Spirit's action, voluntarily went forward, some to read a chapter, others to pray' (p. 165). For examples of Roberts being interrupted see *Evening Express* (29/12/1904), p. 2; 'Awstin', *Religious Revival*, no. 3, p. 22.

48 *Evening Standard* (9/1/1905); G.T.B. Davies, 'Evan Roberts and the Welsh Revival', *The Independent*, 59 (1905), 441–2.

49 'Awstin', *Religious Revival*, no. 3, p. 6.

50 'Awstin', *Religious Revival*, no. 3, p. 26.

51 'Awstin', *Religious Revival*, no. 3, p. 28.

52 Morgan, *Religious Revival*, p. 170. On John Vyrnwy Morgan see E.G. Millward, 'John Vyrnwy Morgan', *Cylchgrawn Llyfrgell Genedlaethol Cymru*, 12 (1961–2), 198–200.

53 J.J. Morgan, *Cofiant Evan Phillips* (Liverpool, Hugh Evans, 1930), p. 334. Phillips posited a more mundane motivation, noting the grandmother's excellent cakes.

54 Bois, *Réveil*, p. 316.

55 On Rhos see R. Jones, 'The Revival in Rhos', *British Weekly* (5/1/1905), p. 352; 'The Revival', *Cambrian News* (20/1/1905). On Liverpool: *Liverpool Echo* (6/2/1905); C. Fort, *Lo!* [1931], reprinted in T. Thayer (ed.), *The Books of Charles Fort* (New York, Henry Holt & Co., 1941), p. 665.

56 Ezekiel 13: 2, 3. Cf. Jeremiah 23: 16, 26. For a contemporary commentary on this passage, see

G. Cunningham Joyce, *The Inspiration of Prophecy: An Essay in the Psychology of Revelation* (Oxford University Press, 1910), pp. 124–32.

57 'Spiritism' translated, C.C. Massey, *Light* (22/8/1885).

58 On the foundation of the Society for Psychical Research see J. Cerullo, *The Secularisation of the Soul* (Philadelphia, ISHI, 1982); J. Oppenheim, *The Other World: Spiritualism and Psychical Research in England, 1850–1914* (Cambridge University Press, 1985). On the invention of the subconscious as a strategy for policing prophecy see R. Hayward, 'Popular Mysticism and the Origins of the New Psychology, 1880–1910' (unpublished Ph.D. thesis, University of Lancaster, 1995), ch. 2; Simon Schaffer, 'Cleaning Up', *London Review of Books* (1–14/7/1982), 10.

59 F. Podmore, *Modern Spiritualism* (2 vols, London, Methuen, 1902), vol. 2, pp. 91–4.

60 Flournoy, *From India to the Planet Mars*, ed. S. Shamdasani (Princeton University Press, 1899, repr. 1994). For Flournoy see Édouard Claprède, 'Théodore Flournoy, sa Vie et son Oeuvre, 1854–1920', *Archives de Psychologie*, 18 (1921), 1–125.

61 On the Highlands investigation see J. Campbell and T. Hall, *Strange Things: The Story of Fr. Allan McDonald, Ada Goodrich Freer, and the Society for Psychical Researches into Highland Second Sight* (London, Routledge and Kegan Paul, 1968).

62 Miss X, 'On the Apparent Sources of Subliminal Messages', *Proceedings of the Society for Psychical Research*, 5 (1888–9), 486–501; 'Experiments in Crystal Vision', *Proceedings of the Society for Psychical Research*, 11 (1895), 114–44.

63 'The Magic Mirror', *The Monist*, 1 (1890–1), 116–17.

64 P. Price, 'Double Revival in Wales/Vigorous Attack on Evan Roberts', reprinted in *The Rev. Peter Price and Evan Roberts* (Cardiff, Western Mail, 1905), pp. 1–2. On Peter Price (1864–1940) see D.J. Roberts, *Cofiant Peter Price* (Swansea, John Penry, 1970).

65 W.F. Alexander, 'Revivalism', p. 359. C.F. Rogers, 'The Psychology of Revivalism', *The Interpreter*, 55 (1905), 511–17.

66 Lewis, *Miners*, p. 16; Phillips, *Evan Roberts*, p. vi; 'S.F.S[mith],' 'The Welsh Revival,' *The Month*, 105 (May 1905), 453. This common strategy of tracing xenoglossic and glossolalic productions back to childhood experience is discussed in M. Yaguello, *Lunatic Lovers of Language* (London, Athlone, 1991), p. 28.

67 On this phenomena see Fryer, 'Psychological Aspects', p. 91; J. Morris Jones, 'The Welsh Revival', *British Weekly* (2/2/1905), p. 448; E. Lombard, 'Essai d'une classification des phénomènes de glossolalie', *Archives de Psychologie*, 7 (1907), 6–8, 45; Bois, *Réveil*, pp. 230–2. Bois drew an explicit comparison with the speeches produced by Flournoy's patient, Hélène Smith.

68 J. Rouges de Fursac, *Un Mouvement Mystique Contemporain* (Paris, Félix Alcan, 1907), ch. 8; Bois, *Réveil*, pp. 202–10. For Bois, Professor of Theology at Montauban, see *Who's Who* (1918), p. 235. For a brief introduction to Rouges de Fursac, Superintendant at Seines Asylum, see B. Hall, 'Two French Contributions to the History of the Revival' in S. Evans and G. Roberts (eds), *Cyfrol Goffa Diwygiad 1904–5* (Caernarfon, Llyfrfa'r Methodistaidd Calfinaidd, 1954).

69 Fryer, 'Psychological Aspects', p. 102 (Mrs Jones); p. 86 (Evan Roberts). See also the contributions of Fryer and S. Oliver to an SPR debate on the subject: 'Private Meeting for Members and Associates,' *Journal of the Society for Psychical Research*, 12 (July 1905), 107–8.

70 [S.F.S.], 'Welsh Revival', p. 465. 'S.F.S.' was probably Sidney Fenn Smith (1843–1921), one-

time editor of *The Month* and Professor of Theology at St Beuno's College: *Who Was Who*, vol. 4 (1921–30).

71 Rouges de Fursac, *Mouvement*, p. 102 – he notes the similarity between Roberts and Flournoy's patient Hélène Smith.

72 Bois, *Réveil*, pp. 408–22; D.M. Phillips devotes twelve chapters of his biography of Evan Roberts to detailing the mental and spiritual influences in the evangelist's childhood, which led to his spiritual awakening.

11

PROVIDENCE, SAVIOUR FIGURES AND WOULD-BE GODS: PROPHECY AND THE FRENCH EXTREME RIGHT

P. Davies

If prophecy is a political grammar which is 'peculiarly flexible and can produce discourse suitable to virtually any context or purpose' and into which 'highly subversive ideas can be inserted',[1] we need look no further than the murky fringes of far-right politics in France to locate a tradition awash with prophecies, prophets and prophetic language. Over two centuries, the extreme 'rights' to which France has given birth have often been characterized by their recourse to mystical language. Thus, far-right discourse has been dominated by talk of 'Providence', 'Saviours' and also would-be 'Gods'. The 'apocalyptical crises' of 1789, 1871 and 1940 in particular have given rise to a whole array of prophetic visions and claims.

In many ways the French extreme right of the last two centuries can be likened to a family, with its own intriguing and highly complex genealogy. This is particularly significant, not least because within this 'family' there is, and always has been, a constant tendency for important political figures to read back over French history and also to honour and uphold previous luminaries. For example, the Ultras in the Restoration period (1814–30) looked to the writings of Joseph de Maistre for their doctrinal inspiration. And, in this century, the top personnel at Vichy were heavily influenced by 150 years of counter-revolutionary thinking, and also by the 'new' nationalist ideas that emerged, around the turn of the century, in the works of Maurice Barrès and Charles Maurras. Within this important far-right tradition, therefore, it is possible to identify a strong prophetic element: an emphasis on the past and on the future, on key works and on important historical indicators.

Across two centuries of fascinating and highly diverse far-right history, it is also possible to identify strong and recurring prophetic attitudes. Thus, in the first half of this study, analysis will centre on two quite consistent and profound far-right positions. First, the idea that 'Regeneration will come', and, second, the related belief that 'Our Divine Saviour has arrived'. Each, to a greater or lesser degree, reflects a prophetic impulse discernible on the extreme right. Thereafter, in the second main section, the focus will shift to the modern-day embodiment of the extreme right, namely the Front National of Jean-Marie Le Pen. With on average 15 per cent of the French vote, this party is not only a key political actor in contemporary France, but also a movement draped in its own type of prophetic discourse. Thus, whether it is Le Pen's self-identification with Joan of Arc as an heroic 'Saviour' figure or the party's use of prophecy as a rhetorical tool – most notably in connection with Islam and homosexuality – the message is that France is in danger and a God-like figure must 'save' her.

Perhaps the most obvious attitude that links the far-right tradition in France to the idea of prophecy is, put simply, the belief that, ultimately and providentially, 'Regeneration *will* come'. For many reasons this is a recognizable attitude, not least because over two centuries the various different types of movement on the extreme right in France have consistently thrived on 'crisis' conditions or what they perceive as such. It has been natural, therefore, for far-right theorists to regularly assert that 'the future', in a certain indefinable sense, 'will be better' and that in national terms 'regeneration will come'. This is particularly the case with Joseph de Maistre, in the late eighteenth century, and to a lesser extent, Charles Maurras at the beginning of this century.

In the history of monarchist, counter-revolutionary thought, de Maistre and Maurras are colossal figures. While de Maistre personified the intellectual counter-attack against the French Revolution – and as such has been viewed by historians as the 'founding father' of right-wing ideas in France – Maurras, a hundred years later, attempted to reformulate the 'monarchist' idea. He fused notions of nationalism and monarchism to create what René Rémond has called a 'unique synthesis'.[2] Curiously, both men wrote their most celebrated works in *fin-de-siècle* climates. In 1796, seven years on from the Fall of the Bastille, de Maistre had put pen to paper to produce *Considerations on France*[3] – a highly emotive analysis of, and retort to, the 'wrongs' and 'sins' of the Revolution. One hundred and three years later Maurras was still vociferously discussing and vehemently opposing the values and fundamental rationale of 1789. His *Dictator and King*[4] was a stinging rebuke to the French Republic, but also a highly articulate blueprint for change and renaissance along monarchist lines.

What both writers had in common, in their respective eras, was their concern for the future. More specifically, both saw the need for – and at times actually delineated or prophesied – 'regeneration'. In the case of de Maistre this future renaissance took a definite shape: counter-revolution and the return of the Bourbon dynasty. Jacques Godechot argues that de Maistre wanted 'a renovated, rejuvenated form of society, based upon theocracy'; he says that for the author of *Considerations*, the 'counter-revolution will be accomplished at the hour willed by God; but it cannot fail to come'.[5] Moreover, when one examines and analyses the 'visionary thought'[6] of de Maistre, it becomes obvious that there is no role for mortals in counter-revolutionary change:

When men form theories about counter-revolution, they too often make the mistake of arguing as if this counter-revolution should and could be only the result of some popular deliberation. *The people are afraid*, it is said; *the people want, the people will never consent, it is not agreeable to the people*, and so on. It is a pity, but the people count for nothing in revolutions, or at least they play a part only as a passive instrument. Perhaps four or five people will give France a king. . . . If the monarchy is restored, the people will no more decree its restoration than they decreed its downfall or the establishment of the revolutionary government[7]

Here, there is not only an élitist, dismissive tone to de Maistre's strictures, but also, in an important sense, a predilection for 'envisaging' or 'foretelling' the future. In particular, there is a strong belief in the power of Providence – what Michel Winock has called de Maistre's 'theological dialectic'[8] and what Paul Beik has termed 'the providential interpretation'.[9] De Maistre argues that 'divine justice' rather than the influence of 'distinguished intellectuals' is the key to understanding history.[10] This faith in 'the lessons that Providence was teaching mankind' – the belief that some kind of all-powerful 'invisible hand' was guiding France and Europe towards 'salvation', and away from the 'evils' of Revolution – is a dominant theme in all of de Maistre's writings.[11] France, he argues, has 'pervert[ed] her vocation . . . it is not surprising that terrible means must be used to set her on her true course again'.[12] John Murray sums up de Maistre's views on this subject as follows: 'The counter-revolution would inevitably come about, "the date alone is doubtful". . . .'[13]

If de Maistre's prophetic overtones are quite obvious – Charlotte Muret claims that de Maistre and his likeminded contemporary Bonald 'have been aptly called the "prophets of the past"' – Maurras's are only slightly less so.[14] Both men, in their different ages, were convinced monarchists, but if the end was identical, the means were different. Maurras, like de Maistre, demands a royalist restoration and quite obviously predicts one too, but in a sense, Maurras assumes rather than prophesies. Looking into the future, Maurras appears to trust in logic rather than Providence. His preamble to *Dictator and King* reads as follows:

The undersigned, being royalist writers, expressing their personal views only, but drawing not only upon the traditions and constitutions of the former monarchy of France . . . affirm that the head of the House of France is in their opinion the dictator which the nation needs as well as being its legitimate king.[15]

In effect, therefore, there is an assumption in Maurrasian writings that a 'dictator-king' figure *will* come and *will* lead France to safety and glory. In near-prophetic tones, Maurras argues: 'France needs the monarchy, if . . . it does not satisfy this need . . . this will be the end of France.'[16] In this respect, therefore, Maurras exhibits a real sense of impending doom: only a king can save France from an apocalyptical fate. Maurras states: 'The royalist constitution is thus the proper, natural and rational constitution of the country at last restored, and the reign of the king is no more than the return to our true order.'[17] The key word here is 'rational'. As Brogan argues, Maurras maintained that politics was propelled by 'certain laws'[18] – and it is certain that one such Maurrasian 'law' was the need for strong monarchical leadership.

If de Maistre and his Ultra friends were 'born' monarchists, whose 'ideas were based on the conviction that a providential order exists', Maurras was of a different breed.[19] He had 'converted' to royalism in the 1890s, and soon after converted the Action Française to royalism too.[20] For Maurras, however, royalism was a convenient but potentially excellent expedient, the best solution to a given problem – and henceforth his brand of belief was labelled 'neo-royalism' to distinguish it from the more principled de Maistre-style variety. 'To sum up', wrote Maurras, 'the state, represented by royal power in all remote and lofty questions of general policy which lie beyond the capacity and the knowledge of individual citizens, will be re-established in its natural and rational prerogatives – namely independence and authority.'[21] Maurras' historical investigations convinced him, therefore, to see the future in clear, rational and logical terms.

Thus, envisaging a post-republican future for France – in de Maistre's case post-First Republic, and in Maurras's situation post-Third Republic – both right-wing intellectuals foresaw serious counter-revolutionary change, with a king, eventually, emerging as a symbol of this transformation. There is also a more general way in which both Maurras and de Maistre foresaw renaissance. Maurras in fact considered the very basics of society and argued that 'liberties' will be returned to 'families', 'towns and villages' and 'important hinterland regions'.[22] 'This,' Maurras states, 'is what the king will do for liberties. He will restore them to the citizens. He will be their guarantor, their defender, their policeman.'[23]

In arguing against the need for a 'Westminster-type parliament'[24] but in favour of 'royal authority . . . at the apex of the whole structure of civil liberties', Maurras is certain that change is needed – and will come.[25] Throughout his works a definite confidence, or arrogance, is evident in his views. One section of *Dictator and King* begins, 'Royalist dictatorship having resolved this crisis . . .'.[26] There is no doubt in his mind that the future for France is assured:

> Whatever critics may say, this hope of a French renaissance is no chimera, for the nation's vitality, if menaced, does not seem to us to be fundamentally impaired, morally, physically and economically. . . . We are royalist because we consider that hereditary monarchy alone is capable of administering the necessary treatment.[27]

Ernst Nolte has gone on to argue that Maurras's demand for a 'soldier-king' and his 'call for a leader' give his doctrine a 'fascist quality'.[28] Nolte also cites

Maurras: 'We lack the man at the helm; we lack him, the man, and that's all.'[29] Here, for Nolte, there is further evidence of Maurras's fascistic, dictatorial tendencies, and for us, there is a further indication that Maurras was, to a significant extent, 'willing' the emergence of a new leader.[30]

The language used by de Maistre in his works is much more emotive and vivid than that utilized by Maurras. There is, for example, talk of 'divine justice',[31] 'vengeance'[32] and 'great crimes' which 'unfortunately demand great punishments'.[33] Beik identifies a 'high prophetic note'[34] within the pages of *Considerations*, and in many ways de Maistre does imply that counter-revolution is inevitable: 'Everything that is laid down must accomplish its destiny: there will be no disobedience until the judgement is fulfilled.'[35]

If in far-right circles it is possible to identify an attitude that predicts or pre-empts 'regeneration' or 'salvation', it is also evident that, at given times too, the dominant, prevailing belief is that 'Our Divine Saviour has arrived'. It is clear moreover that the mentality and temperament of leaders and activists on the extreme right – in all its many guises – is particularly prone to the adoration and adulation of a 'saviour'.

If we are looking for divine political opportunities on the far right of French politics, or those perceived as such by leaders or movements on the extreme right, it would be productive to examine two key years in particular: 1815 and 1940. As W.D. Halls has argued in a different but related context,[36] these watershed dates have much in common. For us, it is sufficient to note that both stand as landmarks in the history of counter-revolution in France. Both dates can be viewed – and have been viewed – as 'beginnings'. Each has been interpreted as a 'dawn', and each in a very general sense has come to be represented by a 'heroic', 'saviour' figure. Charles X, although he acceded to the French throne in 1824, is intrinsically connected with the Restoration 'idea' of 1814–15, and the person of Marshal Pétain is innately associated with the Vichy administration established in 1940.

The significance of these two figures is emphasized by the fact that both, in their different eras, were seen by their supporters and entourage as 'messiah' figures, whose coming, in a very non-specific way, had been much awaited and foreseen, if not actually predicted. As such, the arrival in power of each man was laced in a language high in prophetic and mystical content. In power, both Charles X and Pétain used religion and their own personal vanity to reinforce their authority. And, although both men were to provoke widespread opposition, they did attempt to launch grandiose and highly personal policy 'revolutions' while in power.

It would not be too controversial to assert that the Restoration of the Bourbon dynasty – and key moments in its consolidation (the 1814 Charter, the Second Restoration of 1815 and the accession of Charles X in 1824) – was draped in a highly religious discourse. The message implicit in this discourse was that the 'natural' kings of France had returned and all was again well. Although there had been slight hiccups – in a famous remark on the eve of emigration, the Comte d'Artois (the future Charles X) had said that he and his royalist cohorts 'would be back in three months'[37] – the essence of Restoration rhetoric, post-1814, was proud, confident and self-justifying in tone. The keynote Charter of 1814, for example, began with the words: 'Divine Providence, in bringing us back to our realm after a long absence. . . .'[38] Inherent in such language was the belief that the counter-revolution – as represented, for right-wing forces, by the return of the Bourbons – was inevitable, pre-ordained and divinely inspired. The providential language used by de Maistre and the theocrats had, it was argued, been vindicated.

However, in maintaining that God *had* eventually 'willed' the counter-revolution envisioned by the 'religious prophet'[39] de Maistre, many on the counter-revolutionary right actually ignored the fact that the diplomatic situation in 1814 and the intervention of the Allies[40] were the real stimuli behind the Bourbons' return. Evident still in the early years of the Restoration was thus a naïve, blasé belief that Providence *had* won the day and the counter-revolution, through its own power and prowess, *had* triumphed.[41] The 1814 Charter was particularly 'guilty' in this respect. Ignoring the reality of the revolutionary tumult that had changed France so profoundly in the years following 1789, the document ended with the sentence: 'Given at Paris, in the year of our Lord one thousand eight hundred and fourteen, and of our reign the nineteenth.'[42] Thus, for the Bourbon establishment, the kings had 'never been away'. It was implied that 'salvation' had at last arrived.

It could quite easily be argued that a similar mood was prevalent in 1940. Although Pétain was a highly controversial figurehead for the administration of the Southern Unoccupied Zone, he was also a man whose elevation to power was, in the eyes of some, a mystical occurrence. Some historians argue that Pétain had, in a very practical fashion, been preparing for government throughout the unstable and crisis-ridden 1930s.[43] Agreeing fully with such a verdict, however, would be to underestimate and actually denigrate the very profound manner in which the Marshal 'assumed' power. As James McMillan has stated: 'Philippe Pétain appeared as the country's saviour in its darkest hour, a supreme patriot summoned to assume the burdens of high office at the age of 84'.[44] As this quotation implies, some kind of 'spiritual force' did appear to propel Pétain into power, and thereafter, as Kedward notes, a 'cult' and a 'myth' did surround the aged leader.[45]

For those who located themselves on the extreme right, there was something particularly special and awe-inspiring about Pétain. The case of Charles Maurras is especially poignant. We have already noted how Maurras had spent his whole political career advocating the need for a 'Dictator and King' – a man who would lead republican France to regeneration and renaissance via a monarchical restoration. And for us, it is particularly interesting to note how sharply Maurras's 'prophetic' musings come into focus when Pétain actually arrives in power. For, in 1940, Maurras was in absolutely no doubt that 'the moment' had come. Alexander Werth quotes the words of the writer René Benjamin, who witnessed a deeply significant encounter between Maurras and Pétain:

> He [Maurras] bowed deeply to the guards [at the Hôtel du Parc], respectful as he is of all authority. . . . He was clad in a strange cloak which seemed to have been made of lion skin . . . and on his head he wore a small round hat, of the existence of which he was hardly aware. For Maurras attaches little importance to the things he buys. He bought this hat because laurel wreaths are no longer sold in shops. . . . And then he entered the Marshal's apartments. . . . The moment the Marshal saw Maurras he rose. Maurras leapt forward, put his hand in the Marshal's, bowed with deep reverence, then smiled radiantly. Their eyes met. They were like two flashes of lightning. . . . The light of respect. The flame of admiration. The Marshal was saying to himself: 'Here is the mind that for forty years has been guiding and giving courage to the best men in France,' and Maurras wanted to cry out: 'Saviour, oh magnificent saviour!'[46]

After recounting the brief conversation that, Benjamin claims, the two men thereafter indulged in, Werth quotes Benjamin again: 'Maurras was in the seventh heaven. For thirty years he had been calling for the Sovereign: now he had seen him for a whole evening!'[47]

In 1824 and 1940, therefore, a longed-for 'Saviour' figure had been identified. Accompanying this was an obvious and outrageous vanity – in both Charles X and the Marshal. This self-obsession adds to the impression that the two men were not only perceived as 'divine', 'saviour' figures, but actually perceived themselves as such. Pétain, for example, is notorious for his proud and arrogant personality. Not only did he sign all official decrees in grandiose royalist language – 'Nous, Philippe Pétain, Chef de l'État'[48] – but as if to acknowledge and actually encourage excessive adulation, he became the willing focal point of a new, adapted version of the Lord's Prayer[49] and also a series of flagrantly vain propaganda posters.[50] As Werth has written: 'In . . . all [the] confusion [of 1940] there was Pétain, nearly ninety, incredibly vain and fancying himself the Man of Providence.'[51]

'Providence' was of course a word that had been used consistently by Joseph de Maistre in his late eighteenth-century writings, and a word also that indicated the mystical and, at times, prophetic nature of the counter-revolution. When the Bourbons 'returned' in 1814 and when, ten years later, Charles X ascended the French throne, it was a sign to many on the royalist right of Providence. Roberts quotes the royalist journal *Le Drapeau Blanc*: 'The throne is occupied by an *émigré*, one of those princes who from exile addressed to their faithful servants those calls to which they have responded so nobly. . . .'[52] Not only was the profound significance of the emigration emphasized by the new authorities, but for Charles X and his closest colleagues in government after 1824, there was also a powerful belief in divinity and in particular the 'divine' nature of their rule.

Thus, in the same way that de Maistre in his *Considerations* talked about a 'divine law'[53] propelling history, Villèle, one of Charles's prime ministers, claimed he was 'born to end revolution'.[54] For his part, the new monarch sent out a fundamental message in his 1825 coronation. This ceremony witnessed 'the sight of the king prostrate before the archbishop'[55] and for one historian the whole coronation episode was notable for 'its theatrical and ludicrous echoes of old France, and above all its overwhelmingly religious atmosphere and trappings'.[56] The Reims ceremony implied in essence that the 'Saviour' *had* indeed arrived – and Charles was not a man to argue with destiny.

Despite the domestic opposition unleashed by their very similar accessions to power, both Charles X and Marshal Pétain were able to use their new-found authority to institute very personally inspired 'moral' agendas. Pétain's was the much more overt and rounded, and as such took the name 'National Revolution'.[57] The fact that most practical policy measures in the three main spheres of 'Work', 'Family' and 'Country' were outright failures does not hide the fact that on acquiring the reins of power, the Marshal judged the conditions right to launch what, in his terms, was nothing less than a crusade. This 'crusade' was inspired by God – a new emphasis on Catholic teaching and morality exemplified by anti-abortion and pro-family initiatives – and also by the person of Pétain himself. As such, children in schools were taught to recite pro-Marshal verses, Vichy posters made an example of Pétain's inspiring and unrivalled patriotic credentials, while the man himself lambasted the 'corruption' and 'decadence' of the pre-1940 regime. Essentially, Pétain's 'prophecy' was that France would be re-born under his 'revolution in values' and his paternalistic guidance – a prophecy that remained unfulfilled.

Perhaps more haphazard and less strategically planned was the political and religious 'revolution' personified by Charles X. Only months after coming to the throne he revealed a reactionary programme, and the new king gave the real impression that Providence had both willed his accession and inspired his governmental programme. Thus, in addition to controversially compensating the *émigrés* – the 'desire to heal the last wounds of the Revolution'[58] – he also passed the infamous Sacrilege Law of 1825. Although this law was thoroughly impractical and existed in theory only, its main thrust – that 'the profanation of consecrated vessels and of the consecrated wafers constitutes the crime of sacrilege'[59] – illustrated Charles's desire to create a theocratic state, in which there would be no constraints on the power of the Catholic Church. For the royalist right in general, events like the coronation and the introduction of the

Sacrilege Law proved that Charles X was indeed the 'Divine Saviour' that Providence had always promised. Thiers, writing the day before Louis XVIII died and Charles X became king, confirmed that this feeling existed:

> The fact is everyone is expecting the reign of the priests. On all sides one is told, 'The clerics are in!' The ultras make no attempt to hide their satisfaction. They evince notorious glee all around, and appear to flatter themselves that their long wait is at last ending, and about to give way to enjoyment of all the good things they have been longing for.[60]

Across two centuries there was significant evidence of prophetic discourse on the extreme right of French politics. Together, de Maistre's writings on the counter-revolution and Maurras's musings on the need for a new authoritarian king are clear illustrations of this phenomenon. Furthermore, when Charles X, in 1824, and Marshal Pétain, in 1940, assumed ultimate power, the words, the vanity and the neo-religious mysticism surrounding them left many of their supporters in no doubt that Providence had at last revealed itself.

In the Fifth Republic era, it could be argued that the new embodiment of far-right politics, the Front National of Jean-Marie Le Pen, has also used prophecy in its discourse and in its day-to-day rhetoric. Indeed, the FN is renowned for its unusual but often highly controversial political propaganda, consistently dramatizing political issues. Thus, in this second section we will examine the areas in which Le Pen and his colleagues do emerge as political actors keen to exploit the nature and potential of prophetic discourse. First, it is vital to examine the FN's perspective on their primary political symbol, Joan of Arc. Here Le Pen indulges in grandiose hero-worship, which at times can evolve into a highly distinct brand of prophecy. Another, very different strategy can be identified in the FN's day-to-day political discourse. In this sphere, the FN leader is a widely acknowledged master of language. Not only does he lace his language with emotive and evocative vocabulary, but he also raises the spectre of apocalypse in a variety of forms – and often in spectacular and exaggerated fashion.[61] These scare tactics are particularly evident when Le Pen's focus shifts to two of his favourite topics: immigration and homosexuality. Le Pen lambasts both immigrant and homosexual communities in France and, for differing reasons, he argues that their continued existence amounts to a grave danger to the nation. For Le Pen, the end, it seems, is always nigh.

The most fundamentally prophetic figure for the FN is Joan of Arc. Like many previous leaders, writers and movements on the far right,[62] Le Pen and the FN are eager to exploit the story of Joan of Arc – to read it, and see signs in it for their own political purpose. More poignantly perhaps, the story of Joan introduces an important prophetic element into French history – an element upon which the FN, with its own sense of national destiny, also seeks to trade. Here, prophecy is about the past and the future.

Although it is not necessary to delve into all the details of this celebrated historical tale, it is important to establish the main aspects of the episode. Firstly, it is vital to recognize that Joan, a small peasant girl from Lorraine, was thrust into the political and military world of fifteenth-century French via a series of 'voices from God' which, she claimed, drove her to act on behalf of the Dauphin and expel the English occupiers from France. In truly heroic fashion, Joan *did* fulfil this mission, but was ultimately burnt at the stake by the prevailing authorities. In time, Joan emerged as a martyr and saint.[63]

Even though this simplistic depiction of the Joan of Arc story ignores important historical nuances, and sidesteps many complex dimensions to French and European politics in the fifteenth century, it is still possible to delineate how, and in what manner, Le Pen and his colleagues have analysed the Joan of Arc story for their own benefit. Not only have they been able to exploit the visions and prophecies of Joan – intimating that both Joan and Le Pen have supernatural faculties – but they have also been able to laud and glorify, in a highly abstract and spiritual sense, the saviour-like qualities of the historical Joan. More profoundly, there is also a sense in which the men and women of the FN believe, quite genuinely and quite innocently, in the coming arrival of the eternal Joan as France's twentieth-century saviour. Within FN discourse, the terms Joan and Jean-Marie are often used in a mutually exchangeable fashion.[64] Hence, it is Le Pen who is viewed as the man who could 'save' France, and as a consequence some FN supporters look upon him as some kind of 'proxy' for the teenage saint.

To begin with, however, it is highly illustrative to centre on the figure of Joan. In May 1987, twelve months prior to presidential elections in which Le Pen would be a candidate, the FN leader spoke at his party's special Fête de Jeanne d'Arc.[65] Addressing the teenage saint directly, and at the same time saluting her, Le Pen proclaimed: 'I will meet you here for the national festival next year. Elected President of the Republic, it is to you firstly, symbol and image of *la patrie*, that I will render my main homage.'[66]

In this passage from Le Pen's keynote speech, there are several clues to the true manner in which he and the FN regard Joan. Apart from the significance of the homage – which indicates the party's unadulterated adoration of the girl – and the emphasis on Joan as a symbol of patriotism and nationalism, the way in which Le Pen talks to the historical figure is of profound importance. Le Pen, it could be argued, views Joan as a living person, and a figure who is still exerting a powerful influence on contemporary France. He was not only predicting an election victory for himself in 1988, but also, in a sense, assuming and prophesying that Joan still has a presence in France – five centuries and more after her death.[67]

The belief that the influence of Joan is still at work, and that the saint still has a role to play in modern France, is also clearly evident in a poem written by Pierre Dudan and published in the FN newspaper *RLP Hebdo*. There are several significant lines in the poem:

> Return for us to marvel . . .
> Living flame with a name so sweet . . .
> France needs you . . .
> Deliver us from disarray . . .
> Preserve us always from the invader[68]

In general terms, the message implicit in this poetry is that Joan still has a mission to fulfil. More specifically, the poem implies that Joan of Arc is the figure that the FN adores and reveres most. If this point is clearly obvious from the first two lines quoted above, it can also be discerned from the three other lines that Joan's presence is required to solve a particular contemporary problem. The use of the words 'disarray' and 'invader' suggests that the FN is especially conscious of the immigration issue. Joan is seen as a 'saviour-figure' in this situation, and in blunt terms Dudan almost demands the 'intervention' of the female saint to ease the nation's plight.

To a significant extent leaders and members of the Front National not only yearn for, but actually foresee, her eventual coming. Although FN leaders do not in any way predict the emergence of Joan, they do envisage – and perhaps even fantasize about[69] – a contemporary entrance for their teenage heroine and her message.[70]

It could be argued that this predilection for prophecy – or for 'seeing the future' in a very general way – is extremely unusual in a modern-day political party. It is indeed true that Le Pen has been ridiculed for his 'obsession' and 'hero-worship',[71] but it should also be said that the FN – the third political force in modern-day France and a movement that now consistently attracts the votes of 10 to 15 per cent of the French population – shows no real sign of lessening its attachment or 'homage' to Joan.[72] As such, it is a fascinating area to explore and analyse further.

On the surface, as we have noted, the FN position – if we can call it that – is that Joan will come again to save France. For the party she is a symbol, but also a living reality. Beyond this rhetoric – heartfelt for many FN spokesmen and members[73] – is the belief that Le Pen's destiny is to 'save' France, just like Joan did in the fifteenth century. Le Pen, an incredibly vain man unlikely to reject the most grandiose of comparisons, has consequently expended much energy trying to substantiate this analogy.

The FN leader and his cohorts have been known to 'dress up' as Joan and 'play' at *being* the female icon.[74] On more serious occasions, they have also tried to 'justify' the Le Pen-Joan parallel. In fundamental terms, the FN argument centres on patriotism and on protecting the nation from the 'invader'. On this theme, party supporters hold that Le Pen and Joan of Arc are united: foreigners must be 'expelled' from France. In September 1995 Serge de Beketch – editor of the FNJ newspaper *Agir* – articulated this relationship to me:

She [Joan] gave her life and she was hostile to foreigners – it is just the same today. She wanted to fight against the very physical invader. It is the same principle today – foreigners must respect the 'house' they visit. . . . Joan of Arc incarnates everything that the FN wants for France. When you like the Joan of Arc idea you are a nationalist.[75]

Here, de Beketch is equating the English 'invaders' of the fifteenth century to the immigrant 'invaders' of the late twentieth century. Implicit in Le Pen's speech to his party's annual Fête Jeanne d'Arc in May 1986 was the same general idea:

Joan, your work at the time was political, patriotic and spiritual. You forcefully led the *redressement* of political power; you called the people to stand up to the foreign invader . . . you were at the head of the army, incarnating the popular resistance to foreign occupation and your word of order . . . '*bouter les anglais hors de France*' . . . is one of the phrases which retains immense importance in our history books.[76]

The parallel put forward here by both de Beketch and Le Pen is intriguing and highly significant, but, it would appear, ultimately flawed. FN leaders, and Le Pen in particular, do have a definite penchant for offering historical analogies that are often simplistic and misleading.[77] In this case, no account is taken for the two contrasting historical contexts – five hundred years and more apart – nor any awareness shown of how today's so-called immigrant 'occupation' is totally different, in a variety of ways, from the 'occupation' of the English in the fifteenth century. There is also the view – put forward by ex-Socialist *premier* Michel Rocard, among others – that the concept of 'nation' and 'nationhood' is entirely modern, and that in the fifteenth century Joan of Arc would not have had any national loyalty in the same sense as Le Pen does today.[78]

The FN, however, is happy to pedal the view that Joan's story is important and entirely apposite for modern-day nationalists. This belief was embodied in the FNJ slogan of 1986, '*Le Pen – Jeanne d'Arc – Même Combat*',[79] and also, more recently, by the FN newspaper, *National Hebdo*:

Legitimacy . . . [the] independence of France, the identity and security of all French people, the unity of national forces, vigorous action against the enemy. Faith in the future. Such were her [Joan's] principles and objectives. They are the same as ours nearly six centuries later.[80]

If FN supporters are prone to compare the aims and motivations of Le Pen, their leader, and Joan, the teenage saint, they also draw parallels between the two figures' personal backgrounds. Thus, while an array of glossy FN publications glorify the humble family origins of Le Pen[81] – and depict his lowly Breton roots in an idyllic manner[82] – the party likewise emphasizes Joan's modest upbringing. At the 1990 Fête de Jeanne d'Arc, Le Pen exemplified this strategy:

> Six centuries ago, Joan lived as a simple shepherdess in her village of Domrémy, motivated by voices from the sky. She went to meet the Dauphin to expel the English from France. And now today it is the FN that pursues the mission that was Joan's. . . . We are inspired by her example. . . .[83]

Implicit in this passage of *Lepéniste* rhetoric, as in many others on the subject of Joan, is the idea of purity. In Le Pen's opinion, not only did Joan fight in her era for a pure, unoccupied country – devoid of an English presence – but on account of her obscure origins, her sacrifice and her religious convictions, she also stands as the personification of human purity.[84] While the FN leader is naturally reluctant to use words such as pure to describe his controversial career, or his vision of France, it is clear from reading between the lines of Le Pen discourse that he does look back on his military and political career as a laudable example of service and sacrifice.[85] Much more significantly, he is always eager to use the slogan '*France aux Français*' (or variants on this theme) to clarify what for him is the ultimate political goal.[86]

In his 1995 interview de Beketch asserted that 'Joan of Arc is the symbol of the little person who has done everything for his or her country'.[87] Le Pen argues that he too is the 'small man', from humble surroundings, who has done everything for France. In an overtly populist manner, Le Pen therefore attempts to highlight the similarities that in his opinion link Joan and himself – so much so in fact that it is now quite commonplace to see pictures of Le Pen juxtaposed with images of Joan. Whether or not we locate tactics such as these within the orbit of marketing or propaganda, they do take their place as part of a well thought-out political strategy. It has been written that:

> Many commentators have . . . made great play of the bonds that link Le Pen and his fifteenth-century idol: one, for example, compared Joan, the young shepherdess who became commander-in-chief, to Le Pen, the son of a fisherman who became 'the admiral of the extreme right'; the somewhat contrived argument goes on to claim that whereas Joan heard 'voices', Le Pen has had defined 'visions'![88]

Here again – even as Le Pen is being gently ridiculed – we see that the FN leader, attempting to claim a mantle that his vanity naturally covets, has actually become renowned for his 'visions' or 'prophecies'! It is highly significant, as regards the idea of prophecy generally, that in the 1980s and 1990s any public figure indulging in anything close to prophecy or foretelling the future is regarded with suspicion.

It is equally the case that any contemporary politician attempting to glorify the work and mission of an age-old historical figure – as Le Pen attempts to do with Joan of Arc – is left open to criticism. This is manifestly the case with the FN leader and his imaginative efforts to 'use' Joan. It is true, for example, that Rocard has voiced his opposition to the way in which Joan 'has been recruited too often to the service of causes which could not be hers'.[89] Likewise, the author Marina Warner has argued that Le Pen has tried to 'pervert' the true meaning and message of Joan's story.[90] As if to synthesize these two important 'attacks' on FN thinking, *Le Matin* in 1984 poured scorn on the party's 'manipulation' of history. It referred, sarcastically, to the *'admirables persévérants et courageux de la cause nationale'* whom the FN seemed to pluck out of French history in an attempt to illustrate and somehow 'legitimize' its 'patriotic', 'nationalistic' and often 'exclusionist' ideals.[91] It should be noted in passing that twenty-four years after its formation, in 1996, the FN was still making efforts to co-opt the 'services' of important French historical figures. As the French nation celebrated the 800th anniversary of the death of Clovis, Le Pen's party was making an extraordinary effort to 'capture' the old king's memory![92]

If the FN is happy to glorify the memory and mission of historical figures like Joan of Arc – and also Clovis – it would also be accurate to say that it is highly sensitive to the criticism and ridicule that this tactic often provokes. Indeed, as recently as May 1996, the FN newspaper *National Hebdo* confronted the issue head on. Juxtaposed with a 1917 image of Joan was the big bold headline '*A QUI APPARTIENT JEANNE D'ARC?*' (TO WHOM DOES JOAN OF ARC BELONG?) Attached to the image and the headline was a typically combative FN-style tirade:

> *A qui appartient Jeanne d'Arc?* To France and to history, reply people of common sense who wish to avoid all polemics. But numerous voices within the political establishment periodically accuse Jean-Marie Le Pen of wanting to appropriate her. And of deforming her image for partisan ends . . . far from appropriating her fraudulently, *les nationaux* celebrate all important national figures quite naturally. . . .[93]

While Le Pen and his colleagues do not claim to have a monopoly over Joan of Arc, and invite others to join them in their peculiar historical and prophetic cult, they remain, as a political party, alone in the wish to glorify Joan. In his 1990 speech, the FN leader demanded: 'How can one be a partisan of Joan while at the same time serving the interest of foreigners in France?'[94] The obvious implication of this remark is that Le Pen sees the other political parties – the PS, PCF, RPR and UDF – as fundamentally 'anti-national'[95] in their doctrinal outlook; hence his view that only the FN can legitimately claim Joan's political inheritance.

It is not only on the issue of Joan of Arc that the FN talks in prophetic terms. If we focus on Le Pen's rhetoric further, we can detect a definite strategy: essentially, the use of prophecy as a tool or technique designed to exaggerate and scare, and ultimately, to bring French people round to his way of thinking. On two important social and political topics – immigration and homosexuality – Le Pen is powerful and potent in his use of prophecy as a rhetorical device.

First, on the issue with which the FN is most intimately associated – immigration – the FN leader is dramatic and apocalyptic in his language and intentions. Much has been written by FN authors on the subject of immigration,[96] and much too has been written on the FN–immigration relationship by political scientists.[97] The fact is, however, that Le Pen's fundamental perspective on the highly contentious and controversial issue of immigration remains simple. It can be summarized as follows: 'France is in danger!' This judgement lies at the bottom of every *Lepéniste* utterance on the immigration topic. Moreover, this is so much the case that, at times, the discourse of Le Pen and his FN colleagues has evolved into what could be termed the scare tactics of prophecy.

Take, for example, one extremely important FN tactic. As a party it is particularly sensitive to political developments in the Middle East and the Maghrèb – from where most of France's current immigrant population originates – and in its various newspapers and magazines it has become particularly adept at using provocative stories from the Muslim world to good domestic political effect, and to heighten fears about the future of France. As such, the FN has seized upon several highly significant statements made by Islamic leaders in recent years. It has, for example, exploited words of Hizbollah leader, Hussein Moussawi, which were uttered in 1986. An FN propaganda poster now highlights his 'prediction' that: 'In twenty years it is certain that France will be an Islamic Republic.'[98] In a similar way, the FN writer Max Cabantous has quoted Lebanese Shi'ite leader, Sheikh Mohammed Hussein Fadlallah: 'We are planning to establish an Islamic Republic in France where we have four million Muslims. . . . I demand an Islamic Republic not only in Lebanon, but all over the world.'[99] On the surface, therefore, such statements contain significant predictions. They warn of a calamitous future for France, and as such, they can be used by the FN to help depict, or prophesy, an impending apocalypse. Le Pen argues that only an FN government could stop this scenario becoming reality.

Eric Iorio, a party official, also reflects the FN's fundamental fear of the future. In an interview in 1991, he raised the spectre of a nation losing its identity. He said:

France is a product of its history and its past, but France is changing – there are more immigrants, Muslims and mosques. In short, it is not the same France as before. Of fifty million people half will soon be Catholics and half

Muslims, with possibly fifty per cent immigrants. Yes, you can still call it France, but it is another France.[100]

In exaggerating the situation of France in the 1990s, Iorio is not only predicting a traumatic future for his country, but also seeking to alarm and intimidate his wider audience.

It is clear also that FN rhetoric on the recent *foulard* and mosque-building controversies has been particularly significant.[101] Even as recently as June 1996, the party's deputy leader Bruno Mégret was responding to the 'threat' of more mosque developments by proclaiming: 'France is not a "land of Islam". . . . In only a few years Islam has become the second religion practised on French soil. This is an incredible evolution given the constant determination of our ancestors. . . .'[102] This open hostility to Islam and this only partially concealed sense of impending doom is a constant undercurrent to FN discourse. The same attitude is also evident in the party's historical analyses. Here, the prevailing view is that Islam and Christianity are doomed to 'endless conflict'.[103] As FN writer Jean-Yves Le Gallou has written: 'It is wise to learn the lessons of history . . . no pacific coexistence is possible between Muslim and Christian worlds.'[104]

If in the FN view conflict between civilizations is inevitable, if not actually predictable, it is clear also that 'apocalypse' awaits in another sphere. On the moral plane, the FN proffers the view that France is 'suffering' from *SIDA* (AIDS). In a particularly vindictive party poster, four main symptoms of *SIDA* are emphasized. Whereas the '*S*' on the poster stands for '*Socialisme*', the '*I*' naturally indicates '*Immigration*'.[105] Two important points arise out of this propaganda tactic. First, the use of AIDS as a metaphor for French decline implies the incurability of the disease.[106] Second, AIDS and immigration are linked – immigrants are held responsible for bringing the killer virus into France. In consequence, the party would deal severely with all carriers of the virus if it was ever in a position to pass governmental legislation.[107]

The FN's taste for apocalyptic rhetoric is also evident in adjacent areas of its discourse. As a party that sees itself as highly traditional and extremely moralistic, the FN has become passionately opinionated on the ethics involved in family and population-related issues. In 1984, for example, as part of a typically simplistic and provocative tirade, the FN leader argued, and at the same time prophesied, that homosexuality, on account of its implications for national demography, would usher in 'the end of the world'.[108]

It would appear that the aim of this prediction-cum-prophecy was to emphasize the virtues inherent in the FN's pro-family, pro-*nataliste* stance and also to reinforce the idea of a 'pure' and 'exclusive' France profoundly sensitive to groups of people who are deemed 'foreign' or 'impure' by the party leadership. In this sense, homosexuality is viewed by Le Pen as 'a biological and social anomaly . . . that . . . should not occupy the higher moral ground, nor seek converts'.[109] The fact that, in the FN's view, homosexuals are more liable than heterosexuals to spread the AIDS virus is an added reason why the party mistrusts and demonizes the gay community in France.[110]

We have, therefore, examined at least two highly distinct forms of prophecy on the French extreme right. With de Maistre and Maurras, we see two men 'waiting' for change, and at times predicting and prophesying movement towards the counter-revolutionary ideal. Further, in the persons of Charles X and Marshal Pétain, we can detect two leaders who were perceived – by their followers, and by themselves – as providential God-like Saviour figures, born to rescue France *and* to deliver a new destiny for the country. By contrast, in the contemporary context, it is clear that the extreme-right movement of Jean-Marie Le Pen is home to an array of unusual prophetic attitudes. Whether it is party followers begging Joan of Arc to 'return' and 'save' France, or whether it is Le Pen blaming immigrants and homosexuals (among others) for an impending national 'apocalypse', there is obvious recourse to the idea of prophecy – even if, in the modern era, it is utilized in a cynical and twisted form.

It is vital to understand, however, that, as the editors of this volume point out, 'prophecy' can be an extremely loose, vague and complex concept. As we have discerned, it *is* possible to identify prophetic language and attitudes on the French extreme right, but in doing this it appears that as many questions as answers are raised.[111] The French extreme right always belonged to the liminal fringes of French politics and has long expressed ideas directly aimed against the enlightenment and the age of reason. Prophecy and the reading of a national mystical destiny through the life story of 'la pucelle', the virgin warrior, or through an identification with royal figures form the core of these fringe politics.

Notes

1 B. Taithe and T. Thornton, 'The Language of History', introduction to this volume, p. 3.

2 R. Rémond, *The Right-Wing in France* (Philadelphia, University of Philadelphia Press, 1969), pp. 233–53.

3 J. de Maistre, *Considerations on France* reprinted in J. Lively (ed.), *The Works of Joseph de Maistre* (London, George Allen & Unwin, 1965).

4 C. Maurras, *Dictator and King* reprinted in J. McClelland, *The French Right* (London, Jonathan Cape, 1971).

5 J. Godechot, *The Counter-Revolution: Doctrine and Action 1789–1804* (London, Routledge & Kegan Paul, 1972), p. 94.

6 Ibid.

7 De Maistre, *Considerations*, pp. 86–7.

8 M. Winock, *Histoire de l'extrême droite en France* (Paris, Seuil, 1993), p. 32.

9 P. Beik, *The French Revolution Seen from the Right* (Philadelphia, Transactions of the American Philosophical Society, 1956), p. 66.

10 De Maistre, *Considerations*, p. 50.

11 J. Hayward, *After the French Revolution* (London, Harvester Wheatsheaf, 1991), p. 49.

12 De Maistre, *Considerations*, p. 50.

13 J.C. Murray, 'The Political Thought of Joseph de Maistre', *Review of Politics*, (1949), 63–86.

14 C. Muret, *French Royalist Doctrines since the Revolution* (New York, Columbia University Press, 1933), p. 31.

15 Maurras, *Dictator and King*, p. 215.

16 Quoted by E. Nolte, *Three Faces of Fascism* (London, Weidenfeld & Nicolson, 1965), p. 102.

17 Maurras, *Dictator and King*, p. 217.

18 D.W. Brogan, *French Personalities and Problems* (London, Hamish Hamilton, 1946), p. 58.

19 M. Denis, 'Que faire de la Révolution Française?' in J.F. Sirinelli (ed.), *Histoire des droites en France* (Paris, Gallimard, 1992), p. 33.

20 See M. Curtis, *Three Against the Third Republic* (Westport, Greenwood, 1975), p. 74.

21 Maurras, *Dictator and King*, p. 229.

22 Maurras, *Dictator and King*, pp. 218–19.

23 Maurras, *Dictator and King*, p. 220.

24 Maurras, *Dictator and King*, p. 227.

25 Maurras, *Dictator and King*, p. 231.

26 Maurras, *Dictator and King*, p. 216.

27 Maurras, *Dictator and King*, p. 234.

28 Nolte, *Three Faces*, p. 112.

29 Nolte, *Three Faces*.

30 Nolte, *Three Faces*, p. 133.

31 De Maistre, *Considerations*, p. 50.

32 De Maistre, *Considerations*, p. 53.

33 De Maistre, *Considerations*, p. 54.

34 Beik, *The French Revolution*, p. 67.

35 De Maistre, *Considerations*, p. 54.

36 W.D. Halls, 'Church and State: Prelates, Theologians and the Vichy Regime' in F. Tallett and N. Atkin (eds), *Religion, Society and Politics in France 1789* (London, Hambledon, 1991), p. 168.

37 See J. Roberts, *The Counter Revolution 1787–1830* (Basingstoke, Macmillan, 1990), p. 5.

38 See text of the Charter in I. Collins, *Government and Society in France 1814–1848* (London, Edward Arnold, 1970), p. 10.

39 R. Soltau, *French Political Thought in the Nineteenth Century* (London, Benn, 1931), p. 22.

40 See Roberts, *The Counter Revolution*, ch. 5.

41 See N. Hudson in *Ultra-Royalism and the French Restoration* (London, Cambridge University Press, 1936).

42 Collins, *Government and Society*, p. 15.

43 R. Griffiths, *Marshal Pétain* (London, Constable, 1970), p. 239.

44 J.F. McMillan, *Twentieth-century France* (London, Edward Arnold, 1992), p. 135.

45 H.R. Kedward, *Occupied France: Collaboration and Resistance 1940–1944* (Oxford, Basil Blackwell, 1989), p. 19.

46 A. Werth, *France 1940–55* (London, Robert Hale, 1957), p. 66.

47 Ibid.

48 See McMillan, *Twentieth-century France*, p. 135 and also Werth, *France*, p. 52.

49 Werth, *France*, p. 41.

50 In one such poster a picture of Pétain is accompanied by the words: '*Êtes-vous plus français que lui?*' (Are you more French than him?).

51 Werth, *France*, p. 54.

52 Roberts, *The Counter Revolution*, p. 95.

53 De Maistre, *Considerations*, p. 72.

54 Roberts, *The Counter Revolution*, p. 98.

55 A. Jardin and A-J. Tudesq, *Restoration & Reaction 1815–1848* (Cambridge University Press, 1988), p. 64.

56 Roberts, *The Counter Revolution*, p. 99.

57 See R. Paxton, *Vichy France: Old Guard, New Order* (London, Barrie & Jenkins, 1972).

58 Speech by Martignac, Minister of State, in Jan. 1825, quoted in Collins, *Government and Society*, p. 41.

59 The text of the Sacrilege Law is quoted in J. Stewart, *The Restoration Era in France* (Princeton, Van Nostrand, 1968), pp. 153–4.

60 Quoted in Collins, *Government and Society*, p. 40.

61 On the immigration question, for instance, Le Pen uses many words with powerful historical connotations, e.g. 'colonization', 'invasion' and 'occupation' – to name but three.

62 See P. Contamine, 'Jeanne d'Arc dans la mémoire des droites' in Sirinelli, *Histoire*, and also M. Warner, *Joan of Arc: The Image of Female Heroism* (Harmondsworth, Penguin, 1987).

63 For more on the 'history' of Joan see, for example, V. Sackville-West, *Saint Joan of Arc* (Harmondsworth, Penguin, 1955).

64 See *National Hebdo* (11–17/5/1989). This, and many other associated points are explored more thoroughly in P. Davies, 'The Political Symbolism of Joan of Arc in Front National Discourse', *Politics*, 13 (1993), 10–17.

65 The FN's *Fête Jeanne d'Arc* is held each May in Paris. For more information on this see *National Hebdo* (2–10/5/1989).

66 *Le Figaro* (11/5/1987).

67 Le Pen did not win the 1988 Presidential elections, but did perform creditably, gaining 14 per cent of the national vote and finishing in fourth place.

68 *RLP Hebdo* (10–17/2/1984).

69 See the *Independent* (11/5/1988).

70 The FN's Michel Collinot has described Joan as 'the French heroine *par excellence*'. See *National Hebdo* (no. 94, p. 6).

71 *Independent* (11/5/1988).

72 In the most recent national poll – the Presidential election of 1995 – Le Pen scored 15 per cent in the first round.

73 Gabriel de Monalivet, an FN militant in Paris, told me that the FN's glorification of Joan of Arc is a symptom of the nationalist 'revival' in the 1990s.

74 *Independent* (11/5/1988).

75 The interview took place at the FN's Paris headquarters. FNJ stands for Front National Jeunesse – the FN's youth movement.

76 *Le Monde* (13/5/1986).

77 For example, the conflict that, in the FN's view, is ensuing between the French nation and Third World immigrants has been likened to the Crusades.

78 See *Le Monde* (10/5/1990).

79 This FNJ slogan translates as 'Le Pen – Joan of Arc – The Same Battle'.

80 *National Hebdo* (9–15/5/1996).

81 See, for example, the 1995 magazine *Français passionnément! La Vie de Jean-Marie Le Pen en bande dessinée.*

82 A 1991 FN 'New Year's greeting card' depicted Le Pen's home village, la Trinité-sur-Mer, in a beautiful, serene and tranquil light.

83 Le Pen's speech at this event is reprinted in *Le Pen 90* (Saint-Brieuc, Éditions du Présent, 1991), pp. 9–32.

84 The emphasis on Joan's virginity fits well with the imagery of a political party committed to the family and demographic renewal, led by a divorcee, but still ostentiously inspired by Catholicism.

85 See FN brochure *Le Front National C'est Vous!* (*c*. 1991), p. 15.

86 Le Pen's autobiography is entitled *Les Français d'Abord* (Paris, Carrère-Lafon, 1985), as is his new fortnightly newsletter to party members.

87 Interview: Sep. 1995, Paris.

88 See Davies, 'Political Symbolism', 10–17.

89 *Le Monde* (10/5/1990).

90 *Independent* (2/5/1992).

91 *Le Matin* (14/6/1984).

92 See *The Times* (16/4/1996): 'King Clovis is the toast of the far Right'.

93 *National Hebdo* (2–8/5/1996).

94 See *Le Pen 90*, pp.26–7.

95 These parties are lambasted as '*la bande des quatre*' and also castigated by the FN on account of their 'cosmopolitan' political attitudes.

96 Examples include J-P. Stirbois and J-F. Jalkh, *Dossier immigration* (Paris, National Hebdo, 1985), P. Milloz, *Rapport Milloz* (Paris, Front National, 1990), and J-Y. Le Gallou and P. Olivier, *Immigration* (Paris, Éditions Nationales, 1992).

97 See, for instance, S. Mitra, 'The National Front in France – A Single-Issue Movement' in K. von Beyme, *Right-Wing Extremism in Western Europe* (London, Cass, 1988), pp. 47–64.

98 The poster is, significantly, green and white, and also features an 'Eastern', 'Oriental' architectural landscape.

99 M. Cabantous, 'Deux cultures incompatibles', *Identité* (Mar.–Apr. 1990), 9–15.

100 Interview: Jan. 1991, Paris.

101 See the FN press, in particular *National Hebdo*, for Oct.–Nov. 1989.

102 *Les Français d'Abord!* (1ère quinzaine, June 1996), 4.

103 J-Y. Le Gallou, 'La menace est au Sud', *Identité* (Mar.-Apr. 1990), 20–3.

104 Ibid.

105 On this poster, printed *c.* 1990–1, the '*D*' stood for *Délinquance* (Crime) and the '*A*' for *Affairisme* (Corruption).

106 This appears to be a regular far-right tactic. Général Boulanger, in the 1880s, used syphillis as a metaphor for French decline.

107 Proposal no. 30 in the FN pamphlet *Immigration: 50 Mesures Concrètes* states: 'In view of the recent worldwide AIDS epidemic, it would be appropriate to install thorough health controls at all border posts. A negative AIDS test must become obligatory for entry into France, as it is in Russia, the USA, and the countries of South-East Asia.'

108 *Le Figaro* (12/6/1984).

109 *Pour la France: Programme du Front National* (Paris, Albatros, 1985), p. 244.

110 The FN's claims about AIDS – and how the virus is passed on – became highly controversial. See *Le Monde* and *Libération* throughout May 1987.

111 Taithe and Thornton, 'The Language of History', pp. 1–14.

BIBLIOGRAPHICAL ESSAY

B. Taithe and T. Thornton

This bibliographical essay will only cover the texts we found relevant but did not quote from or use in our introduction. We also excluded the texts used by the contributors in their footnotes and we would invite the reader to make use of the relevant section of our index. To organize this essay we have chosen a thematic approach under the following headings: prophecy in literature, history, and social anthropology. We had to be selective and we have in general excluded from our essay prophetic texts and the immense volume of Old Testament biblical scholarship which is mostly concerned with historical debates pre-dating the boundaries of our book. This essay does not claim to be exhaustive but attempts to give a reasonably representative coverage of the volume of published material.

LITERATURE

While the term prophet is often used indiscriminately to refer to mystically inspired authors or even, in an ever-looser meaning of the word, to underline their deep social or political involvement, literary studies have always been interested in prophecy. Prophets speaking the word of God necessarily ask fundamental questions about authorship in any God-dominated systems of belief. For a fairly typical abusive use of the word to enhance the commercial appeal of a conventional biography see M. Geismar, *Mark Twain, an American Prophet* (Boston, Houghton Mifflin Company, 1970); for a more rhetorical use of the word in order to stress the seminal importance of some canonical figures see J. Borie, *Un Siècle Démodé, Prophètes et Réfractaires au XIXᵉ Siècle* (Paris, Payot, 1989), pp. 47–64. G.C.L. LeRoy, *Perplexed Prophets: Six Nineteenth-Century British Authors* (Westport, Greenwood Press, 1971). The reading of a prophetic dimension in literary texts is considerably eased when this dimension is clearly part of the author's inspiration or even the rationale of his/her writing. By extension literary critics have tended to assimilate concerns about time, history and prophecy. Representative of this type of study are works on, in chronological order, *Piers Plowman*, Dante, Spenser, Shakespeare, Milton, Swift, Blake, Wollstonecraft and Shelley. See E. Kaulbach, *Imaginative Prophecy in the B-Text of Piers Plowman*, Piers Plowman Studies VIII (Cambridge, D.S. Brewer, 1993) and T.L. Steinberg, *Piers Plowman and Prophecy: An Approach to the C-Text*, Garland Studies in Medieval Literature 5 (New York and London, Garland Publishing, 1991); R.N. Ferrall, *The D.X.V. Prophecy, Dante and the Sabbatum Fidelium: An Introductory Study in the Allegorical Interpretation of the Divine Comedy* (New York, Haskell House, 1966); K. Borris, *Spenser's Poetics of Prophecy in the Faerie Queen V*, English Literary Studies 52 (Victoria (B.C.), University of Victoria Press, 1990); J.T. Watt, 'The Prophecy of the Hero's Children in English Renaissance Epic: A Study of Heroic Futurity in Spenser, Milton and Relevant Antecedents' (Unpublished Ph.D. thesis, The University of North Carolina at Chapel Hill, 1977), pp. 101–231; A. Oz, *The Yoke of Love: Prophetic Riddles in The Merchant of Venice* (Newark, University of Delaware Press,

1995); S. Marx, 'The Prophet Disarmed: Milton and the Quakers', *Studies in English Literature 1500–1900*, 32 (1) (1992), 111–28. D. Norbrook, 'Levelling Poetry: George Wither and the English Revolution, 1642–1649', *English Literary Renaissance*, 21 (2) (1991), 217–56. A.D. Chalmers, *Jonathan Swift and the Burden of the Future* (Newark, University of Delaware Press, 1995); E.S. Hamblen, *On the Minor Prophecies of William Blake* (New York, Haskell House, 1968); T.A. Hoagwood, *Prophecy and the Philosophy of the Mind: Traditions of Blake and Shelley* (University of Alabama Press, 1985); M.W. Carpenter, 'Sybilline Apocalyptics: Mary Wollstonecraft's *Vindication of the Rights of Woman* and Job's Mother's Womb', *Literature and History*, 12 (2) (1986), 215–28; D.L. Clark (ed.), *Shelley's Prose or The Trumpet of a Prophecy* (London, Fourth Estate, 1966). These texts usually present a much more balanced account of the role of prophecy in the creative process. The notion of authorship which is so central in literary studies does not receive the same attention in history and is often overlooked. As Michel Foucault pointed out in 'What is an Author?', the *corpus* composed of layers of writing and interpretation grows constantly and eventually becomes detached from the biography of the author or even from its persona, the more so when the text has a prophetic dimension.

HISTORY

Historians have also often used the term prophecy in a rhetorical manner, often to emphasize the long-term consequences of the period addressed or to stress the fervour of a movement. See for instance: A.B. Ulam, *In the Name of the People: Prophets and Conspirators in Pre-Revolutionary Russia* (New York, The Viking Press, 1977). Biographers are especially keen partisans of this abusive use which proves that, while sex commands a significant premium in academic sales, 'prophet' and 'prophecy' to signify authority and political importance bring an aura of commercial viability. At another level the life of the subject of biographies could also be invested with the sort of portentous meaning which is usually associated with saints and martyrs. See M. Elliott, *Wolfe Tone: Prophet of Irish Independence* (New Haven, Yale University Press, 1989); I. Deutscher, *The Prophet Unarmed: Trotsky: 1921–1929* and *The Prophet Outcast: Trotsky 1929–1940* (London, New York, Toronto, Oxford University Press, 1959–63); P. Stern, *C.J. Jung: The Haunted Prophet* (New York, G. Braziller, 1976). Historians of ideas, following the latter model, used the prophetic category to label teleological philosophy and programmatic works. A good instance of this can be found in F.E. Manuel, *The Prophets of Paris* (Cambridge, Harvard University Press, 1962). A certain sensitivity to historic change and 'for reading the signs of the times' also induced many authors to attribute the title of 'prophet' to figures such as Lamennais. See A.R. Vidler, *Prophecy and Papacy: a Study of Lamennais, the Church and the Revolution* (London, SCM Press Ltd, 1954), pp. 275–7.

At a more interesting level some historians chose to deal seriously with the political and social implications of prophecies; R. Taylor, *The Political Prophecy in England* (New York, Columbia University Press, 1911) paved the way. For further references on the political historiography of prophecy see Tim Thornton's and Lesley Coote's papers. The influence of the Joachim de Fiore's prophetic work became the centre of particularly lively scholarship, a coverage which justifies its intermittent treatment in this book. Joachimite ideas are nevertheless at the heart of our analysis because they articulated best an hermeneutic theology of history. On Joachim and millenarianism the reader will usefully refer to the following: E. Anitchkof, *Joachim de Fiore et les Milieux Courtois* (Roma, Collezione

Meridionale Editrice, 1931); H. Mottu, *La Manifestation de l'Esprit Selon Joachim de Fiore, Herméneutique et Théologie de l'Histoire d'après le 'Traité sur les Quatres évangiles'* (Neuchâtel, Paris, Delachaux and Niestlé, 1977); Marjorie Reeves's work on Joachim is especially important and, although already abundantly cited in the above essays, is worth mentioning in full: M. Reeves, *The Influence of Prophecy in the Later Middle Age: A Study in Joachimism* (Oxford, Clarendon Press, 1969); M. Reeves and B. Hirsch-Reich, *The Figuræ of Joachim de Fiore* (Oxford, Clarendon Press, 1972); M. Reeves, *Joachim of Fiore and the Prophetic Future* (London, SPCK, 1976); M. Reeves and W. Gould, *Joachim of Fiore and the Myth of the Eternal Evangel in the Nineteenth Century* (Oxford, Clarendon Press, 1987). The latter places Joachimism at the heart of Western modern literature and reinforce the a-temporality and ubiquity of the prophetic language. See A. Williams (ed.), *Prophecy and Millenarianism: Essays in Honour of Marjorie Reeves* (London, Longman, 1980). Also see B. McGinn, *The Calabrian Abbot: Joachim de Fiore in the History of Western Thought* (New York, Macmillan Publishing Company, 1985); D.C. West and S. Zimdars-Swartz, *Joachim of Fiore: A Study in Spiritual Perception and History* (Bloomington, Indiana University Press, 1983); D. West (ed.), *Joachim of Fiore in Christian Thought: Essays on the Influence of the Calabrian Prophet* (2 vols, New Franklin & Co., 1975). On the theory of prophecy in the Middle Ages see J.P. Torrell, *Recherches sur la Théorie de la Prophétie au Moyen Age* (Fribourg, Éditions Universitaires de Fribourg, 1992). For the post-Joachimite use of prophecy see W.S. Reid, 'The Four Monarchies of Daniel in Reformation Historiography', *Historical Reflections*, 8 (1) (1981) 115–35. On prophetic interpretations of Luther see R. Scribner, 'The Reformer as Prophet and Saint: Sixteenth-Century Images of Luther', *History Today*, 33 (1983), 17–21, and 'Incombustible Luther: the Image of the Reformer in Early Modern Germany', *Past and Present*, 110 (1986), 38–68. On post-annexation prophetic and messianic reactions in Portugal see J. van den Besselaar, 'A Profecia Apocaliptica de Pseudo-Metodio', *Luso-Brazilian Review*, 28 (1) (1991), 5–22. F. Gil, 'La Preuve de la Prophétie', *Annales, Économies, Sociétés, Civilisations*, 46 (1) (1991), 25–44. P.C. Almond, 'Henry More and the Apocalypse', *Journal of the History of Ideas*, 54 (2) (1993), 189–200. B. Andersson, 'The German-Swedish Prophetess Eva Margaretha Frlich (d. 1692) and her National Eschatology', *Lutheran Quarterly*, 6 (2) (1992), 175–86.

Other less important prophets within the Church receive renewed attention, for instance: F.C. Mather, *High Church Prophet: Bishop Samuel Horsley (1733–1806) and the Caroline Tradition in the Later Georgian Church* (Oxford, Clarendon Press, 1992). M. Hennell, *Sons of the Prophets: Evangelical Leaders of the Victorian Church* (London, SPCK, 1979). R. O'Day, 'Hugh Latimer: Prophet of the Kingdom', *Historical Research*, 65 (158) (1992), 258–76. S.W. Gilley, 'Newman and Prophecy, Evangelical and Catholic', *Journal of the United Reformed Church History Society*, 3 (5) (1985), 160–88. Along these lines more emphasis has been put on the art of prophesying through sermon and following the seventeenth-century meaning of the word more fully explored in this book by Gwylim Games. See T. Toulouse, *The Art of Prophesying: New England Sermons and the Shaping of Belief* (Athens and London, University of Georgia Press, 1987). J.E.C. Hill, *Antichrist in Seventeenth-Century England* (London, Oxford University Press, 1971); J.A. Dawson 'The Apocalyptic Thinking of the Marian Exiles' in M. Wilks (ed.), *Prophecy and Eschatology*, Studies in Church History, Subsidia 10 (Oxford, Blackwell, 1994), pp. 75–91; R.H. Popkin, 'Jewish Messianism and Christian Millenarianism' in P. Zagorin (ed.), *Culture and Politics from Puritanism to the Enlightenment* (Berkeley, University of California Press, 1980), pp. 67–90.

On prophetic disputes see: N.I. Matar, 'The Controversy Over the Restoration of the Jews in English Protestant Thought: 1701–1753', *Durham University Journal*, 2 (1988), 241–56. D. Heffner, 'Regnum vs. Sacerdotium in a Reformation Pamphlet', *Sixteenth Century Journal*, 20 (4) (1989), 617–30.

For the influence of prophetic discourse on radicalism, apart from the work of Edward P. Thompson and Iain McCalman cited in the introduction, see W.H. Oliver, *Prophets and Millennialists: The Uses of Biblical Prophecy in England from the 1790s to the 1840s* (Auckland University Press, Oxford University Press, 1978). S. Pollard and J. Salt (eds), *Robert Owen, Prophet of the Poor: Essays in Honour of the Two-Hundredth Anniversary of his Birth* (London, Macmillan, 1971), esp. W.H. Oliver, 'Owen in 1817: The Millennialist Moment', pp. 166–87. Further discussions of Owen and millennial ideas must include J.F.C. Harrison, *Robert Owen and the Owenites in Britain and America: The Quest for the New Moral World* (London, Routledge & Kegan Paul, 1969).

On the fusion between science and prophecy see M. Stubbs, 'John Beale, Philosophical Gardener of Herefordshire: part 1, prelude to the Royal Society (1608-1663)', *Annals of Science*, 39 (5) (1982), 463–89. M. Davies, 'Frederick Soddy: the Scientist as Prophet', *Annals of Science*, 49 (4) (1992), 351–67. G. Carlton, *Friedrich Engels: the Shadow Prophet* (London, Pall Mall Press, 1965); for a critical discussion of the prophetic nature of scientific Marxism see K.R. Popper, *The Open Society and its Enemies, Volume II: The High Tide of Prophecy: Hegel, Marx, and the Aftermath* (1945; 3rd, revised, edition, London, Routledge & Kegan Paul, 1957).

On the social history of prophetic movements, apart from H. Schwartz's work, see among other things: T.A. Kselman, *Miracles and Prophecies in Nineteenth-Century France* (New Brunswick, Rutgers University Press, 1983); J.A. Beckford, *The Trumpet of Prophecy: a Sociological Study of Jehovah's Witnesses* (Oxford, Basil Blackwell, 1975); W.R. Singelenberg, '"It Separated the Wheat from the Chaff": the "1975" Prophecy and its Impact among Dutch Jehovah's Witnesses', *Sociological Analysis*, 50 (1) (1988), 23–40. O. Niccoli, *Prophecy and People in Renaissance Italy* (Princeton University Press, 1990); W. Frijhoff, 'Prophétie et Société dans les Provinces Unies aux XVIIᵉ et XVIIIᵉ Siècles' in M. Dupont-Bouchat, W. Frijhoff, R. Muchembled, *Prophètes et Sorciers dans les Pays-Bas XVIᵉ-XVIIIᵉ Siècle* (Paris, Hachette, 1978). A.C. Fix, *Prophecy and Reason: the Dutch Collegiants in the Early Enlightenment* (Princeton University Press, 1991).

On the diffusion of prophecies see W.T. Hayes, 'The Peaceful Apocalypse: Familism and Literacy in Sixteenth Century England', *Sixteenth Century Journal*, 17 (2) (1986), 131–43. P. Russell, '"Your Sons and Daughters shall Prophesy. . .": the Pamphlet Literature of Southwestern Germany to 1525', *Archiv für Reformationsgeschichte*, 74 (1983), 122–40. N. Nelson, 'Lady Elinor Davies: the Prophet as Publisher', *Women's Studies International Forum*, 8 (5) (1985), 403–9. Anthony P. Dunbar, *Against the Grain: Southern Radicals and Prophets, 1929–1959* (Charlottesville, University Press of Virginia, 1981). The southern radicalism of the 1930s had Christianity as one of its bases; many of its leaders had attended Protestant theological seminaries, and the prophetic tradition allowed them to tackle segregation head on, rejecting previous gradualist approaches.

The history of revolutions has also stimulated a certain amount of research in the history of prophecy: H.M. Davies, 'Morgan John Rhys and James Bicheno: Anti-Christ and the French Revolution', *Bulletin of the Board of Celtic Studies*, 29 (1) (1980), 111–27. M. Caffiero, 'Prophétie, Millennium et Révolution: pour une étude du Millénarisme en Italie à l'époque de la Révolution Française', *Archives de Sciences Sociales des Religions*, 66 (2) (1988), 187–99. J. Frankel, *Prophecy and Politics: Socialism, Nationalism and the Russian Jews, 1862–1917* (New York, Cambridge University Press, 1981).

ANTHROPOLOGY AND SOCIOLOGY

In the history of ideas largely reflecting the considerable input of social anthropology see M. De Certeau, *The Writing of History* (New York, Columbia University Press, 1988) which, as mentioned in the introduction and in Rhodri Hayward's piece, is one of the most stimulating approaches to the study of prophecy. Also see C.G. Williams, *Tongues of the Spirit* (Cardiff, University Press of Wales, 1981); I.M. Lewis, *Ecstatic Religion: an Anthropological Study of Spirit Possession and Shamanism* (Harmondsworth, Penguin Books, 1971; 2nd Edition, London, Routledge, 1989); D.M. Anderson, 'Black Mischief: Crime, Protest and Resistance in Colonial Kenya', *Historical Journal*, 36 (4) (1993), 851–77. T.W. Overholt, *Channels of Prophecy: The Social Dynamics of Prophetic Activity* (Minneapolis, Fortress Press, 1989); Armin W. Geertz, *The Invention of Prophecy: Continuity and Meaning in Hopi Indian Religion* (Berkeley, Los Angeles, and London, University of California Press, 1994). In Hopi Indian religion, prophecy is used to assimilate and ultimately defuse the effects of cultural confrontation, as when the Hopi were faced by the Euro-American presence. D.H. Johnson, 'History and Prophecy among the Nuer of the Southern Sudan' (unpublished Ph.D. thesis, University of California at Los Angeles, 1980). During the second half of the nineteenth century the Nuer people experienced both migration and increasing contacts with other peoples. Their culture showed an greater emphasis on the spiritual: certain men became inspired by new forms of divinity, and through them the Nuer were able to confront the new challenges caused by social dislocation and religious confusion. On a more abstract level see: E. Ardener, *The Voice of Prophecy and other Essays*, ed. Malcolm Chapman (Oxford, Basil Blackwell, 1989), 'The Voice of Prophecy: Further Problems in the Analysis of Events', pp. 134–54.

For a more sociological approach see L. Festinger, H.W. Riecken, and S. Schachter, *When Prophecy Fails* (Minneapolis, University of Minnesota Press, 1956). M. West, *Bishops and Prophets in a Black City: African Independent Churches in Soweto/Johannesburg* (Claremont, Cape Province, and London, David Philip and Rex Collings Ltd., 1975).

INDEX OF AUTHORS' NAMES

Names of authors mentioned in the text, notes and bibliographical essay are indexed; names given in full are explicitly discussed in the text.